# An Introduction to English Poetry

To Edwin

# An Introduction to English Poetry

Fifteen poems discussed
by
Laurence Lerner

Edward Arnold

© Laurence Lerner 1975

First published 1975
by Edward Arnold (Publishers) Ltd
25 Hill Street, London W1X 8LL

Cloth Edition ISBN: 0 7131 5789 5
Paperback Edition ISBN: 0 7131 5790 9

Printed in Great Britain by
Billing & Sons Ltd, Guildford and London

# Contents

# Acknowledgements

The publishers and author gratefully acknowledge permission granted by the following for the use of copyright material:

Faber & Faber Ltd and Random House Inc. for W. H. Auden's "City Without Walls" from *City Without Walls*, and 36 lines from "The Ascent of F.6" and Sonnet XIX from *Sonnets from China* (formerly *In Time of War*); John Murray Ltd for John Betjeman's poem "Middlesex"; the Trustees of the Hardy Estate, the Macmillan Company of Canada Inc., Macmillan Ltd, London & Basingstoke, and the Macmillan Publishing Company Inc., New York for "The Ruined Maid" and "The Ballad of Love's Skeleton" from *The Collected Poems of Thomas Hardy:* copyright in the United States of America © 1928 by Florence E. Hardy and Sydney E. Cockerell, renewed 1956 by Lloyds Bank Ltd; Wm Heinemann Ltd, Lawrence Pollinger Ltd and The Viking Press Inc., New York for "Vengeance is Mine" from *The Complete Poems of D. H. Lawrence;* Faber & Faber Ltd and Random House Inc. for "To an Old Philosopher in Rome", "The House was Quiet and the World was Calm", one stanza from "Le monocle de mon oncle", 21 lines from "Esthétique du Mal" and six lines from "Sea Surface full of Clouds" from *The Collected Poems of Wallace Stevens.*

# Preface

I must apologize for the title of this book. There is only one kind of introduction to English poetry, and that is the reading of English poems. This book is an introduction to the *study* of English poetry, and if I were not afraid of seeming long-winded I would have called it that.

The difference is important: for to read and appreciate poems is not the same as to study and discuss them. Reading poetry is a receptive, delighted and silent process: its natural consequence is the wish to savour the rightness of the words, to allow ourselves to be moved by them, not to want to change anything, not even to want to say anything about them, just (perhaps) to hear them again. Anyone who has never known the satisfaction of just *receiving* a poem, just hearing it in all its uniqueness, is unfit to talk about literature.

But after a while we find there are things we want to say. After all, the poets themselves did not rest in the silent contemplation of their experiences. To Raleigh his anger must have seemed something incommunicable, like Marvell's playfulness or Wordsworth's grief; but then they set themselves to put it into words. If they were willing to try to understand and express the quality of experience, we can set ourselves the more modest task of understanding and describing the experience of reading the poems.

The first aim of these essays, then, is to describe what each poem is trying to say, and what there is in its language that gives it its own peculiar quality. But of course we don't read poems in isolation from one another; so as we reflect on our reading we begin to compare, contrast and classify, and we find that one poem helps us to see more clearly what is happening in another. And so my further aim is to build the discussion of the poems into a discussion of English poetry. For this to be possible, the poems must be chosen with care: I hesitated and changed endlessly before arriving at the final list. The list will seem unusual to many readers, since I have avoided most of the familiar favourites. This is not because I think *Lycidas* or the *Ode to a Nightingale, The Canonisation* or *Sailing to Byzantium,* are overrated, but simply because I felt they needed a rest—not a rest from being read, nor even perhaps from being talked about, but a rest from having more essays written about them. There is so much wonderful poetry in English that I had no problem in finding fifteen very fine but less familiar poems, and there are a hundred and fifteen others I could have chosen. First and foremost, I chose them because I admire them, but I have also tried to represent the main kinds and styles of English poetry of the last four hundred years or so. A few words on why I chose these particular poems will therefore be a kind of introduction to the discussion of English poetry.

Obviously there had to be a spread in time, and so the poems are dated and discussed in chronological order: to read the book through from the beginning to end or (better still, perhaps) to begin by reading the poems through, without the commentary, is thus inevitably to see something of the development of English poetry. The date is the date of composition, not publication, since some of them (*The Dream, The Ruined Maid*) were not published until many years after they were written; but we do not of course always know this accurately, and some of the dates, especially the earlier ones, are guesses. The only poem that is out of chronological order is *Peter Grimes*: it happens to have been written after the Wordsworth, but Crabbe clearly needs to be discussed along with the eighteenth-century tradition he belongs to—as I have tried to indicate in the essay. The history of English poetry is not, of course, simply a matter of dates: it is best thought of as a number of movements that succeeded one another, and I have tried to represent them all. *Clerk Saunders* is probably the earliest poem in the book, though scholars are so uncertain of the origin of the ballads that we cannot be sure of this; we can however be sure that its roots are in the popular balladry of the late Middle Ages, and since I did not want to go back to the times that present linguistic difficulties, it is the only specimen of medieval poetry. Very roughly, we can divide the last four centuries into five movements, Renaissance, Metaphysical or Baroque, Augustan or neo-classical, Romantic, and Modern, and there are at least two examples of each.

But there are other ways of classifying poems as well as by time. At least as important is the division into kinds, and primarily into the three traditional kinds, or genres, lyric, narrative and dramatic. It is not difficult to decide whether a poem is narrative or dramatic, that is, whether it tells a story or has a clearly identified speaker. There is one pure example of each genre, *Peter Grimes* and *Johannes Agricola in Meditation*, and in the essay on the latter I have discussed the nature and value of the dramatic. It is also possible to tell a story dramatically, through the mouths of one or more characters, as the ballads are so famous for doing; and both the ballads in this book, *Clerk Saunders*, the traditional ballad, and *The Ruined Maid*, the modern imitation, can be called dramatic narratives.

Things are more complicated with the lyric. If we insist (as critical tradition often has insisted) that there are only three kinds of poetry, then everything which is not narrative or dramatic is lyrical; but strictly speaking the term "lyric" suggests a poem that retains some connection with music, and is the direct expression of emotion: some might even insist that it be simple enough to be sung. This point is discussed in the essay on *The Dream:* here I add a few words to broaden the discussion to the rest of the book. Only one of the poems quite clearly falls within this strict definition, the *Stanzas Written in Dejection,* but there is little doubt that *A Picture of Little T.C.* and the Shakespeare sonnet are also, basically, lyrics, and there are several other border-line cases. It is clear that we need terms for one or two other kinds of poem that merge into the lyric. There is the poem in which the author conveys his feelings in a much more intellectualized form, so that he appears to be reflecting on a theme, almost discussing it: we might call such a poem a meditation, and *To an Old Philosopher in Rome* and *City Without Walls* would both be examples of this. Then there is satire—a term with very fluid meaning, the main characteristic being an attack on individuals, real or fictitious or thinly disguised, or on institutions, or on the whole state of society. Traditionally, satire is relaxed, even conversational in tone, as in *To Mr Fortescue,* but the quite unrelaxed passion of the *The Lie* could also be called satiric. However, I have preferred in this case to use the term "complaint", and since a complaint is essentially a direct expression of anger or indignation, it can be considered a branch of the truly lyrical. If we are going to separate out some emotions, and say that poems which express them take on marked characteristics that turn them into a genre of their own, then to anger we can add grief, and regard the elegy (which for the last two hundred years has meant a poem concerned with death, and usually the death of an individual—what the Renaissance called a funeral elegy) as a further kind: Wordsworth's *Elegiac Stanzas* is our one example of this.

Then there is classification by metrical form, and I have tried in my choice to show the wide range of metres in English poetry, and the rich variety of effects they can yield. There is the simple ballad stanza of *Clerk Saunders,* and an equally simple stanza with a refrain in the *The Lie*; a rather more formal stanza, still with alternating rhymes, but with longer lines, in the *Elegiac Stanzas,* and something more elaborate but still regular in *The Bunch of Grapes.* The most elaborate stanzas are those of Donne and Marvell, who both loved to show off their technical versatility. Then there are the heroic couplets of the two eighteenth-century poets, two sonnets, and the two twentieth-century poems, both of which approach free verse:

Stevens writing something very like traditional blank verse, and Auden in a metre whose significance is discussed in the essay. I am sorry there is no poem in irregular free verse, and no poem in the short octosyllabic couplets that produced so much beautiful lyric verse in the seventeenth century, but both these forms do appear in other poems or passages quoted.

Finally, there is classification by poet, and here of course I was limited to fifteen. It would have been absurdly artificial to try and mention something by every great English poet in the course of the essays, so though I have compared freely, I have not been able to do anything for Spenser or Marlowe or Ben Jonson, Vaughan or Dryden or Dr Johnson, Blake, Keats or Tennyson, Yeats or Emily Dickinson or T S Eliot—enough material for another volume.

The place of general reflections is after, not before the particular discussions, so it is time now to turn to the poems themselves. Readers of a theoretical turn of mind might, however, like to keep a few general questions in mind as they read, not only the questions of literary history and genre sketched in the last paragraph, but also questions of how to write a critique of a poem: how far in discussing poems are we describing our response to the words in the page, and how far are we placing it in a wider context, as part of the poet's work or of the history of English poetry? This and much else is discussed in the Conclusion, which is an attempt to reach out from these fifteen chapters and offer suggestions on how one might write about any poem.

But there is no real need to ask these theoretical questions while reading, unless they suggest themselves: for what matters is the poems, and the main aim of every essay is to serve the poem it deals with. I would prefer to think of readers reading the whole book, rather than the one or two essays that deal with poems they are interested in, since only in this way can they gain the general picture of English poetry I have tried to build up; but even this is not essential, and the only indispensable qualification for reading any of the essays is to have read its poem, preferably many times.

And now to the poems, the froth being out of the bottle.

# 1

## Clerk Saunders

Clerk Saunders and may Margaret
  Walked ower yon garden green;
And sad and heavy was the love
  That fell thir twa between.

"A bed, a bed," Clerk Saunders said,
  "A bed for you and me!"
"Fye na, fye na," said may Margaret,
  "Till anes we married be.

"For in may come my seven bauld brothers,
  Wi' torches burning bright;
They'll say—'We hae but ae sister,
  And behold she's wi' a knight!' '

"Then take the sword frae my scabbard,
  And slowly lift the pin;
And you may swear, and safe your aith,
  Ye never let Clerk Saunders in.

"And take a napkin in your hand,
  And tie up baith your bonny een;
And you may swear, and safe your aith,
  Ye saw me na since late yestreen."

It was about the midnight hour,
  When they asleep were laid,
When in and came her seven brothers,
  Wi' torches burning red.

When in and came her seven brothers,
  Wi' torches burning bright;
They said, 'We hae but ae sister.
  And behold her lying with a knight!'

Then out and spake the first o' them,
  "I bear the sword shall gar him die!"
And out and spake the second o' them,
  "His father has nae mair than he!"

[1] See short glossary of obsolete words at end of poem.

And out and spake the third o' them,
   "I wot that they are lovers dear!"
And out and spake the fourth o' them,
   "They hae been in love this mony a year!"

Then out and spake the fifth o' them,
   "It were great sin true love to twain!"
And out and spake the sixth o' them,
   "It were shame to slay a sleeping man!"

Then up and gat the seventh o' them,
   And never a word spake he;
But he has striped his bright brown brand
   Out through Clerk Saunders' fair bodye.

Clerk Saunders he started, and Margaret she turned
   Into his arms as asleep she lay;
And sad and silent was the night
   That was atween thir twae.

And they lay still and sleeped sound,
   Until the day began to daw;
And kindly to him she did say,
   "It is time, true love, you were awa'."

But he lay still, and sleeped sound,
   Albeit the sun began to sheen;
She look'd atween her and the wa',
   And dull and drowsie were his een.

Then in and came her father dear,
   Said—"Let a' your mourning be:
I'll carry the dead corpse to the clay,
   And I'll come back and comfort thee."

"Comfort weel your seven sons,
   For comforted will I never be:
I ween 'twas neither knave nor lown
   Was in the bower last night wi' me."

The clinking bell gaed through through the town,
   To carry the dead corse to the clay;
And Clerk Saunders stood at may Margaret's window,
   I wot, an hour before the day.

"Are ye sleeping, Margaret?" he says,
   "Or are ye waking presentlie?

Give me my faith and troth again,
   I wot, true love, I gied to thee."

"Your faith and troth ye sall never get,
   Nor our true love sall never twin,
Until ye come within my bower,
   And kiss me cheik and chin."

"My mouth it is full cold, Margaret,
   It has the smell, now, of the ground;
And if I kiss thy comely mouth,
   Thy days of life will not be lang.

"O cocks are crowing a merry midnight,
   I wot the wild fowls are boding day;
Give me my faith and troth again,
   And let me fare me on my way."

"Thy faith and troth thou sall na get,
   And our true love sall never twin,
Until ye tell what comes of women,
   I wot, who die in strong traivelling?"

"Their beds are made in the heavens high,
   Down at the foot of our Good Lord's knee,
Weel set about wi' gillyflowers:
   I wot sweet company for to see.

"O cocks are crowning a merry midnight,
   I wot the wild fowl are boding day;
The psalms of heaven will soon be sung,
   And I, ere now, will be miss'd away."

Then she has ta'en a crystal wand,
   And she has stroken her troth thereon;
She has given it him out at the shot-window,
   Wi' mony a sad sigh, and heavy groan.

"I thank ye, Marg'ret; I thank ye, Marg'ret;
   And aye I thank ye heartilie;
Gin ever the dead come for the quick,
   Be sure, Marg'ret, I'll come for thee."

It's hosen and shoon, and gown alone,
   She climbed the wall, and followed him,
Until she came to the green forest,
   And there she lost the sight o' him.

"Is there ony room at your head, Saunders?
  Is there ony room at your feet?
Or ony room at your side, Saunders,
  Where fain, fain, I wad sleep?"

There's nae room at my head, Marg'ret,
  There's nae room at my feet;
My bed it is full lowly now:
  Among the hungry worms I sleep.

"Cauld mould is my covering now,
  But and my winding sheet;
The dew it falls nae sooner down,
  Than my resting place is weet.

"But plait a wand o' bonnie birk,
  And lay it on my breast;
And shed a tear upon my grave,
  And wish my saul gude rest.

"And fair Marg'ret, and rare Marg'ret,
  And Marg'ret o' veritie,
Gin e'er ye love another man,
  Ne'er love him as ye did me."

Then up and crew the milk-white cock,
  And up and crew the grey;
Her lover vanish'd in the air,
  And she gaed weeping away.

*Author unknown    (perhaps sixteenth century)*

In all the other poems in this book the spelling has been modernized: for the archaic and scholarly interest of seeing a poem in its original spelling has little place in an Introduction to English Poetry. But to modernize this poem would have been to write a new one, translating it out of the early form of Scottish it is now in; it must be left as it is, and fortunately it is not very difficult, once we have got to know it. A few words do perhaps need explaining, so here is a short glossary:

*ae* one; *and safe your aith* without breaking your oath; *birk* birch; *boding* announcing; *een* eyes; *fain I wad* I long to; *frae* from; *gar* make; *gin* if; *lown* (loon); *boor* man of low birth *presentlie* now; *thir twa* the two of them; *traivelling* child-birth; *twin* separate; *wa'* wall; *ween* believe, consider; *weet* wet.

The story is simple: two lovers sleep together, anticipating marriage; the girl's brothers discover them, and kill the man; waking up, she finds a corpse lying next to her, and refuses to be comforted; then her lover comes back from the dead to visit her. That is all. And the details of the telling are equally clear and striking. Most important is the dramatic quality. Who is Clerk Saunders? Who is Margaret? How did they come to meet? How long have they known each other? We are told none of these things, but are plunged in without any preface; it is not their whole story we are given, but a single episode only. And even in the telling of this episode, we are given no commentary and very little narrative: almost all the poem is in dialogue, so that we hear the voices of the characters, not the voice of the poet. All this adds force and immediacy to the telling: look for instance at the move from the sixth to the seventh stanza. After Clerk Saunders has suggested his trick for letting him in so that she can still pretend to be innocent without actually lying (perhaps this is to reassure her of his love, or perhaps they are superstitious enough to believe such literal-mindedness is important), we are not given her reply but a series of three stanzas that parallel the previous three, in which Margaret does just what he has suggested. No words are being wasted, by her or by the poem; if we want to know her thoughts, we must construct them for ourselves. She had refused to let him in, through fear of her brothers; now she does exactly what he says. Do we imagine her doing it silently and fearfully, wishing she had said no? or so devoted to Saunders that, once she is reassured, her only wish is to carry out his wishes exactly as he uttered them? Either reading is possible, and the power of the poem derives from the way it shows us the events from the outside, invites us to think about what is passing within her mind, but says nothing. The effect is weighty with suggestion, compelling, somehow enigmatic.

There is a very similar effect in the stanzas about her brothers. Just as Margaret had feared, they come in and find them together: this means danger. One by one they speak, and we realize that all may be well: they are touched by what they see, by the devotion and youth of the lovers, they feel uneasy about killing a sleeping man, and it looks as if they will let him go. The movement from the first to the sixth is like a train of thought, and what we are shown is not so much six separate individuals each giving his view, but the whole group, as it were, making up its mind. But the seventh brother, who is inexorable, does not wait to discuss: he draws his sword and kills Saunders. We are not told anything about this brother, but the action clearly invites us to read his thoughts: he is the uncompromising one, filled—is it with hatred? or with justice? And because he is uncompromising he acts immediately, undeterred by what the others have said—perhaps all the more determined because of their relenting. That is what such men do.

The realism of this is startling; and the natural effect of dialogue and swift transitions is certainly realistic. Yet in one important way, *Clerk Saunders* is not at all realistic. There is speech, but much of it is formal and stylized. The very first words show this:

> "A bed, a bed," Clerk Saunders said,
> "A bed for you and me."

"A bed is what we need"; or "a-bed (meaning "to bed" or "in bed") is where we should be": the phrase could be read either way, and is no doubt meant to suggest both. Most striking about it however is the tone, which is both colloquial and formal. Clerk Saunders speaks as he would in life, but the repetitions suggest not only the urgency of speech but also a kind of ritual formula. Stanza three is certainly formalized, with the torches that accompany the brothers burning bright to add to the poem's vividness, and above all as a stock descriptive detail, rather than because they are relevant to what Margaret is then saying. Margaret is not speaking in her own personal voice, but through her the inevitable doom is being announced: that is why the very same words are repeated in the tenth stanza, when the brothers actually do appear. Repetition is in fact the main device by which speech is formalized, and when it is systematic it produces an effect of parallelism: thus the remark of each brother is introduced by the same 'out and spake" formula, and even narrative details appear in parallelism, as when Margaret wakes up and says to Saunders that it is time for him to go, looks, and realizes he is dead: it is not difficult to divide this into successive stanzas, and begin each with the same phrase, in this case, "They/He lay still and sleeped sound"; and the effect of pausing and doubling back on the events slows us down and adds solemnity.

A poem that concentrates on a single climactic episode in the story, and tells it dramatically, with no commentary and a great deal of dialogue; in vivid speech that is both colloquial and stylized—these are the characteristics of the ballads, of which *Clerk Saunders* is one of the most famous. No one knows who wrote this or any other traditional ballad, nor where it came from, nor when it was composed. They were transmitted orally, perhaps for several centuries, and began to be written down in the eighteenth century. The famous collection of Bishop Percy, *Reliques of Ancient English Poetry*, included a number of what have become the most celebrated of the ballads; but *Clerk Saunders* was first published in a later and equally important collection, *Minstrelsy of the Scottish Border*, edited by Sir Walter Scott (1802–3). But to know when a ballad was first published tells us nothing about its age and origin; and we can say no more about the origin of *Clerk Saunders* than about any other ballad. Tradition has ascribed most of the oral ballads to the border country in the fifteenth and sixteenth centuries, but recent scholars have begun to question both the place and the time. There turns out to be very little evidence that points to the border country as the place, though it is clear from their language that a good number, including *Clerk Saunders*, are Scottish; and it has become commoner to place them later in time as well, from the late sixteenth to the mid or later seventeenth century. We know that ballads were a phenomenon of the later Middle Ages all through Europe, but there is little evidence to trace any of our existing texts so far back.

The scholarly arguments are involved and, you may feel, of no great concern to the reader whose aim is simply to understand and enjoy the poems; but it is impossible to dodge the problem of the text. A ballad has no author: for it was handed down over generations by singers who changed and rearranged it to their own taste and that of their audience. If we can find reference to a historical figure or event in a ballad, we may feel we know when it began; but even this is uncertain, for it was always possible to add topical references to existing ballads, or to compose a ballad on an episode that happened some time ago. We are to think of the text of a ballad as constantly changing, shedding some stanzas, adding one detail if sung in one place, a different detail elsewhere. The ritual phrasing is a sign of this kind of transmission; the ballad-singer had a mind well provided with stock descriptions that helped him to compose. If you are making up the brothers' remarks as you sing, then the "line out and spake the fifth of them" gives you time to decide what the fifth should say. But to the twentieth-century reader it might be misleading to think of the ballad-singer composing his own poem, for to us the writing of poetry suggests great originality of language, a personal style different from what anyone else could write, whereas composing a ballad consisted largely of rearranging traditional details. That is why the same poem seems to keep its identity over a number of versions, each of which, however much it changes the details, remains faithful to the spirit of what went before.

The usual source for the text—or texts—of a ballad is the five volumes of F. J. Child's great collection, *The English and Scottish Popular Ballads* (1882–98). Child gives us six different versions of *Clerk Saunders,* plus a few variants, and one very similar ballad about "an ensign and a lady gay". It is impossible to say which of these is the oldest, and meaningless to ask which is the "correct" version. Some are, of course, better than others, and the oldest may not necessarily be the finest poetically. Some variants may be due to an early editor, and even these cannot be dismissed—nor sometimes, spotted. We may not care for "improvements" that reveal the eighteenth-century taste of Bishop Percy, but the hand of Scott refashioned some of his material with scholarly unscrupulousness and poetic genius. In the case of *Clerk Saunders* he tells us that he took it from "Mr Herd's manuscript, with many corrections from a shorter and more imperfect copy in the same volume, and one or two conjectural emendations in the arrangement of the stanzas." Child, after consulting the manuscripts of David Herd, the eighteenth-century collector, was able to state that Scott altered and rearranged with much more freedom than his note admits. But since he understood the ballad spirit perfectly, and was probably as fine a poet as any of his anonymous predecessors, it may well be that what we admire in *Clerk Saunders* is due partly to him.

It was necessary to choose a version, and I chose Scott's. To see how the text of a ballad can vary, we should now put another version next to it: so here is the one which Child calls D, recorded "from the recitation of Mrs Thomson" by one Motherwell:

> "O I have seven bold brethren,
>     And they are all valiant men,
> If they knew a man that would tread my bower
>     His life should not go along wi him."
>
> "Then take me up into your arms,
>     And lay me low down on your bed,
> That ye may swear, and keep your oath clear
>     That your bower-room I did na tread.
>
> "Tie a handkerchief round your face,
>     And you must tye it wondrous keen,
> That you may swear, and keep your oath clear,
>     Ye saw na me since late yestreen."

But they were scarsely gone to bed,
    Nor scarse fa'n owre asleep,
Till up and started her seven brethren,
    Just at Lord Saunders' feet.

Out bespoke the first brither,
    'Oh but love be wondrous keen!"
Out bespoke the second brither,
    "It's ill done to kill a sleeping man."

Out bespoke the third brither,
    "We had better gae and let him be;"
Out bespoke the fourth brither,
    "He'll no be killd this night for me:"

Out bespoke the fifth brother,
    "This night Lord Saunders he shall die;
Tho there were not a man in all Scotland,
    This night Lord Saunders he shall die."

He took out a rousty rapier,
    And he drew it three times thro the strae;
Between Lord Saunders' short rib and his side
    He gard the rusty rapier gae.

"Awake, awake, Lord Saunders," she said,
    "Awake, awake, for sin and shame!
For the day is light, and the sun shines bricht,
    And I am afraid we will be taen.

"Awake, awake, Lord Saunders," she said,
    "Awake, awake, for sin and shame!
For the sheets they are asweat," she said,
    "And I am afraid we will be taen.

"I dreamed a dreary dream last night,
    I wish it may be for our good,
That I was cutting my yellow hair,
    And dipping it in the wells o blood."

Aye she waukened at this dead man,
    Aye she put on him to and fro;
Oh aye she waukend at this dead man,
    But of his death she did not know.

*

"It's I will do for my love's sake
   What many ladies would think lang;
Seven years shall come and go
   Before a glove go on my hand.

"And I will do for my love's sake
   What many ladies would not do;
Seven years shall come and go
   Before I wear stocking or shoe.

Ther'll neer a shirt go on my back,
   There'll neer a kame go in my hair,
There'll never coal nor candle-light,
   Shine in my bower nae mair."

What are the main differences between these two versions? We need
not pay great attention to the absence of the opening stanzas in
version D: perhaps Mrs Thomson did not know them, or for some
reason they were not recorded: it is obvious that something is missing
at the beginning, and that we have not got a complete text. Nor need
we pay much attention to the fact that the language is so much less
markedly Scottish: that may be due to the way it was transcribed,
and is not in this case of much artistic significance. Nor to the fact
that Clerk Saunders has become a lord: this does not happen in any
other version, and is no doubt a touch of sentimentalizing by Mrs
Thomson or someone who taught her (in some versions his name is
even familiarized into "Sandy").

Version D makes less of the tricks for letting Clerk Saunders in.
They are not quite the same tricks (she is to carry him so as to swear
"that your bower-room I did na tread" instead of lifting the latch
with his sword), and not surprisingly there are other versions that
include all three tricks; more important is the absence of the repetition,
so that we are not given the parallelism between what Saunders
suggests and what Margaret does. I have already remarked how
suggestive this is, and its absence also diminishes the force of a main
ironic effect. Saunders's precautions are typical of folk tale, the kind
of prevarication that enables you to keep an oath while breaking it,
and in this story they turn out to be totally useless. We are left to
notice this for ourselves, and the solemnity of the repetition, followed
by the complete ignoring of the whole question, makes the point
with silent eloquence.

The speeches of the seven brothers are better handled in the Scott
than in the Motherwell version—or for that matter in any other

version. Though there are always said to be seven, sometimes only five speak; and in no other version except Scott's do we find the brilliant touch of the silence of the last brother, the one man who acts instead of speaking.

In Margaret's discovery of Saunder's death, there is one savagely realistic detail that Scott omits, and Motherwell retains a reference to:

> "Awake, awake, for sin and shame!
> For the sheats they are asweat," she said . . .

In another of Child's versions we find this stanza:

> "This night," said she, "the sleepiest man
>   That ever my twa eyes did see
> Hay lyen by me, and sweat the sheets;
>   A wite they're a great shame to see."

Here we have a touch of ironic sexual humour: Clerk Saunder's deep sleep and apparent copious sweating, the signs of his death, are taken by Margaret for signs of his sexual prowess, on which she teases him. Only half the point is kept by Motherwell, but Scott leaves it out completely, along with Margaret's dream, with its haunting detail of cutting her yellow hair, and dipping it in the "wells o' blood."

The most important differences concern the ending. Margaret's refusal to be comforted is very powerful poetically:

> Comfort weel your seven sons,
>   For comforted will I never be:
> I ween twas neither knave nor lown
>   Was in the bower last night wi' me.

Here is Margaret defending the rank of her lover, as if that justified what she had done. When we notice that in one version she goes on to call him "Clerk Saunders, that good earl's son", and in another her father says that if she leaves off mourning,

> "I'll wed you to a higher match
>   Or ever his father's son could be",

it begins to look as if Mrs Thomson may not have been merely sentimental in calling him Lord Saunders. There may have been a version in which Saunders was considered to be beneath Margaret socially, and killed for that reason rather than because of the unchastity. Yet perhaps it is equally effective to think of her asserting that he is neither knave nor lown (both terms that primarily indicated social inferiority, but can be generalized in meaning) simply out of the intensity of her grief and love: his real social position does not matter to her.

A similar intensity, this time of anger, is contained in the first line of the stanza, whose power might not be immediately obvious: "Comfort weel your seven sons." It is a rejection of her father, telling him to take his comfort elsewhere, but it is also a taunting of the brothers. No one has thought of comforting them: she is suggesting that they need it more than her, and this can only be because they are going to repent of what they have done, or even that they will be punished by God.

Then, in the Motherwell version, Margaret is given a repetitive statement of her grief and willingness to mourn. It is completely in the style of the rest of the ballad with its parallelisms, its ritual seven years, its details of self-denial; and in other versions she is given similar statements. But in the Scott there is none of this; instead, his version ends with the return of Clerk Saunders from the grave to ask for his faith and troth again. The point of that is not quite clear: he might be seeking his own release from earthly ties, or he might want to set Margaret free for her sake, so that she can marry someone else. At any rate, she refuses, and to pledge her faithfulness she kisses him, asks him questions about the other world, and makes him a gift—traditional ways of putting yourself in the power of a ghost, and ensuring your own quick death. The poem could end there, at the end of stanza 26, but we are then given abother episode, in which she follows him into the forest, and pleads with him. Her plea is one of the most direct and moving stanzas in the poem:

> "Is there ony room at your head, Saunders?
>     Is there ony room at your feet?
> Or ony room at your side, Saunders,
>     Where fain, fain, I wad sleep?"

This produces an exchange that is characteristic of ballads about the supernatural, in which Saunders answers her in parallelism. He tells her to lay a birch wand on his breast (birch is the tree that is often said to grow in the other world), and she is in the end left weeping.

This ending is certainly found in the Herd Ms from which Scott took his text, but not in any other version. Child therefore suggests that it is not part of *Clerk Saunders* at all, and he is clearly right, for there is another ballad called *Sweet William's Ghost*, of which this is a version. Here is *Sweet William's Ghost* as printed in Percy's *Reliques* (Percy took the text from a collection made by Allan Ramsey in 1740):

> There came a ghost to Margret's door,
>     With many a grievous groan,
> And aye he tirled at the pin,
>     But answer made she none.

> "Is that my father Philip,
>     Or is't my brother John?
> Or is't my true-love, Willy,
>     From Scotland new come home?"

> "Tis not thy father Philip,
>     Nor yet thy brother John;
> But 'tis thy true-love, Willy,
>     From Scotland new come home.

> "O sweet Margret, O dear Margret,
>     I pray thee speak to me;
> Give me my faith and troth, Margret,
>     As I gave it to thee."

> "Thy faith and troth thou's never get,
>     Nor yet will I thee lend,
> Till that thou come within my bower,
>     And kiss my cheek and chin."

> "If I should come within thy bower,
>     I am no earthly man;
> And should I kiss thy rosy lips,
>     Thy days will not be lang.

> "O sweet Margret, O dear Margret,
>     I pray thee speak to me;
> Give me my faith and troth, Margret,
>     As I gave it to thee."

> "Thy faith and troth thou's never get,
>     Nor yet will I thee lend,
> Till you take me to yon kirk,
>     And wed me with a ring."

> "My bones are buried in yon kirk-yard,
>     Afar beyond the sea,
> And it is but my spirit, Margret,
>     That's now speaking to thee."

> She stretched out her lilly-white hand,
>   And, for to do her best,
> "Hae, there's your faith and troth, Willy,
>   God send your soul good rest."
>
> Now she has kilted her robes of green
>   A piece below her knee,
> And a' the live-lang winter night
>   The dead corp followed she.
>
> "Is there any room at your head, Willy?
>   Or any room at your feet?
> Or any room at your side, Willy,
>   Wherein that I may creep?"
>
> "There's no room at my head, Margret,
>   There's no room at my feet;
> There's no room at my side, Margret,
>   My coffin's made so meet."
>
> Then up and crew the red, red cock,
>   And up then crew the gray:
> "Tis time, tis time, my dear Margret,
>   That you were going away."
>
> No more the ghost to Margret said,
>   But, with a grievous groan,
> Evanished in a cloud of mist,
>   And left her all alone.
>
> "O stay, my only true-love, stay,"
>   The constant Margret cry'd;
> Wan grew her cheeks, she closed her een,
>   Stretched her soft limbs, and dy'd.

We cannot know if it is merely coincidence that the heroine is here also called Margaret; though if it is, then that might explain how the two ballads were joined together. *Sweet William's Ghost* is a fine ballad, but of a different kind from *Clerk Saunders,* for it is entirely concerned with the supernatural. The effect of Margaret not realizing at first that her lover is dead is, of course, lost when it is attached to *Clerk Saunders.* The faith and troth are returned in *Sweet William's Ghost,* and the lines in which it is done ("God send your soul good rest") suggest that it is for his sake not hers. There are Scandinavian versions in which the dead lover is not able to lie easy in his grave as long as his living mistress continues to weep for him.

It is almost invariable in popular ballads that giving way to the wish of a ghost, or following him to his grave, proves fatal; so it is not surprising that *Sweet William's Ghost* ends with Margaret's death. It is probable that the last two stanzas are more modern than the rest, but the ending is so much in keeping with tradition that we may feel sure that what they replaced was very similar. The concluding stanzas in Scott's version, however, are almost certainly by Scott himself: they are extremely effective, but perhaps in a way that has begun to lose touch with popular feeling. The final effect, of the lover vanished and Margaret going weeping away, shows us the emotional power of the scene, and allows us to see—and imagine —her grief, without being too explicit about it: so far, quite authentic. But by concentrating on this, the poem returns to her grief for Saunders's death, and we are allowed to forget the actual effect of following a ghost. That last stanza could almost stand as the ending of the original ballad, without the ghost story:

> Then up and crew the milk-white cock,
>     And up and crew the grey;
> Her lover vanished in the air,
>     And she gaed weeping away.

It is a brilliant ending, but it suggests the literary craftsman rather than the popular ballad singer.


Having looked at all these versions, we ought to end by reminding ourselves that (apart from the grafting on of *Sweet William's Ghost*), they are variants of a single poem. True, the verbal differences between Motherwell and Scott are almost as great as those between two Elizabethan sonnets on the same theme, by different poets; or even between two love lyrics by (say) two Georgian poets, or two Beat poets. But we have no difficulty in knowing that in the one case we are dealing with variants, in the other with separate poems, for the ballad sets up such different expectations. The prominence of refrain and parallelism, the lack of that kind of concentrated verbal originality for which so much modern poetry is distinguished, sets up a high tolerance of variation: we realize that this is the kind of poem that will be able to keep its identity amid the shifts from one version to another. Listeners to the ballads when they were still carried on by oral tradition must often have had the experience of recognizing instantly that they knew the ballad, and then sitting back with interest to find what that particular singer would make of it.

Yet although this general unity of various versions is the most important characteristic of the ballad, it should not lead us to neglect the differences of talent that must have existed from one bard to another; and perhaps there never was a bard who had more natural feeling for the possibilities of the form than Sir Walter Scott. In the Introductory Remarks to his *Minstrelsy*, Scott remarks that "it is, no doubt, highly desirable that the text of ancient poetry should be given untouched and uncorrupted", but he clearly realizes that this demand cannot be too strictly made. The text of a poem by Chaucer or Villon means, more or less unambiguously, the final revision by the poet himself, and the editor's task is to reproduce that as accurately as it can be discovered; there is no such unambiguous text of a ballad. Scott took far more liberties than Child, because he was a poet first and a scholar second; but we have seen that on almost every point on which his version differs from that of Motherwell it is artistically superior. I believe it to be by far the best version of *Clerk Saunders*, though there is clearly a case for detaching the second ballad—if we could have Scott himself to fashion us an alternative ending!

# 2

# Sonnet 34

Why didst thou promise such a beauteous day,
And make me travel forth without my cloak,
To let base clouds o'ertake me in my way,
Hiding thy bravery in their rotten smoke?
'Tis not enough that through the cloud thou break,
To dry the rain on my storm-beaten face,
For no man well of such a salve can speak,
That heals the wound, and cures not the disgrace.
Nor can thy shame give physic to my grief;
Though thou repent, yet I have still the loss.
Th' offender's sorrow lends but weak relief
To him that bears the strong offence's cross.
Ah but those tears are pearl which thy love sheds,
And they are rich, and ransom all ill deeds.

*Shakespeare* (*about 1595*)

This is a poem of reproach. The poet is addressing someone who has committed a mean act, and then repented: but the repentance was not enough to compensate for the meanness, and so he continues to feel betrayed, and to tell his friend that he seems less attractive than he was. Thus much is clear, but, as far as the facts go, not much more Who is the friend and what has he done? Narrative always arouses curiosity, and the shadow of narrative that lies behind this poem can easily make us curious, but the poem does not answer these questions. Perhaps it was intended for readers who already knew the facts. Perhaps the poet felt that the details did not matter and that the poem was clear without them, for he was concerned to express his disappointment and bitterness, not to recapitulate what had given rise to it. The result is a poem that any of us could apply to a situation in which we feel betrayed: for poetry, after all, takes the particular and universalizes it.

This is also a sonnet: that is, a poem of fourteen lines written according to a set of fairly rigid rules, governing its rhyme-scheme. The rules for this kind of sonnet demand four quatrains, rhyming alternatively, and a final couplet—or, to represent the rhyme-scheme by letters, ABAB CDCD EFEF GG. The poet has stuck to the rules, and a moment's reflection shows us that they are not merely rules for rhyming. The whole movement of the poem is adjusted to this pattern: it makes three measured, bitter statements, each in four lines, and then a final concluding remark in a different tone. The first quatrain is the initial rebuke: why did you begin so well and then behave so meanly? The second quatrain admits that the trouble is now over, and that the friend is once more smiling on him, but asserts that this is not enough to undo the damage. The third quatrain admits further that the friend has repented and shown shame, but this too is not enough: "I have still the loss." Apologies do not really atone, in the eyes of the offended party. Only in the last couplet is there anything that looks like a real concession by the poet, a final brief but ringing admission that when such a friend repents we have to yield, for "those tears are pearl".

Clearly form and content are well fitted to each other. The succession of three parallel assertions is perfectly appropriate to the measured, mounting rebuke of this poem, and the regularity of each quatrain suggests that control of voice that makes anger impressive; and the climax of the final couplet is equally well suited to a turn and a concession at the end. The sonnet form itself might have been invented to enable this poet to write just such a poem.

There are two complications, however. One concerns the poem's language. There is a stylistic change in this poem that does not correspond to the metrical pattern. It begins—as so many poems do —by using imagery: that is, its statements are made by means of comparisons. The subject is a man's actions and emotions, the words actually refer to the sights and sounds of nature. The basic comparison—for this is a single extended image, not a series of different ones—is between the friend and the sun. His initial goodwill is the sun shining; his meanness is the sun going behind rain-clouds; his renewed goodwill is the sun reappearing. It is clear that we have a poet who loves writing about nature, and does so with skill and knowledge—and then half-way through the second quatrain the imagery ceases. The subject remains the same, but now the language is abstract; instead of cloaks, clouds, rain and weather, we hear of shame, disgrace, sorrow and relief. This startling change of style—surely any reader feels it as he reads the poem, even though he may not realize at first just what it is he is noticing—does not correspond to the division into quatrains, or affect the content. It is still a poet reproaching his friend, only in different terminology.

And then right at the end we have a brief reversion to imagery: "those tears are pearl." Brief, even cursory: not lingered on lovingly as in the opening lines. And not only cursory but conventional:

plenty of poets have compared tears to pearls. Is it not an anticlimax, to do so scrappily what at the beginning was so fully done? I believe it is an anticlimax, and a deliberate one, and to explain it we must look again at that last couplet. When I first mentioned it, I cheated; I called it a brief but ringing admission, but did not ask whether it rings true or false. If the climax sounds perfunctory, it may be that it was meant to sound perfunctory: that the concluding note of praise is ironic, and is meant to be read in a deliberately unconvinced voice. One or two touches in its syntax fit well with this reading: that initial "Ah" in so restrained and sophisticated a poem sounds very like an invitation to mockery, and the clumsy construction of the last line ("and . . . and . . .") can easily accompany a smile of self-deprecation. Even the unobtrusive "all" of "all ill deeds" sounds, when we stop to think of it, too good to be true, and if it is stressed in the reading will make the irony very clear. Four quatrains of rebuke then, and a couplet of sarcastic praise—but only mildly sarcastic, of course, for the poem keeps its calm and dignified movement.

We could linger on details, no doubt, but on the whole that is all there is to say about this poem in isolation. Sophisticated, carefully controlled but with intense feeling underneath, written with panache and (in the end) with subtlety. It is a fine poem, and has much to offer the reader who knows nothing of time, place or author. But if we now turn to place it in a context, we shall find there is more to say.


First let us place it in the very general context of its form. It is a sonnet, and writing a sonnet is not an arbitrary thing to do. Why should a poem have fourteen lines rather than (say) thirteen or fifteen? There are two main answers to this question, which I will call the organic and the classical. The organic answer claims that poets have found forms naturally suited to what they want to say: the fact that for so many centuries European poets wrote in sonnets proves that there is something about that length well (or organically) suited to the sort of poem they were writing—love poems usually, sometimes political poems, sometimes (as here) explorations of a personal situation. Organic theories of form are often very useful but I think it is straining matters to apply them to the sonnet. Of course poets have made marvellous use of the fourteen lines length, but we should not underestimate their skill: if the conventional length had been thirteen or fifteen lines they would have devised ways to make equally marvellous use of that.

The obvious reason for writing a poem of fourteen lines is because other people have written them. This is not as banal as it sounds. By giving a name to the length, and constructing rules for the rhyme scheme, poets issue a challenge and an invitation: a challenge to solve the technical problems, an invitation to follow previous example. Each new poet who writes sonnets is accepting the invitation, and announcing that his poem belongs to an established tradition. The tradition began in Italy, above all with Dante and Petrarch, and later sonneteers are in one sense inviting comparison with their predecessors. Of course once the form is accepted for this classical reason—i.e. as a way of following earlier masters—the poet will use, and perhaps even devise, ways of fitting its form most effectively to what he has to say.

There have been two such ways developed, giving us two kinds of sonnet. The original Italian sonnets had the rhyme scheme ABBAABBA CDECDE. This is much tighter than the poem we have looked at, since the first two rhymes have to be used four times instead of twice; and it divides the poem into two parts of eight and six lines (the division is so well known that the terms octet and sestet have grown up). This is clearly a natural and convenient division, splitting the poem more or less into two halves—statement and counterstatement, problem and resolution, upward and downward movement—and the fact that the first part is longer is convenient too: to set forth our situation, to make some general statement about women, seems to need more space than the way out, or the ensuing compliment to a particular woman. And the tight rhyme-scheme of the octet had advantages too, since it gives a coherence and unitary force to the opening statement, after which the sestet can be briefer and more suggestive—so it is not surprising to learn that its rhymes CDE can be arranged in virtually any order.

This form of sonnet is known as the Petrarchan, and the best illustrations of it would obviously be in Italian. It was used by Sir Thomas Wyatt, one of the earliest English sonneteers, and by Sir Philip Sidney in the 1580s, but by the time sonnet-writing became a craze in the 1590s it had been replaced by the Shakespearean form, as it is called, of three quatrains and a couplet. Here is an example of the Petrarchan form in English.

> You that do search for every purling spring
> Which from the ribs of old Parnassus flows,
> And every flower, not sweet perhaps, which grows
> Near thereabouts, into your poesy wring;
> Ye that do dictionary's method bring
> Into your rimes, running in rattling rows;

You that poor Petrarch's long-deceased woes
With new-born sighs and denizen'd wit do sing;
You take wrong ways; those far-fet helps be such
As do bewray a want of inward touch,
And sure, at length, stol'n goods do come to light.
But if, both for your love and skill, your name
You seek to nurse at fullest breasts of Fame,
Stella behold, and then begin to indite.

This is no. 15 of Sidney's sonnet sequence *Astrophel and Stella*, and the subject as it happens is a favourite one with Sidney. Other poets can go in for learned allusions, classical or Italian predecessors, and overingenious verbal patterns, can use "dictionary's method" and write with the help of "denizened wit", i.e. naturalized but originally foreign wit. Such far-fetched aids to wiritng poetry are a sign that inward inspiration is missing; and would be quite unnecessary if the poets would simply look at Stella. The poem is partly a game, a self-refuting joke: Sidney himself is following in Petrarch's footsteps by writing this kind of sonnet, and he clearly enjoys showing us that he can himself perform the tricks he is condemning: attacks on ingenuity are in one way less sincere if ingeniously written, but in another way they are more genuine, for they actually perform the renunciation they assert.

It is clear that this poem falls inevitably into two parts; and the first, developing its contemptuous but ingenious description of the "denizened wit", ought to be the longer and more elaborate. The sestet has a much simpler statement to make, so its first three lines are used to make explicitly the reproach that was implictit in the octet: "you take wrong ways" sums up what we have just heard, and then we are given the reason in general terms. And having said that these tricks show "want of inward touch" it is easy and obvious to move to the compliment.

This is a poem about poetic method; not an exploration of personal emotion in the raw. There is as much sophistication in Sidney's technique as in "Why didst thou promise", but it is not brought to bear directly on a human situation in the same way. Perhaps what we feel most in the contrast is Sidney's lack of urgency. And it is also possible to feel (and this is the immediate point of the comparison) how different is the whole movement of the two poems because of their different patterning: eight plus six feels altogether different from four plus four plus four plus two. I have already tried to show how well the poem's development fits the series of parallel quatrains; and we can see the effect of the convention when we think of the final couplet. Could the poem seem complete after line twelve? Try reading the first twelve lines and stopping: does it seem that we have stopped in mid-air, or does it add up to a rounded whole that needs no more? I suggest that the answer will depend on how many sonnets we have read. For as far as content goes, the poem could be perfectly complete: there does not need to be either a genuine or an ironic reconciliation. But any reader familiar with sonnets knows that there had to be a final couplet, which has to sum up or in some way alter what has gone before, and the poem of course uses this expectation in making its final ironic admission. Poetic convention, we see, enables a poem to do things very economically.

But there is a more immediate context in which to put this poem. It is not only a sonnet, it is part of a sonnet sequence: it is no. 34 of a series of 154 poems all by Shakespeare that were published together in 1609. Let us put it where it appears to belong, and ask how far our reading of it is changed or enriched when we see it as part of that series.

And now we come up against scholarly problems. For Shakespeare's sonnets, though one of the greatest collections of poetry ever published, is also one of the most tantalizing. We do not know how far they were intended to be read through as a sequence; we do not know whether they were published with Shakespeare's consent, and therefore cannot be sure they are in the right order; we do not know whether they were written as a series, or at various times over a decade or more. If we put an individual stanza of (say) Shakespeare's narrative poem, *Venus and Adonis,* in the context of the whole, then of course it will take on more meaning; and in particular its place in the story will come clear. But this alas is not the case with the sonnets: somewhere behind them is a story of human entanglement and passion, but all we can get is scattered glimpses of this story. There are three main characters: the poet, who constantly refers to himself as old; a lovely boy, or young man, his social superior, whom he loves, whom he urges to marry, who neglects him, and to whom sonnet 34 is certainly addressed; and a woman, the poet's mistress, who is unfaithful to him, whom he loves with degrading intensity though he knows she is neither worthy of his love nor even beautiful —she's usually referred to by commentators as the Dark Lady, but the romantic associations of such a phrase are quite inappropriate, and "Black Woman" would be an apter label. And that is all we know. Attempts have been made to identify the lovely youth—the favourite

...didates are William Herbert, Earl of Pembroke, and Henry ...othesley, Earl of Southampton—but there is no conclusive ...ence, and even if we could know who he is we would be little the ... about the details of the story.

...ourse you should go on to read the rest of Shakespeare's ... —it will give you another 153 poems, all fine and some ...nt. But if we ask how much illumination they will cast on ... v far our experience of it will be enriched and clarified as it ... ve been by reading it in isolation, we may be disappointed. There ... ree things we shall learn, and perhaps no more. First we shall dis... (what we almost certainly would not have realized otherwise) that this poem is written to a man; so the offence committed against the poet cannot simply be sexual infidelity. Further, since he is young, handsome and almost certainly aristocratic, we can see an appropriateness in the comparison with the sun; and we may read the whole poem with a new level of awareness if we know about the social distance between them. Second, we may (but with some hesitation) make a guess at what the offence was—from sonnet 42 for instance.

> That thou hast her, it is not all my grief,  *a*
> And yet it may be said I loved her dearly;  *b*
> That she hath thee is of my wailing chief,  *a*
> A loss in love that touches me more nearly.  *b*
> Loving offenders, thus I will excuse ye,  *c*
> Thou dost love her, because thou know'st I love her,  *d*
> And for my sake even so doth she abuse me,  *c*
> Suff'ring my friend for my sake to approve her.  *d*
> If I lose thee, my loss is my love's gain,  *e*
> And losing her, my friend hath found that loss;  *f*
> Both find each other, and I lose both twain,  *e*
> And both for my sake lay on me this cross.  *f*
>   But here's the joy, my friend and I are one;  *g*
>   Sweet flattery, then she loves but me alone.  *g*

It's clear what has happened here: the young man has stolen the poet's girl. The poem is an ingenious piece of self-torture as he invents complicated explanations of why he does not really mind all that much. We have no way of knowing whether no. 42 is about the same episode as no. 34: if it is, we may read line ten a little differently, for in that case there really has been a "loss", the loss of the woman, and the phrase "I have still the loss" does not refer merely to the psychological damage of loss of trust in the youth. The prominence of the very same word in no. 42, where he plays on the ideas of loss and gain, and loss in love, may of course enrich our reading of no. 34 and render it more likely that the occasion is the same for both. And perhaps this is the time to mention the one textual problem in our poem. In the 1609 text, which is the only one we have, the last word of line twelve is "loss". This must surely be wrong: the rhyme word is not likely to be a mere repetition of the word it is rhyming with. The fact that the line as printed makes good sense is an argument in favour of it being corrupt, since it means that a fairly intelligent compositor, in a moment of carelessness, could repeat the previous rhyme word without noticing that he was making a mistake. "Cross" is the most obvious emendation, and it is reassuring to find the same pair of rhymes, in a similar situation, in no. 42. It seems to confirm both the emendation and the view that the poems refer to the same episode.

One further comment on the technique of no. 42 can lead into our third point. Poem 42 also makes use of the sonnet structure, by moving to a fresh kind of point in the final couplet. For twelve lines it teases out ingenious psychological excuses for the friend's treachery; then in the couplet it moves from the psychological to what we may call the metaphysical, not an exploration into motives and feelings but an ingenious idea—"my friend and I are one"—that yields a different and more artificial kind of justification. When we add to this the mention of "sweet flattery", it is natural to conclude that here too we have an irony, a deliberately perfunctory happy conclusion that is not intended to convince. If you felt sceptical at the claim that the last couplet of no. 34 is ironic, here is another piece of evidence: and as we read through the whole series we find several other such conclusions, all overstated, all a little too flamboyant, all excessively flattering conclusions to poems of rebuke. After we have felt their cumulative impression, we can no longer doubt them to be ironic.


That is all we can learn from the context of Shakespeare's sonnets as a whole; but there is, finally, a more immediate context. Though the order of the sonnets is at times uncertain, there is no doubt that there are groups of poems that quite obviously belong together, and are meant to be read in sequence. The first seventeen, for instance, appear to form such a group; and so do 33, 34 and 35. It is time to read them all together.

Full many a glorious morning have I seen
Flatter the mountain tops with sovereign eye,
Kissing with golden face the meadows green,
Gilding pale streams with heavenly alchemy;
Anon permit the basest clouds to ride
With ugly rack on his celestial face,
And from the forlorn world his visage hide,
Stealing unseen to west with this disgrace.
Even so my sun one early morn did shine,
With all triumphant splendour on my brow;
But out alack, he was but one hour mine,
The region cloud hath masked him from me now.
    Yet him for this my love no white disdaineth;
    Suns of the world may stain when heaven's sun
       staineth.

Why didst thou promise such a beauteous day,
And make me travel forth without my cloak,
To let base clouds o'ertake me in my way,
Hiding thy bravery in their rotten smoke?
'Tis not enough that through the cloud thou break,
To dry the rain on my storm-beaten face,
For no man well of such a salve can speak,
That heals the wound, and cures not the disgrace.
Nor can thy shame give physic to my grief;
Though thou repent, yet I have still the loss.
Th' offender's sorrow lends but weak relief
To him that bears the strong offence's cross.
    Ah but those tears are pearl which thy love sheds,
    And they are rich, and ransom all ill deeds.

No more be grieved at that which thou hast done:
Roses have thorns, and silver fountains mud,
Clouds and eclipses stain both moon and sun,
And loathsome canker lives in sweetest bud.
All men make faults, and even I in this,
Authorizing thy trespass with compare,
Myself corrupting, salving thy amiss,
Excusing thy sins more than thy sins are;
For to thy sensual fault I bring in sense—
Thy adverse party is thy advocate—
And 'gainst myself a lawful plea commence.
Such civil war is in my love and hate,
    That I an accessory needs must be
    To that sweet thief which sourly robs from me.

It is immediately clear that all three poems refer to the same episode; and the fact that we are nowhere told what it is suggests that the poet did not mean us to know—that this bit of universalizing was deliberate, and the effect of the poems depends on their exploration of the betrayal—repentance—resentment situation, not on the narrative basis.

The episode is the same, the poems differ slightly. The first is the simplest: a pure lament for the fact that the young man is "stained", and then a final couplet (in which there seems no trace of irony) asserting that the poet's love for him is undiminished. The second, as we have seen, tells us that the offence was followed by repentance, but that the damage remains: it is more concerned with the poet's response to the meanness, and it is more bitter in tone. And the third continues this progression: attention has now shifted even more from the young man to the poet, and it is a dark, even savage poem of self-examination. Only the first quatrain tells us of the youth's fault, and in language that seems to hold far more resentment and intensity of feeling than anything in no. 33: "loathsome canker lives in sweetest bud." In the second quatrain he suggests that his own conduct is as bad as that of the young man, because of the complicated deceptions with which he justified him, and these deceptions are spelt out in the third quatrain, and summed up in the final couplet, in which with resigned emphasis brought out in the word-play ("sweet . . . sourly") he concludes that the pair of them are in the same plight. There is then a double movement through the three poems: the feeling grows more bitter and the emphasis more and more shifts to include the poet as well as his friend. It is clear that they form not only a group but a carefully unified group.

And there is also a unity of stylistic development. The shift we have already remarked on, from imagery to analytical language, extends over all three poems too, and no. 34 holds a pivotal position. The implicit comparison with the sun is, in the first poem, completely explicit. We start with eight lines of pure nature-poetry, a magnificent poem about the unreliability of the English weather— full of moral terms ("basest", "disgrace"), but in a way that suggests they are merely high-spirited metaphors for the spoiling of the weather. Then in the third quatrian comes the comparison with "my sun" and that too is developed in terms of the same image: he shows and has gone behind the cloud. All that the final couplet has to do is assert the analogy: "suns of the world may stain when heaven's sun staineth.'

It is a shameless use of argument by analogy. The pardon extended in the couplet is based on nothing more than the fact that he has compared his friend with the sun. The more magnificent the nature poetry, the greater is the effrontery with which the poet can make that final assertion. There is a kind of bravura in this poem: he is dazzling us with how brilliantly he can write, and then calmly concluding that because he has drawn the comparison so brilliantly, his friend's fault is excused. As if he was saying, "Look what I can get away with, because I'm such a good poet."

We might not feel this if we had only no. 33: but when we look at the three together, it becomes steadily clearer. For each of them uses less imagery and more argument, and at the same time offers less forgiveness, than the one before: the stylistic movement corresponds to the psychological movement. There is no irony in the final couplet of no. 33, because its bold assertion is to be undermined by what follows. And now if we look at the third poem, we see how well it fits into this scheme. This time there is only one quatrain of imagery and even that is not the single extended image of the sun, but a series of miscellaneous comparisons. Purely moral and psychological terms are used in the second quatrain to say that he is himself to blame in the way he excuses the friend, and then in the third quatrain he actually talks about the writing of the poems: "for to thy sensual fault I bring in sense." ("Sensual", incidentally, suggests that we were right in suggesting that the fault may have been stealing the poet's girl.) "Sense" is ambiguous here. Most obvious it means intellect, and refers to the ingenuity with which he is defending his friend—even in this very line, and the next, with their careful word-play. But in the first poem, he did not really use cleverness to defend the youth, but description and analogy— something more like "sense" in the meaning of "the senses". At the very point of apologizing for his word-play, Shakespeare is using it with special skill.

We have hardly begun to taste the richness of Shakespeare's sonnets. Not only are there dozens of other poems as fine as these three (though perhaps none finer), there are also so many kinds of poems in the series—poems of simple golden eloquence in praise of the young man's beauty and charm (for instance nos. 17 and 18), moving general laments on some of the great traditional themes of lyric poetry, time and death (nos 60, 63, 64, 65), explorations of the complicated personal relationship between the two men (not only these three, but also 87, 88 and 89), and the painful but marvellous group of poems about the emotional degradation of his love for the black woman (nos 127–52). To read Shakespeare's sonnets with full awareness and response is not only to see what can be done with the English language and with the sonnet form; it is to live a lifetime's experience, and emerge at the end moved, sadder and wiser.

## 3

# The Lie

Go, Soul, the body's guest,
Upon a thankless arrant:
Fear not to touch the best;
The truth shall be thy warrant:
Go, since I needs must die,
And give the world the lie.

Say to the court, it glows
And shines like rotten wood;
Say to the church, it shows
What's good, and doth no good:
If church and court reply,
Then give them both the lie.

Tell potentates, they live
Acting by others' action;
Not loved unless they give,
Not strong but by a faction:
If potentates reply,
Give potentates the lie.

Tell men of high condition,
That manage the estate,
Their purpose is ambition,
Their practice only hate:
And if they once reply,
Then give them all the lie.

Tell them that brave it most
They beg for more by spending,
Who, in their greatest cost,
Seek nothing but commending:
And if they make reply,
Then give them all the lie.

Tell zeal it wants devotion;
Tell love it is but lust:
Tell time it is but motion;
Tell flesh it is but dust:
And wish them not reply,
For thou must give the lie.

Tell age it daily wasteth;
Tell honour how it alters;
Tell beauty how she blasteth;
Tell favour how it falters:
And as they shall reply,
Give every one the lie.


Tell wit how much it wrangles
In tickle points of niceness;
Tell wisdom she entangles
Herself in over-wiseness:
And when they do reply,
Straight give them both the lie


Tell physic of her boldness;
Tell skill it is pretension;
Tell charity of coldness;
Tell law it is contention:
And as they do reply,
So give them still the lie.


Tell fortune of her blindness;
Tell nature of decay;
Tell friendship of unkindness;
Tell justice of delay:
And if they will reply,
Then give them all the lie.


Tell arts they have no soundness,
But vary by esteeming;
Tell schools they want profoundness,
And stand too much on seeming:
If arts and schools reply,
Give arts and schools the lie.


Tell faith it's fled the city;
Tell how the country erreth;
Tell manhood shakes off pity
And virtue least preferreth:
And if they do reply,
Spare not to give the lie.

> So when thou hast, as I
> Commanded thee, done blabbing
> —Although to give the lie
> Deserves no less than stabbing—
> Stab at thee he that will,
> No stab the soul can kill.
>
> *Sir Walter Raleigh*    (*about 1596*)

Who is this poem denouncing? The obvious answer is everyone, as stanza after stanza sweeps through one institution after another, lashing out at each in turn. But before the cumulative effect mounts up so remorselessly, we have already been given an impression that it is, above all, attacking those in authority. "Fear not to touch the best," the soul is assured in the very first stanza, and the next few are clearly directed at "the best"—courtiers and churchmen, potentates, men of high condition, those who dress extravagantly. The attack is on the centres of power and the official models of conduct.

In Elizabethan England this chiefly meant the court. The monarchy was the centre not only of political power but also of culture. Under a variety of idealizing names—Cynthia and Gloriana were the favourites—the Queen's praises were sung by every poet interested in success: a cult of what can almost be called queen-worship was widespread and officially encouraged. Spenser's huge unfinished elaborate epic *The Faerie Queene* refers constantly to the court of Gloriana, that was no doubt going to be the setting of its last book, and on one of the poem's various levels of allegory Gloriana is certainly Queen Elizabeth. The Queen's appetite for flattery was immense; the path to political advancement was to go to court; and a wealth of poetic eloquence celebrated the divine influence of the monarch. Some of this eloquence came from Raleigh himself:

> Praised be Diana's fair and harmless light . . .

> Praised be her nymphs, with whom she decks the woods,
>     Praised be her knights, in whom true honour lives,
> Praised be that force, by which she moves the floods;
>     Let that Diana shine, which all these gives. . . .

No contemporary reader would have failed to think of the Queen on reading such lines; and Raleigh's long strange fragment *The Ocean to Cynthia* flatters in language that sounds more like a lover than a courtier:

> What storms so great but Cynthia's beams appeased?
> What rage so fierce, that love could not allay?

In such a world, if you turned away from society in anger and distaste, as *The Lie* is clearly doing, you would naturally denounce the court. We know that Raleigh was one of the most ambitious and ostentatious men of his time, and that he fell into disgrace for marrying one of the Queen's ladies-in-waiting without permission. He spent some time in the Tower, and since we also know that this poem was written about 1596, the time of these events, it is tempting to read it biographically, as the complaint of a courtier who has fallen from grace and turned in bitterness on the court where he once shone. This may well be a true account of how the poem originated: we do not know. But in order to understand it, there is no need to bring in Raleigh's life, for Elizabethan poetry is full of angry writing like this. Raleigh's friend Spenser wrote very bitterly about the envy and backbiting of courtiers in *Colin Clout's Come Home Again,* a poem which was, as it happens, dedicated to Raleigh:

> Where each one seeks with malice and with strife,
> To thrust down other into foul disgrace,
> Himself to raise . . .
> Either by slandering his well-deeméd name,
> Through leasings lewd and feignéd forgery;
> Or else by breeding him some blot of blame,
> By creeping close into his secrecy. . . .

As it happens, these lines too have a biographical origin—Spenser returned from Ireland to go to court in 1589, and left a disappointed man: but if we turn to a play we are unlikely to find any reference to the life of the author (and this play is by an author of whom we know nothing):

> It will confirm me bold—the child o' the court;
> Let blushes dwell i' the country. Impudence!
> Thou goddess of the palace, mistress of mistresses,
> To whom the costly perfumed people pray,
> Strike thou my forehead into dauntless marble,
> Mine eyes to steady sapphires. Turn my visage;
> And, if I needs must glow, let me blush inward,

> That this immodest season may not spy
> That scholar in my cheeks, fool bashfulness—
> That maid in the old time, whose flush of grace
> Would never suffer her to get good clothes.
> Our maids are wiser, and are less ashamed;
> Save Grace the bawd, I seldom hear grace named.

This extraordinary passage is spoken by Vendice, the central character of Tourneur's brilliantly sardonic play *The Revenger's Tragedy:* Vendice is putting on a disguise to go to court, and ironically announces that he will need to take on a correspondingly impudent attitude in order to feel at home in such a world of depravity. With deliberately exaggerated rhetoric—"Strike thou my forehead into dauntless marble"—he strikes a posture of boldness, dramatizing his own action, as characters in Elizabethan plays so often do; and then indulges in verbal ingenuities to mock at his own new wickedness —"let me blush inward", he says, and puns on the term "grace". What emerges from the speech is that "going to court" is an experience in which one takes a savage, self-punishing delight: it is like accepting human wickedness. The idea of court is central to this play—corruption is sophisticated, the corrupt community is small, wealthy, inward-looking; but there is a constant hint that to show up the court is to show up the depravity of human nature.

If we think of *The Lie* against this background, several things become clearer—or rather, since the poem is not obscure, we should say they take on a fuller significance. The poem begins with an attack on authority, and one of its most brilliant images, right at the beginning, is directed at the court:

> Say to the court it glows
> And shines like rotten wood . . .

—an image that Vendice might easily have used; but then as it continues we see that the poet is attacking *everything*. Hence the relentless hammer-blows as he goes through all the professions: "wit", "wisdom", "physic" are not abstract qualities but ways in which men behave—poets, scholars, doctors. We can see that an attack on every institution, by an Elizabethan poet, needs to begin with an attack on the court: one must work from the centre outwards.

The most likely contemporary term for this kind of poem was "complaint"—not used in quite its modern sense, but suggesting something more like "lament": a complaint does not imply that the poet is complaining to anyone, simply that he is setting forth the distress of his situation. A Complaint as all-embracing as this one, in which the condemnation is total, enjoys a great rhetorical advantage over a more moderate or qualified one, as we can see by looking at an anonymous poem which was written as an answer to Raleigh's. It is not really memorable enough to quote in full, but here are a few stanzas:

> Confess, in glittering court
> All are not gold that shine;
> Yet say one pearl and much fine gold
> Grows in that Prince's mind.

> Confess, that many leaves
> Do overgrow the ground;
> Yet say within the field of God
> Good corn is to be found.

> Confess, some judge unjust
> The widow's right delay;
> Yet say there are some Samuels
> That never say her nay.

> Admit some man of state
> Do pitch his thoughts too high;
> Is that a rule for all the rest
> Their loyal hearts to try?

> Your wits are in the wane,
> Your autumn in the bud;
> You argue from particulars,
> Your reason is not good.

How much more reasonable than Raleigh's poem! How full of good sense, how balanced and sober—how much *truer* than *The Lie*! Some people are corrupt, some are honest; not every judge is unjust, not every man of state is overambitious. The speaker of this poem is a sensible man who does not lose his head: but good sense does not produce poetic fire, and these stanzas have none of the cumulative intensity, the eloquent passion, that drives *The Lie* so remorselessly forward. And so in the last stanza quoted above we have what sounds like the judicious man's comment on poetry itself. If your aim is a social survey or a balanced view of human nature, you will not "argue from particulars", that is, generalize from vivid cases that may not be typical: but the aim of *The Lie* is rather to express a white heat of anger with mounting intensity.

The poem, then, offers us a total condemnation of human institutions. Now in the later twentieth century we are used to such condemnations: we live in a sick society, we ought to reject the establishment—or the "system"—totally: it is a familiar cry in the 1970s. To understand such a cry we need to draw distinctions, for there is more than one kind of total indictment. I suggest there are three kinds, which I will call nihilistic, radical and religious.

The nihilistic implies no contrasting values, takes up no standpoint from which human institutions are judged and found wanting. It does not condemn man's activities for failing to reach some desired standard, it condemns human effort itself. It says, for instance,

> Tomorrow and tomorrow and tomorrow
> Creeps in this petty pace from day to day . . .

and it compares life to
>                                 a tale
> Told by an idiot, full of sound and fury,
> Signifying nothing.

It is a common note in modern literature, an expression of revulsion or disgust, of a complete alienation from human achievement—a terrible state to find oneself in, so that the true poetry of despair, like Macbeth's, is some of the most powerful and frightening ever written. But it is also a state which is easy to adopt as a pose, so that superficially held nihilism results in a slick and easy rejection that may produce nothing but irritation in the reader.

The radical rejection is socially based. It condemns society for being wrongly organized, and it implies (it may explicitly state) a revolutionary programme for destroying the old society and replacing it with a new one. If it is Marxist in its basis, it will show how every institution in our society serves the function of keeping the possessing class in power, and will propose a classless society in which this ideological function will no longer taint every activity. Whatever its basis, it will stress the interrelatedness of our institutions, how they all support one another and the status quo, and how they all serve the function of oppression. What makes its basis social is its belief that a better—and utterly different—form of society is possible. It implied goal is revolution.

Now it is surely clear that Raleigh's poem is neither nihilistic nor radical. It expresses anger as well as despair, it castigates with a fervour the very reverse of Macbeth's quiet terrible hopelessness. But it offers no hint of another and better social order: for its standards are not of this world. This point is quite explicit in the first stanza: it is the soul who is to give the world the lie, and the reason for this is that "I needs must die"—death forces on us the possibility of another vantage point from which to judge the world and find it wanting. This other-worldliness, suggested to us in the first stanza, then retreats into the background until it is reaffirmed in the final couplet: the soul's judgement will endure. The condemnation has a religious basis, as has that in *The Revenger's Tragedy,* whose sardonic snarl, like the fiery anger of *The Lie,* describes the corruption of court in a way that hints at a criterion above and beyond the human. After a brilliantly gruesome passage on incest ("O Dutch lust! fulsome lust!") Vendice says mockingly:

> O hour of incest!
> Any kin now, next to the rim o' the sister,
> Is men's meat in these days; and in the morning
> When they are up and dressed, and their masks on,
> Who can perceive this, save that eternal eye
> That sees through flesh and all?

The traditional term for this kind of poetry is *Contemptus mundi*— the despising of the world: the phrase implies a religious standpoint. We can see that it yields a powerful kind of eloquence; and I want to suggest that this kind of complaint has an enormous advantage over the radical condemnation. For to adopt a criterion that is ultimately social makes total condemnation illogical: to denounce "the system" in a way that leads to the despising of all human institutions removes the very basis of one's condemnation. If for instance one finds a class bias in the education system, this ought not to lead the radical to say that education must be wholly condemned, for that would mean condemning teaching people to read or count or (even) criticize institutions; it would mean condemning the very processes of socialization that make us members of one another and able to judge our particular society. Radical criticism of society, being socially based, cannot in consistency be total: and if it launches into the eloquence of Complaint it is too obviously being swept into exaggerated verbal gestures. We will say that if it argues from particulars, its reason is not good. *Contemptus mundi,* on the other hand, is total by its very nature: it is being consistent with itself when it sets out to "give the world the lie".

So far I have spoken of the purpose of the poem, and tried to measure that against other similar purposes; now let us turn from purpose to execution, and look at the poem's technique, at its structure and language.

Both these are very simple. The poem is formal, repetitive, direct. It thrusts powerfully forward in a straight line, not pausing for subtlety or elaboration, building up a series of insistent, parallel stanzas. The refrain varies, often very effectively, but what is most important is that there is a refrain: we recognize the inevitable recurrence of "then give them all the lie" as if it was a fist pounding the table after each fresh example. The poem has no richness of language, no lines packed with complex meaning or fraught with haunting suggestiveness: not even the satiric complexity of Vendice's "let me blush inward", nor the enormously moving resonance of "Life's but a walking shadow, a poor player". So perhaps I need to say explicitly that this does not prevent it from being poetry. We are here presented with a different kind of power from the resonance of Shakespeare or the brilliance of Tourneur—more direct and more rhetorical.

Not only is it not rich, it is not spontaneous: there are effective rhetorical tricks deployed, for the poem is written with careful art—as almost all Elizabethan poems were. A contemporary reader could have named a number of its verbal devices, and though we no longer employ the Latin and Greek terminology of the rhetorical books—no longer refer to such figures of speech as zeugma, proplepsis or catachresis—we can still recognize the effects of parallelism and contrast that are omnipresent in the poem. To the modern reader, such deliberate craftsmanship often suggests a lack of inspiration, for since the Romantics we have tended to assume that the poet who is swept away by emotion will not stop to polish. The Elizabethans believed in inspiration, but they did not see it as sweeping aside one's verbal skills: for rhetorical devices were, after all, simply a systematization of the way feeling naturally manipulated language. This point is one of the main stumbling blocks for the modern reader of poetry in coming to terms with Elizabethan poetic theory: we may respond to the beauty of an Elizabethan lyric, but find it hard to accept that it was written with such a conscious use of figures of speech as contemporary critics often seem to assume. The term "artificial", always derogatory in our vocabulary, was more likely to be a term of praise to the Elizabethan critic.

Clearly what is involved here is the relationship between technique and inspiration, and it is not an easy question to resolve in every age. But we can say that the issue is less urgent for a poem like *The Lie* than for the more purely lyrical, for whereas love and delight do seem to lose something of their immediacy when carefully expressed, anger and indignation can only gain by it. Anger is a mere splutter, condemnation a mere growl of dislike, if they are not expressed in deliberate, steady, mounting units: parallelism and contrast seem to add to the intensity of these emotions.

Let us look to the other extreme: Complaints that lack all strictness of form. D H Lawrence offers us a good example, for what is perhaps his most famous book of poems (though certainly not his best, in my view) contains a series of angry meditations in totally free verse. The book is called *Pansies* (a play on the French *pensée*, meaning "thought" as well as "pansy"), and since I am quoting it as a foil to show up the excellence of *The Lie* it seems only fair to Lawrence—and my readers —to quote a short poem. This one in fact is taken from the posthumous collection, *More Pansies*, and was not published in Lawrence's lifetime:

### Vengeance is Mine

Vengeance is mine, saith the Lord, I will repay.
And the stiff-necked people, and the self-willed people, and
    self-important ones, the self-righteous, self-absorbed
all of them who wind their energy round the idea of themselves
and so strangle off their connection with the ceaseless tree of
    life,
and fall into sharp, self-centred self-assertion, sharp or soft,
they fall victim at once to the vengeance of the unforgiving god
as their nerves are stretched till they twangle and snap
and irritation seethes secretly through their guts, as their
    tissue disintegrates
and flames of katabolistic energy alternate
with ashes of utter boredom, ennui and disgust.

It is the vengeance of the Lord, long and unremitting
till the soul of the stiff-necked is ground to dust, to fertilising
    meal
with which to manure afresh the roots of the tree of life.
And so the Lord of Vengeance pays back, repays life
for the defection of the self-centred ones.

In a way this poem has an immediate appeal; but I believe it is an appeal we soon tire of. It is a poem of anger with the stiff-necked people, and the framework of references to God does not represent a true *contemptus mundi*, for Lawrence is identifying God with his own anger: it is an attack on a particular kind of person whom the poet dislikes, not on the world. Each line represents a new unit of thought, and their irregularity shows that the poem is intended to be a direct transcript of how the feeling wells up in the speaker. This means that none of the compelling, inevitable movement of *The Lie* is possible, none of the effect of controlled power. No doubt Lawrence would admit this: in choosing to use free verse he sacrificed the effects that strict form makes possible, hoping this would be compensated for by a certain immediacy and freshness. In the case of a love poem, or a lyric of joy, this might happen: different readers will feel differently on that point. But in a Complaint it never seems to happen, for freshness and spontaneity so easily degenerate then into mere abuse. It is surely no accident that Lawrence's poem piles up insults in cliché as if it wasn't able to stop ("self-important, self-righteous, self-absorbed"), that it clumsily repeats the same verbal point ("self-centred self-assertion": repetition, so powerful when in tight form, can be so flabby when simply poured out), that it retreats into awkwardly private terminology, as if showing off ("katabolistic energy"), and ends the paragraph on a mere string of well-known abstractions. It is the voice of an ordinary man voicing ordinary insults.

In contrast to this, here is another Elizabethan Complaint that uses strict form to increase the emotional impact, that deploys rhetorical devices with powerful results:

> Tired with all these, for restful death I cry,
> As to behold desert a beggar born,
> And needy nothing trimmed in jollity,
> And purest faith unhappily forsworn,
> And gilded honour shamefully misplaced,
> And maiden virtue rudely strumpeted,
> And right perfection wrongfully disgraced,
> And strength by limping sway disabléd,
> And art made tongue-tied by authority,
> And folly, doctor-like, controlling skill,
> And simple truth miscalled simplicity,
> And captive good attending captain ill.
> > Tired with all these, from these would I be gone,
> > Save that to die, I leave my love alone.

In this sonnet, Shakespeare uses figures of speech that are easily recognizable, including puns ("captive good attending captain ill"), carefully balanced verbal contrasts ("Maiden virtue rudely strumpeted"), alliteration and above all a parallelism as relentless as Raleigh's: but the result, as one gets to know the poem, is an intensity of feeling, even of personal involvement, far greater than the crude anger of Lawrence—so great in fact that to many readers the final complimentary couplet seems a weak addition, and the poem's final impact is that of pure Complaint.

So much for the advantages of rhetorical control. In conclusion, however, we must pay more attention to the individuality of *The Lie*, which is after all exceptional among Elizabethan Complaints in its power. Rhetorical style can be used to greater or lesser effect, and we have not yet looked at the full brilliance of Raleigh's strategies. To do this, let us take a more run-of-the-mill poem to put next to it. An anonymous poem in *Tottel's Miscellany* (an anthology published in 1557) is close enough to *The Lie* for the comparison to be fruitful. Once again, I shall not quote the whole poem. It is called *Totus Mundus in Maligno Positus:*

> Complain we may: much is amiss:
> Hope is nigh gone to have redress:
> These days be ill, nothing sure is:
> Kind heart is wrapped in heaviness.
>
> The stern is broke: the sail is rent:
> The ship is given to wind and wave:
> All help is gone: the rock present.
> That will be lost, what man can save?
>
> Learning is lewd, and held a fool:
> Wisdom is shent, counted to rail:
> Reason is banished out of school
> The blind is bold, and words prevail.
>
> Wily is witty: brainsick is wise:
> Truth is folly: and might is right:
> Words are reason: and reason is lies:
> The bad is good: darkness is light.
>
> Wrong to redress, wisdom dare not.
> Hardy is happy, and ruleth most.
> Wilful is witless, and careth not,
> Which end go first, till all be lost.

> With floods and storms thus we be tost,
> Awake good Lord, to thee we cry.
> Our ship is almost sunk and lost.
> Thy mercy help our misery.
>
> Man's strength is weak: man's wit is dull:
> Man's reason is blind. These things t'amend,
> Thy hand (O Lord) of might is full
> Awake betime, and help us send.
>
> In thee we trust, and in no wight;
> Save us as chickens under the hen.
> Our crookedness thou canst make right,
> Glory to thee for aye. Amen.

This is not a worthless poem. It has a certain epigrammatic neatness, as in the third stanza quoted, where after three parallel complaints on what the abstract nouns represent, it shifts in the fourth line, and instead of beginning with the abstraction which is spurned it begins with the concrete ("the blind") which is doing the damage: that makes an effective climax. But in some stanzas this neatness is ruined by sheer incompetence, as in the limping lines that conclude stanza two, where "present" has to be mispronounced even for approximate scanning, and the balance of the fourth line is only achieved by the clumsy compression of "that which is sure to be lost" into "that will be lost". Once or twice it has a verbal bite that is more than neat, as in "Wily is witty: brainsick is wise"—surely the best line in the poem. The alliteration gives the effect of a proverb, and to the Elizabethan reader "Wily" might have suggested the name of the Vice figure in a morality play as well as functioning as an adjective; and there is verbal liveliness in the play of "brainsick" against "wise". But the poet could not leave well alone, and "Wilful is witless" plays the same verbal trick again, to less effect. And finally, the last stanzas are merely clumsy in their piety, and the explicitness with which they state the religious basis of the poem throws up by contrast the force of Raleigh's restraint.

By seeing what this poet failed to do, we can see very clearly what Raleigh did. It is not only his polish, his steady level of technical competence, that marks him out: it is above all his discovery of a unifying device. His poem forms a coherent whole, as *Totus Mundus* does not, and what holds it together is stated in the title. To give someone the lie—it is essential to realize this—is to accuse him of lying, and in the world of the court, where honour is so important, this is to insult him and perhaps to find yourself challenged to a duel. Readers of *As You Like It* will remember Touchstone's elaborate joke on the seven methods of giving the lie, a parody of the courtier's insistence on his own honour. Since the soul is being sent forth to give everyone the lie, it is behaving like an ill-bred courtier, flaunting the rules of honourable behaviour. The truth shall be the soul's warrant—for it has no ordinary warrant, no reason acceptable to court etiquette, for delivering all these insults. There is a constant suggestion, never wholly absent from the refrain, of the impudence of the soul, as it walks through the world insulting everyone: the sense of mounting outrage should emerge from the emphasis of the lines "Give *every one* the lie", "Then give them *all* the lie." And in the last two stanzas this unifying idea issues in one or two brilliant details that show us that the poem is not so completely lacking in verbal subtleties as I suggested earlier. The first is the use of "tell": in normal usage, this verb always has an indirect object, as it does all through the poem ("Tell potentates", "tell zeal", "tell fortune")—until the penultimate stanza, when it is suddenly used absolutely:

> Tell, how the country erreth;
> Tell manhood shakes off pity
> And virtue least preferreth . . .

Though not unknown, this construction is unusual. Instead of telling its message *to* someone, the soul is now simply "telling" it— to the world at large. It is as if it has finally been swept away by its zeal, and is now shouting its words without even stopping to secure a hearer. Ill-breeding has gone to an extreme. And the transition to this final boorishness shows great verbal skill, for the first use of the absolute "tell" *is* idiomatic ("tell how"), thus leading us more plausibly into the next two lines with their touch of verbal outrage.

And then, finally, in the last stanza the underlying device emerges to the surface again, and the soul is told that it is misbehaving. It has been blabbing—uttering secrets—and so it "deserves no less than stabbing". This ironic line is completely in the vocabulary of honour. The stabbing is probably to be done in a duel, and the soul "deserves" to be challenged because it has offended against court etiquette. It is from this terminology that the final couplet emerges with a clear reminder that the soul is able to behave so badly because its appeal lies elsewhere, not in this world at all. The religious basis of the Complaint, that grows so explicit at the end, has been implicitly present all through: the poem's very conception is a rejection of the court and all its ways.

# 4

# The Dream

Dear love, for nothing less than thee
Would I have broke this happy dream.
     It was a theme
For reason, much too strong for fantasy,
   Therefore thou wakdst me wisely; yet
My dream thou brok'st not, but continuedst it;
Thou art so truth, that thoughts of thee suffice
To make dreams truths; and fables histories;
Enter these arms, for since thou thoughtst it best,
Not to dream all my dream, let's act the rest.

   As lightning, or a taper's light,
Thine eyes, and not thy noise waked me;
     Yet I thought thee
(For thou lov'st truth) an angel, at first sight,
   But when I saw thou saw'st my heart,
And knew'st my thoughts, beyond an angel's art,
When thou knew'st what I dreamt, when thou knew'st when
Excess of joy would wake me, and cam'st then,
I do confess it could not choose but be
Profane, to think thee anything but thee.

   Coming and staying showed thee, thee,
   But rising makes me doubt, that now,
     Thou art not thou.
That love is weak, where fear's as strong as he;
'Tis not all spirit, pure, and brave,
If mixture it of fear, shame, honour, have.
Perchance as torches, which must ready be,
Men light and put out, so thou deal'st with me,
Thou cam'st to kindle, goest to come; then I
Will dream that hope again, but else would die.

               *John Donne*   (*about 1603*)

The poet has been asleep, dreaming of his mistress: waking, he finds
her there. The poem consists of what he then says to her, his delight
at her presence, his reflections on the relation of dreaming to reality,

his praise of her for coming, his regret when she leaves. It is an intricate, at times highly intellectual argument: so we ought to start by establishing just what it is saying.

Nothing could have woken him from his "happy dream" except her presence, because the dream was so strong. Waking life is governed by the reason, which deals in truths; dreams and fables come from an inferior scource, the fantasy; so to pay an extravagant compliment to the lady, the poet reverses this piece of conventional psychology, claiming that to dream of her is "a theme/For reason, much too strong for fantasy". She has so much truth in her, that her presence even in dream or fable converts it to something more like reality. Therefore it was appropriate for her to wake him: he was virtually in the realm of reality already, now he actually is, and finds her there. The last two lines of the stanza are clearly a sexual invitation: the dream appears to have been an erotic one, and if she enters his arms he can continue it in fact.

The second stanza begins with reflections on the waking. It was the light of her eyes that woke him: a straightforward compliment. Then comes a complicated thought. Because she loves truth, he must tell her what he thought at the sight of her: that she was an angel. But then he realized that she must have known his thoughts, since she not only knew that he was dreaming of her, but knew when "excess of joy would wake" him (a new explanation now of why he woke, not her bright eyes but the dream itself!); and having realized this

> I do confess, it could not choose but be
> Profane, to think thee anything but thee.

It is important to understand what these lines are suggesting. Angels cannot read our thoughts, for they lack the power: only God can do this. It was undervaluing her to compare her with an angel; he now realizes that the comparison should have been with God himself.

The third stanza appears to be a response to her saying that she must go now or else she will be caught with him. This makes it clear that they are not married: fear, shame and honour cause her to leave. For this he rebukes her, suggesting that she is not as great as he had thought: "thou art not thou." But in the last four lines he contrives to comfort himself with an analogy drawn from practical knowledge. In one of his sermons, Donne observes "as a torch that hath been lighted and used before is easier lighted than a new torch"—it was clearly a bit of knowledge that had stuck in his mind as useful for analogies, and here the analogy seems to be sexual: he is the torch, and she has aroused and put out his desire so that he is more easily aroused when she next comes. That thought reassures him that she intends to come back, so he will dream of her again— "but else would die". If we accept that "die" in Elizabethan times had the slang meaning of having sexual intercourse, those last four words may hold a kind of threat.

That then is the poem's argument; and by setting it forth at such length I have already indicated its most striking quality as a love-lyric. This is the quality that Donne's admiring contemporaries praise as wit, and that later ages, after a change of taste, condemned as false wit. "He affects the metaphysics," complained Dryden, "not only in his satires, but in his amorous verses, where nature only should reign; and perplexes the minds of the fair sex with nice speculations of philosophy, when he should entertain and soothe them with the blandishments of love." This is the origin of the label "metaphysical" now generally applied to Donne and his followers, and clearly Dryden's view of what a love-lyric should be is something altogether more direct, simple and attractive. There are plenty of such lyrics in Elizabethan poetry: here is one among hundreds:

> Come, O! come, my life's delight,
>     Let me not in langour pine.
> Love loves no delay; thy sight
>     The more enjoyed the more divine.
> O! come, and take from me
> The pain of being deprived of thee.
>
> Thou all sweetness dost enclose,
>     Like a little world of bliss.
> Beauty guards thy looks. The rose
>     In them pure and eternal is.
> Come then and make thy flight
> As swift to me as heavenly light.
>                                    *Thomas Campion*

In this poem (almost exactly contemporary with Donne's) there is nothing to perplex the minds of the fair sex. The melodiousness and regularity of its rhythm are appropriate to a poem meant to be sung; its emotional pattern is simple—a direct appeal for love; its compliments are uncomplicated, and the most memorable lines are those of dignified general praise:

> Beauty guards thy looks. The rose
>     In them pure and eternal is.

In only one respect can Donne's poem be called more direct than Campion's, the fact that he is more openly sexual. He on the other hand does not trouble to praise the lady's beauty; and in comparison to the Campion we see how intricately, even ingeniously argumentative his poem is. Look at the skill with which the first stanza uses the distinction between reason and fantasy to pay a compliment. We can match this in other poems of Donne—in *The Second Anniversary*, for instance, his extraordinary poem of extravagant compliment to the dead daughter of his patron Sir Robert Drury:

> Her pure and eloquent blood
> Spoke in her cheeks, and so distinctly wrought,
> That one might almost say, her body thought.

The human being consists of mind and body: blushing is an act of the body, thinking an act of the mind, and acts of the mind are purer, and take place on a higher level of being. That is mere orthodox Christian belief; and Donne plays with it in order to make a compliment. If you want to show how much purer Elizabeth Drury was than other women, you can do it by suggesting that bodily functions in her are as pure as mental functions in others, so that her blushing is like thinking. It is the same kind of upsetting of the hierarchy of categories as the suggestion that his lady, by appearing in a dream, turns it to reality.

Or look at the second stanza which uses, as you may have noticed, an idea also used by Campion. The comparison between love and religion is old and often used, and Campion is referring to it when (in quite conventional language) he speaks of the sight of his lady as "divine" and compares her coming to "heavenly light". This draws on the familiar comparison in an almost automatic way; whereas Donne's is both more outrageous and more subtle. It is more outrageous because he offers what is really a blasphemous comparison: the lady is compared to God himself, in a stanza that carefully works its way up through a lower comparison (she is an angel) to this shocking climax. But it is more subtle because he never brings it into the open: he relies on his reader's knowledge that only God knows our thoughts. If you do not know this, you may not see the point. The tone of those last two lines is very carefully controlled. They make it clear that the climax of the whole intricate stanza is now coming, first by the preliminary "I do confess", then by the elaborate idiom "it could not choose but be", with heavy stress on "choose", as a more emphatic way of saying "it would certainly be"; finally by the skilfully placed "profane". The knowing reader realizes what is coming—and then it does not come: with a smile, the poet ends the stanza with words that could contain the blasphemous meaning, or could be an innocent compliment.

We could learn a good deal about changing poetic taste in England by asking which ages have preferred Campion and which Donne; for the choice between them reveals contrasting conceptions of lyric poetry. For Dryden, what mattered was that a lyric should be as lyrical as possible: it should be as immediately attractive as the lady no doubt is (or has to be told she is); it should be the direct expression of emotions like joy and longing, or direct and delighted praise. The reader who prefers Donne will believe that thought can enrich such emotions; that to pause and explore analogies, to use one's learning or one's ingenuity, to intellectualize, is not necessarily to abandon emotion for mere cleverness. Certainly there is plenty of mere cleverness in Donne's poetry, especially in the weaker poems, and in many of his followers, but this comparison has shown us the possibility of something else: that by taking a conventional comparison seriously, by exploring how shocking it can be, the poet can offer a richer and more subtle tone, can see the emotion in the context of his whole personality. And so after Donne had gone out of fashion in the mid-seventeenth century, under the influence of a new respect for plainness and for "nature", he came back early in the twentieth under the influence of a new respect for the involved and passionate intellect.

Another poem by Donne will enable us to illustrate this point more fully, and enrich our reading of *The Dream*; and it would clearly be best to take one that explores the same analogy.

### The Relic

When my grave is broke up again
Some second guest to entertain,
(For graves have learnt that woman-head
To be to more than one a bed)
    And he that digs it, spies
A bracelet of bright hair about the bone,
    Will he not let'us alone,
And think that there a loving couple lies,
Who thought that this device might be some way
To make their souls, at the last busy day,
Meet at this grave, and make a little stay?

If this fall in a time, or land,
Where mis-devotion doth command,
Then, he that digs us up, will bring
Us, to the bishop, and the king,
    To make us relics; then
Thou shalt be a Mary Magdalen, and I
    A something else thereby;
All women shall adore us, and some men;
And since at such times, miracles are sought,
I would that age were by this paper taught
What miracles we harmless lovers wrought.

First, we loved well and faithfully,
Yet knew not what we loved, nor why;
Difference of sex no more we knew,
Than our guardian angels do;
    Coming and going, we
Perchance might kiss, but not between those meals;
    Our hand ne'er touched the seals,
Which nature, injured by late law, sets free:
These miracles we did; but now alas,
All measure and all language, I should pass,
Should I tell what a miracle she was.

Once again, we had better begin by summarizing the argument, but I will be briefer this tine. He has fastened a circlet of his lady's hair round his wrist, and he expects it still to be there when his flesh has rotted. If anyone digs up his skeleton, they will presume it to be a lover's token, useful for purposes of recognition on the Day of Judgement. If, however, they are dug up in a time of mis-devotion (which certainly here means Popery), then he and she—bone and hair—will be turned into holy relics. All Donne's readers would have known of the late medieval custom of selling bits of the bodies and garments of saints, even splinters from the true cross, as relics with magical powers. Indignation at what had become a vast commercial swindle was one cause of the Reformation, and a good Protestant reader in the late sixteenth century would certainly have regarded the sale of relics as one of the superstitious abuses of Popery. Since relics were supposed to work miracles of healing, the poet's body will be expected to supply its share of miracles. Hence the poem ("this paper"): he would like the future age to learn from it what miracles they wrought. The final stanza, describing the "miracles", is a more straightforward compliment: they loved, but chastely. That was the miracle they did; even finer is the miracle she was.

The closest comparison with *The Dream* comes in the second stanza, which is also built on a religious analogy, and one that hints at blasphemy. The careful tone that we saw in the second stanza of *The Dream* is exactly matched by

> then
> Thou shalt be a Mary Magdalen, and I
> A something else thereby . . .

A something else? It sounds contemptuous, and no doubt is: in such superstitious times we must expect them to identify us with some of their innumerable saints—and he cannot be bothered to name them. But if we read "something else" not in a tone of dismissal but of awe, or at least of a meaningful hint, then we can notice that metrically it is the exact equivalent of "Jesus Christ". Jesus replaced Mary Magdalen's lovers in her life after her conversion, and the association between them would make the identification natural. We do not need to follow the blasphemous thought that he was her lover in a carnal sense, though Donne is anti-Papist enough to accuse the age of misdevotion of thinking even that; we simply need to see it as an example of how far Roman Catholic idolatry can go.

The religious analogy, the constant hinting at parallels between ordinary human love and Christianity, runs through both these poems. The poet offers it himself in *The Dream,* he attributes it to the age of misdevotion in *The Relic,* but after doing so is clearly glad to use it for his own purposes: he really does want to call their love a miracle. But having said this, we have only described one aspect of the poem: if we look at the opening lines we see something different:

> When my grave is broke up again
> Some second guest to entertain,
> (For graves have learnt that woman-head
> To be to more than one a bed) . . .

That parenthesis is startlingly effective. It is there, of course, as a foil to the last stanza: in a world where women are promiscuous, the chastity of the poet and his lady truly deserves to be called a miracle. But its immediate impact is of a total cynicism. This is achieved in two ways: first, the fact that he is actually talking of the fickleness of graves constantly entertaining new "guests", and throws in the reference to woman's fickleness as a comparison that occurs to him, that we will all accept as we accept that torches lit and used before are easier lighted than a new torch; and second, through the causalness of the tone, the colloquial feel of the language. It is a poem, we see, that uses the speaking voice.

Something very like a speaking voice appears in the last three lines:

> These miracles we did; but now alas,
> All measure and all language, I should pass,
> Should I tell what a miracle she was.

The lines sound extravagant, even exaggerated: this comes from the repetitions and the rhythm. They demand to be read expansively, in the voice of a man paying excessive compliments. The "now alas" prepares us for this note; the second line has to be lingered on extravagantly, and the last word of all, "was", can also be lingered on to bring out the contrast with "did". Indeed, the extravagance is so marked that we can wonder if it is deliberately overdone, if the lines are meant to be read with a smile, an awareness that such compliments are not to be taken wholly seriously. Such questions of tone can seldom be decided without looking at a wider context; and the reader familiar with the rest of Donne's love poems will know that he does sometimes hint at a touch of mockery when paying his finest compliments, as if he is enjoying, quite consciously, his power to lay the flattery on rather thick. Perhaps what we should say about these lines is not exactly that they have a speech rhythm; but that if we read them with a sensitivity to speech rhythm (as other parts of the poem surely invite us to) then we shall be sensitive to their possible irony.

*The Relic,* then, is remarkable for the sensitivity of its rhythms, for its sense of actuality, as well as for its wit; and now turning back to *The Dream* we can see that the same is true of that. There is one point I have not yet made about *The Dream,* though it is perhaps the most obvious of all: that is, that in contrast to the Campion poem, it imagines a particular situation. We know where the poet is, and what he is doing: we know it from the very first moment, for the poem opens dramatically by plunging us into the midst of the situation, and several touches capture the changing tone of his voice. "Enter these arms" is expansive, perhaps even extravagant. "For thou lov'st truth" is an apology in passing, hinting back to his earlier compliment, perhaps also said with a slight smile. "Thou cam'st to kindle, goest to come" has a neat balance as if he is congratulating himself on the cleverness of the consolation he has managed to work out for her departure. Almost every line, when we look at it carefully, is alive with a spoken rhythm, and adds something new to the changes of tone, now vivid, now subtle. When a poem like this is read aloud by a good reader, it takes on a compelling and realistic quality. We hear a human voice speaking. Campion's lyric can—perhaps should —be sung. Here we have a poem that has to be spoken.

One of Donne's contemporaries reported that as a young man he was a great reader of Divinity, a great frequenter of plays, and a great visitor of ladies. It is a fascinating glimpse of the man: and how well it corresponds to the personality we find in the *Songs and Sonnets*. They certainly sound like the poems of a great visitor of ladies, for they are the most brilliant series of love poems in the language, and the most richly varied in mood. Even in these two, we have seen the changes rung on cynicism, sexless compliment, erotic compliment, touches of mockery, and sheer admiration; and elsewhere in the series we find a wider range, from the most playful to the most passionate. And such variety suggests the frequenter of plays, for it suggests a desire to expand, not to narrow, the range of moods, even of personalities, expressed. It is no use, when reading Donne, insisting on a rather narrow and austere concept of sincerity. What we have here is not a man constantly pruning away excesses and imaginative flights in order to be sure that he means what he says; we have instead a delight in the varied roles the same man can play, a delight we naturally associate with the drama.

It is time we introduced the obvious term to describe this realistic quality, this control over speech-rhythms, and called it dramatic. Donne's originality as a love poet consists essentially of two things, his wit (we have seen the brilliance and the mischievous subtlety with which he makes use of his reading in divinity) and his dramatic power. Some of his love poems have a startling reality in their openings that speaks to us immediately over the centuries:

> I wonder, by my troth, what thou and I
> Did, till we loved. . . .
> When by thy scorn, O murdress, I am dead. . . .

How easy it is to imagine Donne in the audience at the Globe theatre, listening to the lovers quarrelling in *A Misdummer Night's Dream,* or to Portia declaring her love for Bassanio, or to Hamlet taunting Ophelia.

I said earlier that the taste which prefers Campion to Donne likes the lyric to be purely lyrical. By his complex reasoning, Donne introduces a note perhaps more appropriate to a reflective or meditative poem; his wit, we may feel, belongs more to satire; and now we see how the speaking voice suggests drama. The complexity of Donne's poetry blurs distinctions of *genre*. Such distinctions are invaluable for telling us what kind of poem we are faced with (this point is further discussed in the Conclusion); but with some poems, and those often the finest, they may fail us in the end. The very fact that Donne's lyrics are not just lyrics results from his being a greater poet than Campion.

# 5

## The Bunch of Grapes

Joy, I did lock thee up: but some bad man
Hath let thee out again:
And now, methinks, I am where I began
Sev'n years ago: one vogue and vein,
One air of thoughts usurps my brain.
I did toward Canaan draw; but now I am
Brought back to the Red Sea, the sea of shame.

For as the Jews of old by God's command
Travelled, and saw no town;
So now each Christian hath his journeys spanned:
Their story pens and sets us down.
A single deed is small renown.
God's works are wide, and let in future times;
His ancient justice overflows our crimes.

Then have we too our guardian fires and clouds;
Our Scripture dew drops fast:
We have our sands and serpents, tents and shrowds;
Alas! our murmurings come not last.
But where's the cluster? where's the taste
Of mine inheritance? Lord, if I must borrow,
Let me as well take up their joy, as sorrow.

But can he want the grape, who hath the wine?
I have their fruit and more.
Blessed be God, who prospered Noah's vine,
And made it bring forth grapes good store,
But much more him I must adore,
Who of the Law's sour juice sweet wine did make,
Ev'n God himself being pressèd for my sake.

*George Herbert   (about 1630)*

What is this poem about? This time, the question is not easy to answer: and that is what it is about.

For it seems to be about two things. On the one hand there are the personal struggles of the poet, his difficulties over prayer and self-discipline, the phase of spiritual dryness he is going through; on the other hand, there is the Old Testament story of the crossing of the Red Sea by the Jews, and their journey to the promised land. Let us look at these two subjects one at a time.

The first five lines seem wholly personal, and describe a setback: he thought his happiness was secured, but he has lost it. The opening words are striking, and subtle: they can be spoken as a cry of puzzled distress—I *thought* my joy was secure—so that the poem starts with great emotional force, plunging us into the painful situation. But they can also be seen as foolish: how *can* anyone hope to lock joy in? Our emotional and spiritual life is not under that sort of control and so when he turns to complain "Some bad man Hath let thee out again", we can feel he is being childish. Why does he need to blame someone, to find a villain whose fault it was, when he had in any case been asking for the impossible?

The despair of the next lines will be familiar to anyone who has passed through painful periods of introspection:

> And now methinks I am where I began
> Seven years ago. . . .

We naturally like to think of our lives as growth and development; so the sensation of being back where one started is one of the most discouraging imaginable. Once again, there is the feeling of something inevitable in this lament: he tried to do the impossible, and escape the limitations of the human condition in which no joy can be relied on to stay with us, so of course he is back where he was, where "one air of thoughts usurps my brain" (this meaning of "air" is now slightly archaic; it is found in phrases like "foul air" or "a grosser air", and refers to the quality of the air when it is contaminated by odours and exhalations).

So far then, the poem seems personal and direct, an account of the spiritual struggles of the poet himself. Now if we read it as part of *The Temple,* Herbert's collection of poems, we shall recognize this as a familiar note, for poem after poem records very similar experiences. The most famous of all is *The Collar.*

### The Collar

> I struck the board, and cried, No more.
> I will abroad.
> What? shall I ever sigh and pine?
> My lines and life are free; free as the road,
> Loose as the wind, as large as store.

Shall I be still in suit?
Have I no harvest but a thorn
To let me blood, and not restore
What I have lost with cordial fruit?
Sure there was wine
Before my sighs did dry it: there was corn
Before my tears did drown it.
Is the year only lost to me?
Have I no bays to crown it?
No flowers, no garlands gay? all blasted?
All wasted?
Not so, my heart: but there is fruit,
And thou hast hands.
Recover all thy sigh-blown age
On double pleasures: leave thy cold dispute
Of what is fit, and not. Forsake thy cage,
Thy rope of sands,
Which petty thoughts have made, and made to thee
Good cable, to enforce and draw,
And be thy law,
While thou didst wink and wouldst not see.
Away; take heed:
I will abroad.
Call in thy death's head there: tie up thy fears.
He that forbears
To suit and serve his need,
Deserves his load.
But as I raved and grew more fierce and wild
At every word,
Methought I heard one calling, *Child!*
And I replied, *My Lord*.

The Collar is a symbol of discipline, and the poem is about his restlessness under the constraints of discipline, his breaking out, his sudden and moving submission. Since we know Herbert was a priest, it is natural to read it as an account of his rebellion against the burden of priesthood; and there are other poems in *The Temple* quite explicitly on that subject. But Herbert was a protestant priest, and would certainly have subscribed to the protestant doctrine of the priesthood of all believers, by which the priesthood are not seen as a dedicated and separate race, but which stresses the similarity between them and the laity. The parson's rebelliousness, then, against his yoke can be seen as an example of the Christian's difficulty in accepting the need of submission to God's will, and the poem is a record of the struggles of every erring believer.

Since its movement is so vividly dramatic (we can see Herbert's poetic debt to Donne in the realism with which the poem embodies the to and fro of feeling), we can take our bearings by dividing it into stages. The first stage, of sudden violent protest against a discipline he seems forced to follow, occupies the first sixteen lines, until "all wasted". The second is his discovery that he does not need to submit but can throw off the yoke, beginning with a note of excited discovery, "Not so, my heart"; then continuing with a series of eager, shouted imperatives, addressed to himself ("Recover . . . Forsake . . . Call in") growing, as he tells us, more and more fierce and wild; and culminating in the dogmatic assertion that to submit and suffer is one's own fault, a kind of assertion of the need for self-discovery and self-fulfilment:

> He that forbears
> To suit and serve his need,
> Deserves his load.

Finally comes the third stage, brief, unforgettable, irresistible, the two marvellous lines in which he hears the voice of his Lord gently reproaching (not even named: we are so close to the experience he is simply "one calling"), and instantly recognizes that his true will is to submit. The modern reader of Herbert, if he is not a Christian, may not feel in sympathy with this doctrine: self-fulfilment is so highly valued a goal in our ethic, that we are reluctant to dismiss it as simple rebellion. But it is clear that Herbert, though his values were different, felt the impulse as strongly: and the poem can even be read as a dramatic conflict between our goal of self-fulfilment and a reassertion of the traditional Christian scheme.

By saying this we show that it is not merely part of the poet's spiritual autobiography: it is an attempt to place his personal struggles in a wider context. That context is itself presented in vividly personal terms, and here we have the main difference between *The Collar* and *The Bunch of Grapes,* which also places personal experience in a wider context. In *The Bunch of Grapes* that context is explicit, and is stated at great length; it is not rendered dramatically, but is explained and discussed, so that the poem has much of the quality of an intellectual exploration.

The habit of reading Scripture allegorically was natural to

Christians for many previous centuries. For the Bible was not seen as a book like other books; it was God's word, and it contained the whole story of humanity and the whole meaning of life. To turn from one's own experience to a biblical analogy would have seemed the most natural thing in the world, not a way of changing the subject but a way of giving it fuller significance. So when Herbert ends the first stanza by doing just this, he is doing more than offering an analogy.

> I did towards Canaan draw; but now I am
> Brought back to the Red Sea, the sea of shame.

This is of course a reference to the wanderings of the Jews after their exodus from Egypt. Canaan is the promised land they are in search of, the Red Sea is the frontier of their shameful slavery to the Egyptians. Of course it *is* an analogy—he is comparing his spiritual journey through life with the journey of the Israelites through their wilderness; and to that extent it operates in the poem as any other analogy might operate—he could have compared himself with Odysseus seeking his home, Jason seeking the Golden Fleece, Julius Caesar seeking power in Rome, and found in those stories apt details to describe his setbacks.

But as we read on we soon realize that no other story would do. To tell his own story by comparison with the Old Testament is to tell it in the one completely meaningful way: the poem is as much about the Bible as it is about the poet, and above all it is about the special relationship between the two. And so the second stanza asserts "Their story pens and sets us down": the Old Testament is about us. Each Christian today can find his journeys spanned ("spanned" is used in the now obsolete sense of "measured out", "having bounds set to it"), because they correspond to, even re-enact, the journeying of the Israelites. We too have to pass through a time of seeking and frustration, on the way from our Egypt to our Canaan.

The Bible must be read allegorically; and our own lives should be seen in biblical terms. This is what the poem is saying, but unless we are familiar with the tradition of scriptural interpretation we may not realize the full complexity of the assertion. It is a tradition that goes back to the Middle Ages, and a Latin couplet by one Nicholas of Lyra sums it up succinctly.

> Littera gesta docet, quid credas allegoria,
> Moralis quid agas, quo tendas anagogia.

There are four meanings to a scriptural text, which Nicholas calls the literal, the allegorical, the moral and the anagogical. The literal tells you what happened ("gesta"); the allegorical tells you what you must believe ("quid credas"); the moral what you must do ("quid agas"); the anagogical whither you are going ("quid tendas"). There is no problem, clearly, about the literal meaning. The allegorical regards the literal events as in some way representing other events, asking you to believe that they are anticipations or symbols of something else. The commonest kind of allegorical meaning was the typical, in which figures or events in the Old Testament were regarded as "types" or anticipations of something in the New. The moral meaning (also known as the tropological) relates the biblical events to the spiritual condition of the individual believer: if you take the Bible as your guide you will learn what you ought to do. Finally, the anagogical meaning concerns God's Kingdom, and tells us about Heaven, Hell and the Day of Judgement. Thus if you read about Jerusalem in the Old Testament, you will on the literal level take it to refer to the actual city; on the allegorical level, to the Holy Church; on the moral, or tropological, to the faithful soul of the individual Christian; and on the anagogical to the life of those dwelling in Heaven.

Sometimes this method of interpretation produced readings of astonishing ingenuity. Most of us are familiar with the one aspect of such interpretation that has survived to our own day, often in almost lunatic form: the habit of predicting events in modern history by reading the Book of Revelation allegorically. Ingenious arithmetical calculations based on the seven angels with their seven plagues, or attempts to identify the great red dragon or the Whore of Babylon, can be used to announce the rise (or fall) of almost any political leader. Only cranks do this nowadays: but to read Herbert is to realize how deeply serious is the purpose such readings of scripture can be put to. For they assume a view of language that the reader of poetry will find himself sympathetic to—that instead of having a single exclusive meaning, a text may function on more than one level. It can be true literally *and* tropologically.

It is clear that Herbert's main concern is with the moral (or tropological) meaning. The third stanza, for instance, opens with the same kind of parallel we have already seen in stanza two: all the details of the wanderings of the Israelites in the wilderness have their equivalents in our life: "We have our sands and serpents, tents and shrowds." A reader familiar with the story as it is told in Exodus, Leviticus, Numbers and Deuteronomy will recognize all these details: he will for instance realize that the scripture dew which drops fast is a reference to Numbers XI. 9: "And when the dew fell upon the camp in the night, the Manna fell upon it." Like the Israelites, we find substance and comfort to help us through our wilderness. But do we also find the same reward? The reward is the Promised Land, and to realize that that is "the cluster" we need to know the thirteenth chapter of Numbers, in which Moses sends scouts to spy out the land of Canaan:

"And they came unto the brook of Eshcol, and cut down from thence a branch with one cluster of grapes, and they bare it between two upon a staff; and they brought of the pomegranates, and of the figs. The place was called the brook Eshcol, because of the cluster of grapes which the children of Israel cut down from thence."

The cluster of grapes is the sign of the fertility of Canaan: if we have to re-enact ("borrow") the sufferings of the Israelites, are we not entitled to expect their reward as well? Where then (and now we begin to see the point of the title) is our bunch of grapes?

So far then, the poem has been about reading the Bible tropologically, drawing a straightforward parallel between the story of the Israelites and our own spiritual quest; but in order to understand the last stanza we need to invoke a third level, the allegorical or typical, that by which Moses is seen as a symbol of Christ, Eve of the Virgin Mary, or the forty days of the Flood as a symbol of Jesus' forty days in the wilderness (medieval stained glass windows often show such symbolism by means of adjacent pictures).

In the final stanza, the poem asserts not only a relationship between the Old Testament story and our condition, but also between it and the New Testament. Grapes give wine, and wine is the blood of Christ: so that the cluster of grapes found in Eshcol is a symbol of another promise besides that of Canaan, a much more important promise (of which Canaan itself can be seen as a symbol), the redemption from the Law by the Gospel, the promise of God's grace through the sacrifice of Christ. "But can he want the grape, who hath the wine?" The poet reminds himself that he is a Christian, that he enjoys a promise, of which wine is the symbol, that is greater even than the promise given in Numbers. Of course Herbert did not invent this analogy between the cluster of grapes and the wine of the Sacrament: it sounds a characteristic piece of metaphysical wit, but it was (like so much of the wit in the religious poems of the metaphysicals) based on a traditional comparison. In medieval iconography, whether in illuminated manuscripts or in stained glass windows, the habit of thinking in analogies can be seen in the way pictures are juxtaposed with each other—the crossing of the Red Sea with the baptism of Christ, or the carrying of the bunch of grapes with Christ carrying the Cross. Indeed, as we read through the last stanza we can see that the habit of drawing analogies is irrepressible, and reaches into other parts of the Bible too. "Noah's vine" is a reference to the ninth chapter of Genesis, in which God told Noah and his sons to be fruitful and multiply and replenish the earth after the flood. There is no image of a vine used in these verses, but in the later part of the chapter the story is told of how Noah planted a vineyard, drank of the wine, and when drunk was seen naked by his children. It looks as if Herbert has taken the image of the vine from that story and applied it to the earlier part of the chapter, in which God causes the family of Noah to multiply and prosper; and in doing this he would be following the orthodox tradition, for the image of the vine was used to expound the meaning of many other passages in both the Old Testament and the New. The point of mentioning this story here is once more to assert the superiority of the New Testament over the Old: if Noah's vine was blessed by God, how much more blessed is something in the Gospel that can be figured by the same image. We can see that the reference to Noah is meant to involve both the fruitfulness and the drunkenness: the latter enables us to think of that vine as producing "sour juice", contrasting with the "sweet wine" of the Gospel promise. The Bible is full of images of a vine, the poem is saying: but nothing in the Old Testament can compare with the picture of God himself becoming flesh and being symbolized as a vine—as is done in St John XV. 1, where Jesus says "I am the true vine, and my Father is the husband-man." And so we are able to complete the meaning of the title: the bunch of grapes is the promise of Canaan to the Israelites, but for us has the truer and greater meaning of our redemption by Christ; and a reference to the Old Testament comes to rest on a Christian statement.

The Old Testament has its literal meanings, and can also be read figuratively; and the possibility of more than one figurative interpretation is central to the understanding of the poem. If we think of the Old Testament as about "future times", then we are being offered the typical meaning (also called the allegorical) by which it prefigures the New Testament (and beyond that the history of the Christian Church). If we think of it as about our "sea of shame" then we have the moral (or tropological) meaning, by which it deals with the spiritual life of the individual believer. And this poem explores the relationship between the two: the historical allegory, or type, imparts a richer value to the moral interpretation.

I began by saying that it was not easy to say what this poem is about, and I hope that remark is now clear. It is about the life of the poet himself, as is *The Collar*, but it has little of the marvellous dramatic power of that poem; if it did have, it would not be able to deal with its other subject, which is the exploration of what the individual life means. For this subject, the crucial line is "A single deed is small renown." The single deed is the individual life only, taken for itself and not placed in a wider context: its "renown" (perhaps the nearest modern equivalent to this word would be "significance") is small, and if we allow "small" to retain its old meaning of "narrow", then the contrast will be clear with "God's works are wide": the Bible story has so much more meaning than the merely individual story, because it reaches out so far.

The whole structure of the poem depends on this point. Thus the first word of the third stanza, "then" (a logical "then", equivalent to "thus") carries on the biblical comparison: because of what happened to the Jews, there must be guardian fires for us too. Similarly, the pivotal terms of the argument of the last stanza, the two uses of "But", both involve the movement from Old Testament to New. Thus we have a completely different purpose to this poem from that of *The Collar*.

It is easy to understand why *The Collar* has become Herbert's most admired lyric: for there is nothing that compels a response so powerfully as the immediacy of personal experience. To receive the full force of Herbert's genius, a modern reader certainly ought to read it, along with such other urgently personal poems as *Affliction*, an anguished, almost self-pitying autobiographical poem:

> Whereas my birth and spirit rather took
> The way that takes the town;
> Thou didst betray me to a lingering book,
> And wrap me in a gown.
> I was entangled in the world of strife,
> Before I had the power to change my life.

If Herbert had not had the power to write with such directness, he would not rank among the great English poets; and it must have been poems like this that he had in mind when he described *The Temple* to his friend Nicholas Ferrar as "a picture of the many spiritual conflicts that have passed betwixt God and my Soul". Yet to pick out these directly personal poems and ignore the rest of Herbert's work is to tear him up from his roots and I have therefore chosen a poem that, beginning with the personal, takes us almost to the other extreme by saying that the merely personal has "small renown", that richness of significance only comes when the individual life is seen as a part of a larger whole that is full of resonant interconnections. *The Bunch of Grapes* can be described as a poem about the meaning of meaning.

# 6

# The Picture of Little T. C. in a Prospect of Flowers

See with what simplicity
This nymph begins her golden days!
In the green grass she loves to lie,
And there with her fair aspect tames
The wilder flowers, and gives them names;
But only with the roses plays;
        And them does tell
What colour best becomes them, and what smell.

Who can foretell for what high cause
This darling of the Gods was born?
Yet this is she whose chaster laws
The wanton Love shall one day fear,
And, under her command severe,
See his bow broke and ensigns torn.
        Happy, who can
Appease this virtuous enemy of man!

O let me then in time compound,
And parley with those conquering eyes,
Ere they have tried their force to wound,
Ere, with their glancing wheels, they drive
In triumph over hearts that strive,
And them that yield but more despise
        Let me be laid
Where I may see thy glories from some shade.

Meantime, whilst every verdant thing
Itself does at thy beauty charm,
Reform the errors of the spring:
Make that the tulips may have share
Of sweetness, seeing they are fair;
And roses of their thorns disarm;
        But most procure
That violets may a longer age endure.

But O young beauty of the woods,
Whom Nature courts with fruits and flowers,
Gather the flowers, but spare the buds;
Lest Flora angry at thy crime,
To kill her infants in their prime,
Do quickly make th' example yours;
        And, ere we see,
Nip in the blossom all our hopes and thee.

                   *Andrew Marvell* (*1645*)

A little girl playing among flowers: that is the subject of the painting the poet is looking at, and by talking about the painting he conveys his feelings about the girl. That is all we need to know in order to respond to this poem, so delicate in tone yet so straight-forward in situation: that an adult man is talking about a little child. So it will be best, once we have got to know the poem, to begin by going through it, stanza by stanza, without, for the moment, stepping outside its world.

The first stanza is simple compliment, based on the conceits in "tames" and "tells". The little girl may be playing with the flowers, perhaps talking to them, naming them and telling them to be good; or she may by her mere presence, the fact that she is somehow lovelier and more innocent than the flowers, be exerting a kind of influence over them. In the first case, taming and telling describe what she is doing, and could be spoken with a sad adult smile that knows it is just a child amusing herself; in the second case the adult is so charmed that *he* feels she is teaching Nature. A mere compliment, no doubt—yet perhaps with a hint that there is something magical about the child's influence, or at least that he is tempted to think so.

In the second stanza the compliment grows more extravagant: T.C. when she is grown up will conquer men's hearts, indeed the God of Love himself will retire defeated before her. More extravagant, and therefore more playful, this fierce picture of her conquests is of course made comic by its contrast with the child's present innocence. Because of this contrast, the end of the stanza can be taken two ways:

               Happy, who can
        Appease this virtuous enemy of Man!

This may describe the future (any man *then* will be lucky to escape) or the present (how fortunate I am now, that I can still tread safely with her). Either way, it is said with a smile.

The extravagance grows even stronger in the third stanza, which quite explicitly relates the present to the future, and builds on both meanings of the previous lines. Because it will be so dangerous to meet the girl's glance when she is grown up, it is best to "parly" with her now. The danger is presented in an even more military image than before, culminating in the magnificent disdain of the heartless conqueror:

> And them that yield but more despise.

Yet after all he will be safe—perhaps as a result of the parly, perhaps simply because he will be old:

> Let me be laid
> Where I may see thy glory from some shade.

That reminds us, certainly, of the gap in their ages. Its main meaning is that he will be out of the battle by then, no longer susceptible to women's charms, and so able to admire from a distance—similar to the distance between them now, when he is no doubt in the battle and she hasn't yet begun. But of course the phrasing hints at a more sinister meaning: he may be wholly out of the battle, in the shade of death. A hint, no more.

The poem having now suggested a greater seriousness than before, it is time to return to the present time and the light-hearted tone, so the next stanza begins "Meantime". Since T.C. has power over nature now, she should use it to good purpose and carry out a few reforms. The reforms are the traditional impossibilities of proverbs—giving scent to tulips, taking the thorns from roses, and above all:

> That violets may a longer age endure.

Playful again: they are all impossibilities, so we are being reminded that she hasn't really any power over nature, it's all a deceiving fancy by the poet. Yet one hesitates to call this mockery: it is as if the poet is more moved by the innocence that drives him to believe this than by the good sense that tells him it's nonsense. And the last wish is especially touching: for just as the previous stanza hinted, though ever so slightly, at the poet's own death, so this one ends by hinting at the possibility of T.C.'s. The reason why this last is to be wished the most is of course that the violet is an analogy to the little girl—small, shy, lovely, and (alas) short-lived.

Perhaps the last stanza begins with a glance back at the picture—perhaps he notices that like any little girl she is picking the flowers, or about to. "But O" could suggest this upward glance, or possibly he is just pursuing his train of thought. Once again the adult is addressing the child, and though smiling he is stern, telling her what she mustn't do. And once again he thinks in analogies: T.C. is a bud, and if she plucks the flowers Flora, Goddess of flowers, will want revenge—or rather perhaps will herself (thinking in analogies too) get an idea from the action and:

Nip in the blossom all our hopes and thee.

The metaphor "nip in the blossom" is not of course invented by Marvell: this is important, for the poem ends by saying that nature *does* think in analogies, they are built into our language. The very familiarity of the phrasing, in that last line, should make the suggestion of danger sound real.

A straightforward enough poem, then: playful, with hints of something more serious and (at the end) almost sinister. All that, surely we can get simply by reading the poem repeatedly and carefully. We may feel immediately that the tone is right and the words suggestive; then with familiarity we may come to see what is being said, what suggested. It seems best, with this poem, to begin by reading it over and over, savouring its delicacy. It is a poem in which the tone is supremely important.

And now, having done that, we can move outwards and set it in a context. First, a context of literary history, relating it to other similar poems that Marvell expects his readers to know. Then, more narrowly, the context of Marvell's work, for he wrote a number of other poems quite as poised and elegant but not quite on the same theme. Then, finally, the specific context of what is, after all, an occasional poem.

There is no doubt that *The Picture of Little T.C.* belongs in a tradition. Its central metaphor, the comparison between love and war, was not invented by Marvell, but goes back at least to Horace. In one of Horace's most famous odes, *Vixi Puellis nuper idoneus* (III. 26), the poet speaks as an ageing lover no longer capable of sexual adventures, and he presents the theme in a sustained military metaphor. Here is the poem as translated by James Michie.

> In love's wars I have long maintained
> Good fighting trim and even gained
> Some glory. But now lyre
> And veteran sword retire

> And the left wall in the temple of
> The sea-born deity of love
> Shall house them. Come lay, here,
> Lay down the soldier's gear—
>
> The crowbar, the tar-blazing torch,
> The bow for forcing past the porch,
> Here is my last request:
> Goddess, ruler of blest
>
> Cyprus and Memphis, shrine that knows
> No shiver of Sithonian snows,
> Whose whip bends proud girls' knees—
> One flick for Chloe, please.

Laying down his weapons, hanging them up in the temple of Venus: the lover retires from campaigning, and describes it by means of a detailed analogy with the retiring warrior. Here we have the beginning of a long tradition. The comparison between love and conquest can of course operate in two ways: the man can be seen as the conqueror, or the woman. In the first case (which we have in Horace) we presume that the woman has yielded sexually, so that the physical act of love is what is seen as conquest; whereas if the woman is seen as the conqueror, her conquest consists of making the man fall in love with her because of her beauty, while resisting his advances. This contrast is inevitable in European culture, in which the male is seen as the dominant sexual partner, who initiates while the woman responds—or resists; we may speculate whether the metaphor would be used differently in another culture (or in our own transformed by the sexual consequences of the complete emancipation of women!), but it can only be a speculation.

For the woman as conqueror we can turn to Spenser, who uses the military analogy frequently in his sonnet sequence, the *Amoretti* (published in 1595). Addressing the Lord of Love in Sonnet 10, the poet says:

> See how the Tyranness does joy to see
> The huge massacres which her eyes do make;
> And humble hearts brings captive unto thee,
> That thou of them mayst mighty vengeance take.

The next two sonnets both use the metaphor of a truce. The poet seeks and sues for peace, "and hostages do offer for my truth", but

"She, cruel warrior" insists on continuing the battle. Sonnet 12 is worth quoting in full.

> One day I sought with her heart-thrilling eyes
> To make a truce, and terms to entertain:
> All fearless then of so false enemies,
> Which sought me to entrap in treason's train.
> So, as I then disarmèd did remain,
> A wicked ambush which lay hidden long
> In the close covert of her guileful eyen,
> Thence breaking forth, did thick about me throng,
> Too feeble I t'abide the brunt so strong,
> Was forced to yield myself into their hands;
> Who, me captivating straight with rigorous wrong
> Have ever since me kept in cruel bands.
> So lady, now to you I do complain,
> Against your eyes, that justice I may gain.

The parallels with Marvell's poem are striking: the "truce" corresponds with his "parley", and in both cases the enemy force against which he needs to protect himself is located in her eyes. Later in *Amoretti* the same image recurs:

> Fair cruel! why are ye so fierce and cruel
> Is it because your eyes have power to kill?
>
> (*Sonnet 49*)

One tradition, two poets. To see the similarity between the *Amoretti* and *Little T. C.* is to observe the continuity of a convention; but how different they are—and to notice this is to be aware of the individuality of each poet. Spenser's poem is a careful, competent and (in the end) rather pedestrian elaboration of the conceit that compares the dangerous glance of her eyes to an ambush. The first quatrain describes the truce; the second the treachery committed by her eyes; the third his capture; and the final couplet is a formal complaint to the lady, presumed to be in command of her eyes. Into this neat structure are inserted a number of simple poetic devices, such as the alliteration in the second, fourth and eighth lines. There is nothing unexpected in the way the conceit is developed, and the poem is in the fullest sense conventional: it is offered as an illustration of one point in the traditional analogy. Marvell, in contrast, writes with a poise and a confidence that announce an individual voice. His rhythms, without departing from the formal stanza pattern, constantly suggest the speaking voice; he uses the conceit in a tone that hovers constantly between the playful, the mock-solemn and an underlying seriousness. His poem is altogether less predictable than Spenser's, and though it belongs in the same tradition it gives the impression of using the conventions for its own purposes, rather than simply illustrating them.

One detail in particular, which as far as I know Marvell was the first to use, marks out the poem as a variant on the tradition: the fact that it is addressed to a child. This is inseparable from the playfulness. The straightforward use of the love-war analogy belongs only in the future; by referring to it now, the poet is reminding us that it does not really apply to the little girl, and that we should not therefore take it too seriously. Yet the future will come, and little girls do grow up, so behind the playfulness there is a potential seriousness. Marvell may have been the first to write about a child in this way, but he was not the last; and if we move forward to Matthew Prior's *To a Child of Quality,* written in 1704, we can find a poem that may have been influenced by Marvell's and which certainly provides an interesting parallel:

> Lords, knights, and squires, the numerous band,
> That wear the fair Miss Mary's fetters,
> Were summoned by her high command,
> To show their passion by their letters.
>
> My pen among the rest I took,
> Lest those bright eyes that cannot read
> Should dart their kindling fires, and look
> The power they have to be obeyed.
>
> Nor quality, not reputation,
> Forbid me yet my flame to tell,
> Dear five years old befriends my passion,
> And I may write till she can spell.
>
> For, while she makes her silkworms beds
> With all the tender things I swear;
> Whilst all the house my passion reads,
> In papers round her baby's hair;
>
> She may receive and own my flame,
> For, though the strictest prudes should know it,
> She'll pass for a most virtuous dame,
> And I for an unhappy poet.

> Then, too, alas! when she shall tear
> The lines some younger rival sends;
> She'll give me leave to write, I fear,
> And we shall still continue friends.
>
> For, as our different ages move,
> 'Tis so ordain'd, (would Fate but mend it!)
> That I shall be past making love,
> When she begins to comprehend it.

The resemblances are clear: in both poems, we are invited to look forward to the time when the little girl, grown up, will make conquests, and the poet will be safe from her because of his age; in both poems there is a playful suggestion (mainly in the first stanza, with Prior) that she is already dangerous. Prior is Marvell's equal in elegance and can capture the tone of the condescending adult in the rhythmic poise of

> And I may write till she can spell.

His irony is well shown by

> Then, too, alas! when she shall tear
> The lines some younger rival sends; . . .

a rueful glance towards the inevitability of the future, and of his own old age, that gives a mocking, but not wholly mocking, tone to the carefully placed "alas". For what it sets out to do, Prior's poem is, surely, as successful as Marvell's; but it sets out to do less. For Prior has not the underlying seriousness of Marvell, and time is not seen as a true threat. He does not hint at death, neither hers nor his own—for "past making love" quite clearly means that he will still be alive: they are to "continue friends". He has written a charming, light-hearted poem; Marvell an equally charming poem with overtones of true sorrow.

And in doing this he is writing in a wholly characteristic way. Perhaps no English poet is so perfect a master of the witty surface with an underlying seriousness as Marvell. His long poem on the country seat of his patron Lord Fairfax, *Upon Appleton House*, is full of examples of this. Here for instance is part of the description of how the meadow is flooded in summer by the nearby river Denton:

> Then, to conclude these pleasant acts,
> Denton sets ope its cataracts;
> And makes the meadow truly be
> (What it but seemed before) a sea.
> For, jealous of its lord's long stay,
> It tries t'invite him thus away.
> The river in itself is drowned,
> And isles th'astonished cattle round.
>
> Let others tell the paradox,
> How eels now bellow in the ox;
> How horses at their tails do kick,
> Turned as they hang to leeches quick;
> How boats can over bridges sail;
> And fishes do the stables scale.
> How salmons trespassing are found;
> And pikes are taken in the pound.

A meadow transformed into a sea by flooding. It is a subject that suggests analogies and ingenuities, and Marvell has enjoyed himself developing them. There are strange juxtapositions, like the fishes in the stables: as it happens, Marvell was not the first to describe these, and he may here be remembering an equally ingenious description of a flood in the first book of Ovid's *Metamorphoses*, in which you catch fish from the top of an elm-tree, and seals lie where goats have recently grazed. There is an opportunity for verbal wit too, so that the salmon are "trespassing", and for unusual verbal effects (the river "isles th' astonished cattle round", where the eccentric use of "isles" as a verb, to mean "makes them into islands", corresponds to the unusualness of what is happening). And there is paradox: the river "in itself is drowned", and the meadow, which the poem had compared to the sea in an ingenious metaphor a few stanzas earlier, now really seems to be one. All this treats the flooding as an opportunity for a verbal game; but the conceit that opens the next stanza can be taken more seriously.

> But I, retiring from the flood,
> Take sanctuary in the wood;
> And, while it lasts, myself embark
> In this yet green, yet growing Ark;
> Where the first carpenter might best
> Fit timber for his keel have pressed.
> And where all creatures might have shares;
> Although in armies, not in pairs.

The poet takes shelter in the wood and compares it to the ark, which was built of timber; this ark is still growing, and can therefore be seen as Nature's own protection against its own flood. Ingenious again; but also an invitation to compare this ordinary English summer flood to the myth of the Flood itself—the definite article in "retiring from the Flood" offers just such an ambiguity, between "this flood" and "*the* flood". Once we make that comparison, all sorts of possibilities open out in our reflection: for it looks as if Nature is re-enacting in an innocent form what was originally a punishment for sin. Is it a parody of the story of Noah, or a repetition of it, or a sceptical interpretation?

That is quite a simple illustration of Marvell's ability to be playful while offering a possibility of seriousness. For a more profound example we can turn to his finest poem, *To His Coy Mistress*, justly famous for its mingling of wit and passion.

> Had we but world enough, and time,
> This coyness lady were no crime.
> We would sit down, and think which way
> To walk, and pass our long love's day.
> Thou by the Indian Ganges' side
> Shouldst rubies find: I by the tide
> Of Humber would complain. I would
> Love you ten years before the Flood;
> And you should if you please refuse
> Till the conversion of the Jews.
> My vegetable love should grow
> Vaster than empires, and more slow.
> An hundred years should go to praise
> Thine eyes, and on thy forehead gaze.
> Two hundred to adore each breast:
> But thirty thousand to the rest.
> An age at least to every part,
> And the last age should show your heart.
> For Lady you deserve this state;
> Nor would I love at lower rate.
>
> But, at my back I always hear
> Time's wingèd chariot hurrying near;
> And yonder all before us lie
> Deserts of vast eternity.
> Thy beauty shall no more be found,
> Nor, in thy marble vault, shall sound

My echoing song; then worms shall try
That long preserved virginity;
And your quaint honour turn to dust;
And into ashes all my lust.
The grave's a fine and private place,
But none I think do there embrace.

Now therefore, while the youthful hue
Sits on thy skin like morning dew,
And while thy willing soul transpires
At every pore with instant fires,
Now let us sport us while we may;
And now, like am'rous birds of prey,
Rather at once our time devour,
Than languish in his slow-chapt power.
Let us roll all our strength, and all
Our sweetness, up into one ball;
And tear our pleasures with rough strife,
Thorough the iron gates of life.
Thus, though we cannot make our sun
Stand still, yet we will make him run.

This poem is arranged like a logical proposition, as the opening words of each section make clear: *if* we had world enough and time, *then* I would woo in the leisurely way your coyness invites; *but* mortality threatens; *therefore* let us sport us while we may. It is the argument of a thousand *carpe diem* poems, that remind us of the passage of time and urge us to seize the passing joys of youth before they fade:

Gather ye rosebuds while ye may,
Old Time is still a-flying.

Marvell spells out the logic of the theme more remorselessly and more explicitly than most; and at the same time he is more extravagantly witty than most. The wild conceits of the first section offer an ingenuity even more dazzling, and more entertaining than the description of the flood: the thought of having hundreds of years in which to make love leads to an equally exaggerated treatment of space, so that they would be able to wander all over the earth's surface while they courted. Impossibilities are touched and toyed with.

And you should if you please refuse
Till the conversion of the Jews.

You should be able to go on refusing for a very long time? You should refuse for ever and remain a virgin (for we know the conversion of the Jews is only a wishful fable)? Your acceptance would be as unlooked for a wonder as that conversion we speak of and hardly believe in? All these meanings are hinted at, none is clear-cut; and there is a similar effect in:

And the last age should show your heart.

It sounds like a splendid climax: or is it a mock-splendour? Does it announce that her heart is a wonder that deserves to be led up to? Or that she has no heart, and hence it will not be shown until the world comes to an end?

The wit and poise of this suggests a poet of high sophistication, who enjoys his mastery over words; yet in the very same poem, without abandoning that mastery, he can move on to a statement about the imminence of death that has haunted readers for centuries. The vast spaces of the earth's surface that were so fascinating in the first section have now become "deserts of vast Eternity", bleak and terrifying. The wit of this second section is no longer playful but deadly:

then worms shall try
That long preserved virginity . . .

The body will in any case be ravished by corruption: is it then worth keeping it chaste with such care? It is the voice of the frustrated male, getting his own back on the woman who has refused to yield to him, and the poem grows, for a moment, sardonic and even sadistic. Then, a moment later, he re-admits that he is threatened as much as she is, and the final snarl of

The grave's a fine and private place,
But none I think do there embrace.

includes them both in an effect that mingles fear with the satisfaction of having spoken out. The third section takes us back to the possibilities of life, but the underlying fear that the poem has pointed to cannot be brushed aside: we are urged to live fully not in order to avoid thinking about death, but because we have remembered its threat.

Even more than *Little T.C.*, this poem is both traditional and individual. Scores of other poets had urged their mistresses to yield because of the shortness of youth, or indeed of life; and Marvell builds on what they said, and expects his readers to realize that his poem is the heir of many others. Yet he is not merely submitting to tradition, he is revitalizing it. He has learned a taste for extravagant wit from Donne, and in sheer brilliance he has equalled his master; at the same time he is prepared to be deadly serious without abandoning the wit, as Donne is at his best. Marvell, who after all wrote much less than Donne, does not often dazzle with bravura displays of ingenuity, but relates his wit to the great commonplaces of lyric poetry, love, time, death, praise. He has a classical polish, a control over his own powers, that he learned from Latin poetry, and that reminds us of an English classicist like Ben Jonson, whom he must also have admired. Donne is the brilliant pathfinder; Marvell the more perfect poet.

It is easy to read the whole of Marvell's small output of English poem's and they yield constantly new delights to those who know them well. *Little T.C.* is a typical specimen, and one of the best; and to appreciate it fully is to cultivate one's sensibility and awareness to what words can say and not quite say, as well as to learn that wit and playfulness are not alternatives to seriousness, but a surface that makes the seriousness all the more moving.

We could stop here, for there is no more to say about the poem as a verbal structure; but there is perhaps something to say about the relation of that structure to the real world. A very convenient way to do this is to ask (the title invites the question, after all) who Little T.C. was.

Marvell does not tell us, but we need not conclude from that that he does not want his reader to know. *Little T.C.*, like most of his poems, was not printed until 1681, after his death, but it must have been read and passed round in manuscript long before then, and it seems reasonable to assume that the original circle of readers knew who the little girl was. And now, thanks to the researches of H M Margoliouth, we know too. It appears that Humphry Cornewall and his wife Theophila had a daughter Theophila, baptized on 23 August 1643, who died two days later; and a second daughter, born on 26 September 1644, was also called Theophila. Since a Theophila Cornewall was married at Ludlow in 1673 (the name can hardly have been common) we may assume that this one lived. A certain kind of curiosity is gratified to know that the poem was addressed to a real child; but the information is of more particular importance than that. For the name Theophila means "beloved by the Gods", so that when she is referred to as "this darling of the Gods", a play upon her name is intended. The poem is saying: you have been named Theophila, I wonder if there is some significance in that—are you, for instance, going to turn out especially beautiful and make conquests? Or are you going to be especially fragile, like a violet, like a bud?

It is at this point that the modern reader must find the poem a little odd—perhaps even in doubtful taste. Suppose a poet today were to write a lyric to a little girl, which means of course that the poem is meant to be read by the parents. If he ended it by speculating on the possibility that she might die, the parents would certainly be surprised, and perhaps offended. We do not expect children to die, and we must wonder if the imagination that broods on such a thought is morbid. This is a point on which it is impossible to think about poetry in isolation from society; for even so apparently timeless a subject as this must be influenced by our changing expectation of child mortality. The drastic reduction in mortality rates can be seen in the language: in the fact that middle-aged parents will today be asked "how many children have you got?", whereas their great-grandparents would more probably have been asked "how many children have you reared?", for it would not have been assumed that all had survived. No morbid imagination was necessary in the seventeenth century to associate Theophila Cornewall with death; and the fact that her elder sister, of the same name, had not lived gives a special poignance to the poem. It is as if it was asking, Are you, at any rate, going to be favoured as the other one wasn't? Her name, we realize, is not necessarily a good omen—and we could have realized this from the name itself, since a proverb tells us that those whom the Gods love die young. So far from being an unnecessary touch of morbidness, the sombre hints on which the poem concludes seem its natural, even its unavoidable, climax.

Poems are made of words, not thoughts; and to respond to a poem we need above all to be sensitive to the words. Yet this example has surely shown us that words do not live in a universe of their own. Their effect on us depends on certain assumptions about human life, and that in turn may depend on social reality, even on such down-to-earth matters as the progress of medical science, or the spread of birth control. Two equally sensitive readers may read this poem differently simply because they are separated by three centuries of social change; and to respond to it today is not only to reflect on our own situation, but to perform an act of historical imagination.

# 7

## On his Blindness

When I consider how my light is spent,
   Ere half my days, in this dark world and wide,
   And that one talent which is death to hide,
   Lodged with me useless though my soul more bent
To serve therewith my Maker, and present
   My true account, lest he returning chide,
   Doth God exact day-labour, light denied,
   I fondly ask; but patience to prevent
That murmur, soon replies, God doth not need
   Either man's work or his own gifts, who best
   Bear his mild yoke, they serve him best. His state
Is kingly. Thousands at his bidding speed
   And post o'er land and ocean without rest:
   They also serve who only stand and wait.

*John Milton*   (*1652*)

The theme of this poem is acceptance of one's lot. It can never be easy to accept blindness, or to escape from the feeling that one has, somehow, been unfairly singled out for suffering; and the struggle which this short poem enacts is between protest and resignation, between bitterness and acceptance. And since it is a Petrarchan sonnet, the natural ordering of the poem is, protest in the octet, acceptance in the sestet.

Yet the poem does not begin with direct anger, with the voice of someone insisting that he's been badly treated, as it might if written by a highly dramatic poet—Donne, say. It begins with a considered statement, a long and complex sentence, the voice of someone controlling his emotion while he explores a difficult situation. Control is important in this poem.

Yet so is personal feeling. As we recite that long opening sentence, we are enacting an argument in which feeling is never quite bottled up, and keeps breaking through but without upsetting the movement of thought. The general structure of what the octet is saying is clear: when I survey my position, I ask "Doth God exact day labour . . . " And for six lines he surveys his position. His life is only half over; he has a talent which blindness has rendered useless; he wants to serve God—he *ought* to serve God—but feels he has been robbed of the power to do so. Just under the surface, we can hear the clamouring emotion: unfair, unfair, unfair! And breaking up to the surface every now and then in an intonation, in a rhythm, a betraying turn of phrase—"ere half my days": each word can be lingered on and stressed. Or "lodged": tremendously emphatic at the beginning of the line, and fraught with bitterness. Or "*more* bent": it can be spoken with a plea in the voice, almost a whine. And so as that long introductory clause comes to an end, and we come to the protest itself, the actual words, we are prepared for the more direct touch of emotion—though still not as an exclamation, but as a question of the "how-can-I-be-expected-to" kind:

Doth God exact day-labour, light denied?

"Day-labour": work done in the day? Work that lasts all day? Perhaps we are meant to think of both meanings. The first could be metaphorical, if daylight is a symbol of that clear illumination, coming from God, needed to carry out the task imposed; if the task needs metaphorical light, and the poet has lost literal sight, then he is not, in fact, incapacitated from doing his duty, but under such emotional stress one does not reason so scrupulously—yet one should, and perhaps that is one of the things that makes the speech "fond", which here of course has its old meaning of "foolish". The second meaning of "day-labour" is also apt, however, because it recalls the parable of the labourers in Matthew XX, all of whom, no matter when they began, toiled till evening for the same wage; and so helps us to think of the work as directly in the service of God.

One important poetic principle is very clearly illustrated by the octet: that emotion is something which affects us more powerfully if kept in check. A sonnet is always a formal structure; and the formal language and elaborate syntax take us far from direct outbursts of feeling. But there is nothing detached or impersonal about this poem, in which intensity of feeling burns its way through the dignified manner.

The second part of the poem (not, strictly, the sestet, for Milton has loosened the sonnet structure a little, and begins the counter-statement half-way through line 8) is spoken by Patience, and its manner and content are deliberately very different. In reply to that complaint, on the verge of becoming petulant, we are given a vision of the grandeur of God's rule in the world, the completeness of God's power, the splendour and complexity of a design in which everyone has an allotted part to play. Because all is decided by God, it does not matter if your task is great or small: what matters is the fidelity with which you carry it out: "They also serve who only stand and wait." In the grandeur of the courts of Heaven, there are messengers and there are sentries, and the line suggests those angels whose duty it is to stand, not to travel: by this reading "wait" will probably mean "attend on". But of course the line also suggests the poet, waiting to be given a task he can carry out. There is something like a play on words here, suggesting that though he seems to be forgotten, the blind, neglected poet may have a ceremonial function in God's plan.

Acceptance, the culminating idea of the poem, is played against another dominant idea, that of dedication. What is the "one talent" which the poet feels it could be death to hide? From the poem itself, we could not know: we could only know it is something he values deeply, and feels he is called into the world to exercise. But to anyone familiar with Milton's work, prose and verse, there can be no doubt of the answer: the talent is poetry. From his earliest years Milton had been preparing himself to write a great poem. Living in studious retirement in the country as a young man, he wrote to his friend Diodati that he was meditating an immortality of fame: "I am letting my wings grow and preparing to fly; but my Pegasus has not yet feathers enough to soar aloft in the fields of air." He spent a long time grooming his Pegasus, turning over the possible subjects for his masterpiece (for a while he favoured the story of King Arthur, and it was not until he finally settled to his great work, blind and disillusioned, that he fixed on a biblical subject). An autobiographical passage in his pamphlet *The Reason of Church Government* reveals how completely the ambition of writing a great poem had taken possession of him, as he tells us how he assented to the urgings of his friends and literary acquaintances

"and not less to an inward prompting which now grew daily upon me, that by labour and intense study (which I take to be my portion in this life), joined with the strong propensity of nature, I might perhaps leave something so written to after-times, as they should not willingly let it die."

The quiet pride of that last phrase is eloquent of the intensity of emotion behind it; and a sense of dedication as strong as this cannot be easy to live with. It must lead to constant brooding on the difficulty of the task, constant self-questioning, and doubts of whether one is going to be able to succeed in such a high destiny. Long before Milton went blind, he was subject to such doubts—the mere fact that one is growing older and hasn't yet begun is cause enough for anxiety; the fact that one has had a birthday can be a reminder.

How soon hath Time the subtle thief of youth
   Stolen on his wing my three and twentieth year!
   My hasting days fly on with full career,
   But my late spring no bud or blossom shew'th.
Perhaps my semblance might deceive the truth
   That I to manhood am arrived so near,
   And inward ripeness doth much less appear
That some more timely-happy spirits indu'th.
Yet be it less or more, or soon or slow,
   It shall be still in strictest measure even,
   To that same lot, however mean, or high,
Toward which Time leads me, and the will of Heaven;
   All is, if I have grace to use it so,
As ever in my great task master's eye.

The construction of this sonnet is very similar to that of "When I consider": an octet of complaint, a sestet of reassurance. The octet, in this case, without any touch of the self-pity that hovers behind the sonorous lines of the other, later poem, is simply an awareness of the passage of time. The opening line should probably be spoken with a sad shake of the head, rather than with bitterness. But the sestet is very similar to that of the blindness sonnet. The splendid inevitability of

Yet be it less or more, or soon or slow,
   It shall be still in strictest measure even . . .

seems to imply just that vision of God's ordered authority in directing the world that sends thoudands posting o'er land and ocean, and the same imaginative acceptance by the poet.

Milton did not have to wait until he was blind to encounter this idea of acceptance. In *Reason of Church Government* he wrote "But were it the meanest underservice, if God by his secretary conscience enjoin it, it were sad for me if I should draw back . . . . "Underservice": Milton did not think, in 1641, that what God would enjoin would be something so like complete inaction. The attitude of acceptance was something he had long held, but in the sonnet on his blindness he faces it with a new intensity. And the intensity, we see, is due to the dedication. Perhaps in 1641 he felt sure that the underservice, however humble, was something that would use his talent: the pain of this great sonnet comes from having to face the possibility that acceptance might involve foregoing his great task.

This is a great deal to draw out of a sonnet. Traditionally, it is a lyric form, devoted to personal themes: most previous sonnets had been about love. Is there not a sense of strain, of loading the form with more than it can bear, in the asking of these cosmic questions, in this vision of God's government of the universe? "Thousands at his bidding speed": no one who saw that line by itself would dream that it came from a sonnet. It has an epic sound.

If Milton had written only sonnets we would feel that his use of the form was eccentric, inappropriate, but strangely impressive. It would be a rare reader, whoever, who read this poem without knowing that Milton did complete the task, that he wrote *Paradise Lost* to justify the ways of God to men. He may have begun it when he wrote this sonnet, though that is unlikely; more probably, he had decided what to write about, and was afraid that blindness would prevent him. But he is writing as a poet who feels his gift to be epic: his sonnets (he wrote twenty-three in English, and a few more in Italian) are a small part of his poetry, a pendant, a minor variation.

In one sense, we cannot view this poem in isolation. It is by the author of *Paradise Lost,* and though complete it is also an appendage to that great work. This faces us with a problem in our discussion. If you have not read *Paradise Lost,* you ought really to stop and do so now. It is after all the greatest poem in English, and it gives meaning to everything else Milton ever wrote. But few readers are likely to squeeze such a demanding experience into the middle of reading an essay like the present one! So you must treat the sonnet as a hint of the splendours to come in your reading, rather than as a comment on what you possess; and moving now to its connections with the great epic, I must inevitably address myself mainly to those who have read it.

Satan's rebellion against God, when he was still Lucifer and had not fallen, is the earliest part of the action chronologically, though it does not occur until Book 5, in the form of retrospective narrative. Satan drew with him, we are told, the third part of Heaven's host; of all his followers, only one refused to join him in defying God. This was the seraph Abdiel, who has a public argument with Satan before going over to God. Satan has asserted in front of his followers that the elevation by God of his Son to rule over the angelic host is a usurpation, and a denial of their traditional freedom. To this Abdiel replies that no one has a right to question God's decrees:

> Shalt thou give law to God? Shalt thou dispute
> With him the points of liberty, who made
> Thee what thou art, and formed the Powers of Heaven
> Such as he pleased, and circumscribed their being?

It is folly for any of them to consider himself equal to God, whose reign makes them more illustrious, not more obscure:

> His laws are ours; all honour to him done
> Returns our own.

Clearly we have here the same doctrine as in the sonnet on his blindness, but spelt out at greater length. Abdiel is asserting the majesty of God's order, and the fact that to accept your place in it, however humble, is to receive honour more than to give it. In the more leisurely lines of an epic argument in Heaven, this theological vision can be more fully conveyed than in a sonnet, and *Paradise Lost* Book 5 shows the main body of work to which it is a pendant. Yet for all the sense of strain, we can see that the sonnet has a poetic function that the epic hasn't: it shows the emotional use of the doctrine. The very fact that a doctrine of such vast scope is brought to bear on the personal situation of an individual shows that it *matters*; and there is a sense in which we really understand the function of the theology better from such a worm's eye view than from all the rolling periods of Abdiel's speeches.

What was the significance of this vision in Milton's opinions as a man living on earth? It is a vision of the sublime rightness of the *status quo,* and therefore (we would expect) conservative in its implications. Yet Milton, who was actively involved in politics, was a radical: a supporter of the parliamentary side in the Civil War, then of the tiny fanatical minority who executed the king. If his lifelong loyalty to Cromwell suffered a strain at the end, it was for the necessary compromises that power imposed on him. Few figures in the seventeenth century more clearly anticipate the more liberal and progressive doctrines of later times than Milton: he believed in religious toleration, and was hostile to authoritarianism in both Church and State. How could a man with such views offer for our approbation a figure such as Abdiel, with his enthusiastic vision of hierarchy and rank:

> . . . the mighty Father made
> All things, even thee, and all the spirits of Heaven
> By him created in their bright degrees,
> Crowned them with glory, and to their glory named
> Thrones, Dominations, Princedoms, Virtues, Powers.

We can draw one conclusion from this about the social function of theology. That is that a man's vision of God's universe need not be a mirror of what he sees on earth, but can be a counterweight to it. Milton saw God as the Supreme Monarch, not because he supported earthly monarchy, but because he opposed it: God's authority was not seen as reinforcing the authority of King Charles (this is how Shakespeare saw it) but as a higher authority to appeal to against the actual king. Hence the situation of Abdiel, who in the poem is a rebel —that is, a rebel against rebellion. He appeals to the "bright degrees" of God's order as a defiance of his own superior, who has behaved like a tyrant. This is a situation very like Milton's view of himself. Progressively disillusioned by politics as he grew older, he began more and more to feel that he was one of the few men in England— perhaps the only one—who had never compromised himself, and so he identified Abdiel's position with his own.

> So spake the Seraph Abdiel, faithful found;
> Among the faithless faithful only he;
> Among innumerable false, unmoved,
> Unshaken, unseduced, unterrified,
> His loyalty he kept, his love, his zeal;
> Nor number nor example with him wrought
> To swerve from truth, or change his constant mind,
> Though single. From amidst them forth he passed,
> Long way through hostile scorn, which he sustained
> Superior, nor of violence feared aught;
> And with retorted scorn his back he turned
> On those proud towers to swift destruction doomed.

These lines are surely the finest in the story of Abdiel. Poetically, the passages asserting God's authority were not very distinguished: they have a certain weighty impressiveness, but seem more like versified theology than true poetry. Here, however, a new excitement has entered the verse: Milton's identification with Abdiel has quickened the emotional beat, and we can feel a more personal urgency. It comes from that mixture of rebellion and orthodoxy that Milton saw as Abdiel's and his own: the loneliness of the defiant individual, isolated in his righteousness, and the despairing confidence with which he rests on a higher authority by which the apparent ruler has (though no one yet knows it) been doomed. Is not this appeal to the invisible law of God against actual power very similar, emotionally, to the appeal in the sonnet: from the self-pity of the man who sees only immediate failure, to the vision of him who sees his ultimate triumph in God's plan, that plan in which

Thousands at his bidding speed
And post o'er land and ocean without rest . . .

There is one other parallel with *Paradise Lost,* a more obvious and a
more famous one: that is with the invocation to light which opens
Book 3, another lament by the poet on his blindness. It is a greater
but more difficult passage, and there is only space for a few introductory remarks on it.

As was customary in epic tradition, Milton opens *Paradise Lost*
with an invocation to the Muse; and follows it at carefully chosen
points with three other invocations. This one comes after we have
left Hell, in which the first two books are set, and are now to be
transported to Heaven, then eventually to earth.

Hail, holy Light, offspring of Heaven first born!
Or of the Eternal coeternal beam
May I express thee unblamed? since God is light,
And never but in unapproachèd light
Dwelt from eternity—dwelt then in thee,
Gright effluence of bright essence increate!
Or hearst thou rather pure ethereal stream,
Whose fountain who shall tell? Before the sun,
Before the Heavens, thou wert, and at the voice
Of God, as with a mantle, didst invest
The rising world of waters dark and deep,
Won from the void and formless Infinite!
Thee I revisit now with bolder wing
Escaped the Stygian Pool, though long detained
In that obscure sojourn, while in my flight,
Through utter and through middle darkness borne,
With other notes than to the Orphean lyre
I sung of Chaos and eternal night,
Taught by the Heavenly Muse to venture down
The dark descent, and up to reascend,
Though hard and rare. Thee I revisit safe,
And feel thy sovran vital lamp; but thou
Revisitst not these eyes, that roll in vain
To find thy piercing ray, and find no dawn;
So thick a drop serene hath quenched their orbs,
Or dim suffusion veiled. Yet not the more
Cease I to wander where the Muses haunt
Clear spring, or shady grove, or sunny hill,

Smit with the love of sacred song; but chief
Thee, Sion, and the flowery brooks beneath,
That wash thy hallowed feet, and warbling flow,
Nightly I visit: nor sometimes forget
Those other two equalled with me in fate,
So were I equalled with them in renown,
Blind Thamyris and blind Maeonides,
And Tiresias and Phineus, prophets old:
Then feed on thoughts that voluntary move
Harmonious numbers; as the wakeful bird
Sings darkling, and, in shadiest covert hid,
Tunes her nocturnal note. Thus with the year
Seasons return; but not to me returns
Day, or the sweet approach of even or morn,
Or sight of vernal bloom, or summer's rose,
Or flocks, or herds, or human face divine;
But cloud instead, and ever-during dark
Surrounds me, from the cheerful ways of men
Cut off, and, for the book of knowledge fair,
Presented with a universal blank
Of Nature's works, to me expunged and rased,
And wisdom at one entrance quite shut out.
So much the rather thou, Celestial Light,
Shine inward, and the mind through all her powers
Irradiate; there plant eyes; all mist from thence
Purge and disperse, that I may see and tell
Of things invisible to mortal sight.

The sonnet on his blindness derived much of its power from the tension between the formal and the personal; and that is even more true of this invocation, in which very intense personal feeling mingles with highly abstract theology and literary theory. It opens with a direct address to light, followed immediately by almost pedantic concern about getting the terminology correct. In a Christian epic, light must be celebrated as God's first gift, hence the reference to the Bible story of Creation: the lines beginning "Before the sun" are clearly built up from the opening verses of Genesis ("And darkness was upon the face of the deep. . . . . And God said, Let there be light, and there was light. . . . .") Having established what light is, Milton turns to his poem, and sees himself as the epic poet, taught by the Heavenly Muse (for unlike his model, Orpheus, he is writing a Christian poem), and feeling that it is a privilege to be allowed

            to venture down
The dark descent, and up to reascend,
Though hard and rare.

(to be, in fact, one of those who "post o'er land and ocean" at God's bidding). An*g* now the movement of the sonnet is reversed: at the very moment of exultation at being allowed to celebrate God, he turns to his own situation, and sees the painful contrast with his loss:

            Thee I revisit safe,
And feel thy sovran vital lamp; but thou
Revisitst not these eyes, that roll in vain
To find thy piercing ray, and find no dawn. . . .

As one grows familiar with Milton's verse, one learns to respond instantly to the surge of personal feeling into a hitherto formal passage, and to realize how central to his poetry such effects are. Here the whole structure of the sentence, and the movement of the rhythm, conveys the intensity of loss: especially the pained lingering on "but thou" at the end of the line, and above all the tremendous emphasis on the verb in "roll in vain", a difficult, frustrated movement contrasting with the confidence and success of his movement "down the dark descent". God has helped him as a poet and punished him as a man; he is celebrating his gifts (his "talent") in writing epic, and then turns all the more movingly to his loss.

One more example of the same tension. After telling us that, despite his blindness, he listens to poetry each night (he tells us this in deliberately artificial language—"wander where the Muses haunt"), he compares himself with the great legendary blind figures of antiquity. Two poets and two prophets are named, but in each case simply for the imposing effect of a pair of names, since virtually nothing is known about Thamyris and Phineus. Maeonides is another name for Homer (the artificiality is still further increased by the unusual name), and Tiresias is the blind prophet who foretold the future with unerring truth, but was never believed (he appears in the most famous of all Greek plays, Sophocles' *King Oedipus*). Milton is invoking his learning to set his own blindness in a context that will take us beyond the merely personal; and then when he goes on to tell us how he still composes poetry, he once more does so in highly formal language: his thoughts "voluntary move harmonious numbers", and the nightingale to whom he compares himself "tunes her nocturnal note". If the passage stopped there it would be learned, dignified, depersonalized, impressive but not urgent—a passage for those who enjoy Latin or Greek poetry, and like the feel of reaching out to classical precedents. And so at this moment (we have learned to expect it by now in Milton) we move to the personal, first by a reflection on the passage of the year, unimpeded by the sorrows of an individual; and for this we drop into simpler and more direct language ("Thus with the year Seasons return"), which prepares us for the sudden surge of feeling as he talks directly about himself. How moving, after the formality that preceded, are the two tiny words "to me", bearing the whole weight of the move to simplicity and directness. Milton is playing his role as epic poet, but he is still John Milton the man—blind, disillusioned, marvellously convinced of his poetic mission, of the one talent which is death to hide.

# 8

# To Mr Fortescue. The First Satire of the Second Book of Horace Imitated

P.   There are (I scarce can think it, but am told),
There are, to whom my Satire seems too bold:
Scarce to wise Peter complaisant enough,
And something said of Chartres much too rough.
The lines are weak, another's pleased to say,
Lord Fanny spins a thousand such a day.
Timorous by nature, of the rich in awe,
I come to counsel learned in the law:
You'll give me, like a friend, both sage and free,
Advice; and (as you use) without a fee.
    F.   I'd write no more.
    P.   Not write? but then I think,
And for my soul I cannot sleep a wink.
I nod in company, I wake at night,
Fools rush into my head, and so I write.
    F.   You could not do a worse thing for your life.
Why, if the nights seem tedious, take a wife:
Or rather truly, if your point be rest,
Lettuce and cowslip wine; *Probatum est.*
But talk with Celsus, Celsus will advise
Hartshorn, or something that shall close your eyes.
Or, if you needs must write, write Caesar's Praise:
You'll gain at least a Knighthood, or the Bays.
    P.   What? like Sir Richard, rumbling, rough and fierce,
With Arms, and George, and Brunswick crowd the verse,
Rend with tremendous sound your ears asunder,
With Gun, Drum, Trumpet, Blunderbuss, and Thunder?
Or nobly wild, with Budgell's fire and force,
Paint angels trembling round his falling horse?
    F.   Then all your Muse's softer art display,
Let Carolina smooth the tuneful lay,
Lull with Amelia's liquid name the Nine,
And sweetly flow through all the Royal Line.
    P.   Alas! few verses touch their nicer ear;
They scarce can bear their Laureate twice a year:
And justly Caesar scorns the Poet's lays,
It is to History he trusts for praise.

F.   Better be Cibber, I'll maintain it still,
Than ridicule all taste, blaspheme quadrille,
Abuse the City's best good men in metre,
And laugh at Peers that put their trust in Peter.
Even those you touch not, hate you.
P.   What should ail'em?
F.   A hundred smart in Timon and in Balaam:
The fewer still you name, you wound the more;
Bond is but one, but Harpax is a score.
P.   Each mortal has his pleasure: none deny
Scarsdale his bottle, Darty his Ham Pie;
Ridotta sips and dances, till she see
The doubling Lustres dance as fast as she;
F— loves the Senate, Hockley Hole his brother,
Like in all else, as one egg to another.
I love to pour out all my self, as plain
As downright Shippen, or as old Montaigne:
In them, as certain to be loved as seen,
The soul stood forth, nor kept a thought within;
In me what spots (for spots I have) appear,
Will prove at least the medium must be clear.
In this impartial glass, my Muse intends
Fair to expose myself, my foes, my friends;
Publish the present age; but where my text
Is vice too high, reserve it for the next:
My foes shall wish my life a longer date,
And every friend the less lament my fate.
My head and heart thus flowing through my quill,
Verse-man or Prose-man, term me which you will,
Papist or Protestant, or both between,
Like good Erasmus in an honest mean,
In moderation placing all my glory,
While Tories call me Whig, and Whigs a Tory.
Satire's my weapon, but I'm too discreet
To run amuck, and tilt at all I meet;
I only wear it in a land of Hectors,
Thieves, supercargoes, sharpers, and directors.
Save but our Army! and let Jove encrust
Swords, pikes, and guns, with everlasting rust!
Peace is my dear delight—not Fleury's more:
But touch me, and no minister so sore.
Whoe'er offends, at some unlucky time
Slides into verse, and hitches in a rhyme,

Sacred to ridicule his whole life long,
And the sad burden of some merry song.
Slander or poison dread from Delia's rage,
Hard words or hanging, if your judge be Page.
From furious Sappho scarce a milder fate,
P-xed by her love, or libelled by her hate.
Its proper power to hurt, each creature feels;
Bulls aim their horns, and asses lift their heels;
'Tis a Bear's talent not to kick, but hug;
And no man wonders he's not stung by Pug.
So drink with Waters, or with Chartres eat,
They'll never poison you, they'll only cheat.
Then, learned sir! (to cut the matter short)
Whate'er my fate, or well or ill at Court,
Whether old age, with faint but cheerful ray,
Attends to gild the evening of my day,
Or Death's black wing already be displayed,
To wrap me in the universal shade;
Whether the darkened room to muse invite,
Or whitened wall provoke the skewer to write:
In durance, exile, Bedlam, or the Mint,
Like Lee or Budgell, I will rhyme and print.
    F.   Alas, young man! your days can ne'er be long,
In flower of age you perish for a song!
Plums and directors, Shylock and his wife,
Will club their testers, now, to take your life!
    P.   What? armed for virtue when I point the pen,
Brand the bold front of shameless guilty men;
Dash the proud gamester in his gilded car;
Bare the mean heart that lurks beneath a star;
Can there be wanting, to defend her cause,
Lights of the Church, or guardians of the laws?
Could pensioned Boileau lash in honest strain
Flatterers and bigots even in Louis' reign?
Could laureate Dryden pimp and friar engage,
Yet neither Charles nor James be in a rage?
And I not strip the gilding off a knave,
Unplaced, unpensioned, no man's heir, or slave?
I will, or perish in the generous cause:
Hear this, and tremble! you who 'scape the laws.
Yes, while I live, no rich or noble knave
Shall walk the world, in credit, to his grave.
To virtue only and her friends a friend,

The world beside may murmur, or commend.
Know, all the distant din that world can keep,
Rolls o'er my grotto, and but soothes my sleep.
There, my retreat the best companions grace,
Chiefs out of war, and statesmen out of place.
There St. John mingles with my friendly bowl
The feast of reason and the flow of soul:
And he, whose lightning pierced th'Iberian lines,
Now forms my quincunx, and now ranks my vines,
Or tames the genius of the stubborn plain,
Almost as quickly as he conquered Spain.
Envy must own, I live among the great,
No pimp of pleasure, and no spy of state,
With eyes that pry not, tongue that ne'er repeats,
Fond to spread friendships, but to cover heats;
To help who want, to forward who excel;
This, all who know me, know; who love me, tell;
And who unknown defame me, let them be
Scribblers or Peers, alike are mob to me.
This is my plea, on this I rest my cause—
What saith my counsel, learned in the laws?
    F.   Your plea is good; but still I say, beware!
Laws are explained by men—so have a care.
It stands on record, that in Richard's times
A man was hanged for very honest rhymes.
Consult the Statute: *quart*. I think, it is,
*Edwardi sext.* or *prim. et quint. Eliz.*
See *Libels, Satires*—here you have it—read.
    P.   Libels and satires! lawless things indeed!
But grave Epistles, bringing vice to light,
Such as a king might read, a bishop write,
Such as Sir Robert would approve—
    F.   Indeed
The case is altered—you may then proceed!
In such a cause the plaintiff will be hissed,
My lords the judges laugh, and you're dismissed.

                                 *Alexander Pope*   *(1733)*

The *Sermones*, or satires, of the Roman poet Horace, written between
40 and 30 B.C., are a collection of informal, personal, rather rambling
poems making fun of leading public figures, usually under fictitious
names. The first satire of the second book, which is eighty-six lines
in length, is in the form of a dialogue between the poet and his friend

Trebatius, a distinguished lawyer, on the arguments for and against writing satire. Horace begins by remarking that some people find his satire too sharp, others find his verses pedestrian, and asks what he should do. Trebatius tells him to stop writing. Horace says he can't sleep; and Trebatius suggests other ways of finding sleep, such as swimming three times across the Tiber. If Horace must write, why not celebrate the heroic exploits of Caesar? No, Horace replies, he has no talent for that. It would be much more prudent, Trebatius points out, than making fun of living men under false names: everyone's afraid it may be him, and hates the author. Then comes the bulk of the poem, a long reply by Horace explaining that everyone has his leaning, and his is to poetry. He has modelled himself on the noble Lucilius, who has left us his whole life-story in verse, who wrote fearlessly and was a friend of great statesmen. He has no desire to look for quarrels, but if attacked he will reply, and fiercely. To cut things short, he concludes that whatever life has in store for him he will go on writing. Trebatius is afraid Horace will not live long, or will get into trouble; Horace replies with another admiring account of Lucilius, his fearlessness, and his friendship with the great men of his time, and claims that of him too envy will have to confess, however reluctantly, that he lived among the great. Trebatius repeats his concern, warning him that the law condemns the writing of *mala carmina*, malicious poems; Horace deliberately misunderstands this and interprets it in the sense of bad poems, and suggests that his poems are not bad but good. In that case says Trebatius, joining in the joke, the indictment will be laughed out of court, and you will get off.

Over 1700 years later, Alexander Pope published a series of poems attacking contemporary customs and individuals, and discussing his own role as a poet. As Horace had looked back to Lucilius as a model, he looked back to Horace, but in a different and much closer fashion: instead of talking about Horace he rewrote his poems in English, in versions that are sometimes very close to the original, sometimes very free, and published these under the title *Imitations of Horace*, clearly intending his readers to know what he had done. To the twentieth-century reader this may seem very odd: we value originality highly, and despise anyone we think of as a mere imitator: lifting material from another poet we regard as stealing, and we have a word—plagiarism—to describe it. If the other poet is living, he may be able to sue us for breach of copyright. So we ought to begin our discussion by thinking for a moment about the very idea of imitation, in order to feel ourselves back into the position of Pope's original readers. Pope did not invent the idea. It was common in the sixteenth and seventeenth centuries and some Renaissance critics suggest that it is normal practice when writing poetry. The qualities required by the poet, says Ben Jonson in his treatise *Timber*, are five: goodness of natural wit (*ingenium*), the exercise of those parts (*exercitatio*), imitation (*imitatio*), exactness of study and multiplicity of reading (*lectio*), and art (*ars*). The most surprising of these, to us, is certainly imitation, which is defined as "to be able to convert the substance or riches of another poet to his own use". You choose your model, and try and equal his skill. Jonson insists that the imitation should not be slavish; we must do it

"not as a creature that swallows what it takes in, crude, raw, or undigested; but that feeds with an appetite, and hath a stomach to concoct, divide, and turn all into nourishment."

Jonson himself (like Pope) is a splendid example of a poet who could turn his models into nourishment; but why have models? To this there are perhaps two main answers.

The first involves our conception of the past. A poet's view of past poetry is not likely to be of a burden that has to be shed, for if he did not love poetry in the first place he would not want to write it himself. He is more likely to think of it as a heritage to be passed on. Think for a moment not of a poet but of a cook: we would be very suspicious of a cook who did not want to learn, and use, the recipes of others— indeed, we might be unwilling to trust our digestion to him. Skill in cooking, once learnt, is clearly worth imitating; and to find recipes in past poets that lead to ravishing verbal dishes is, surely, to want to use them. Of course there is a difference: the true equivalent of the cook using someone else's recipe is, no doubt, the anthologist or editor who hands on the poem as it is, without pretending that he has taken part in its composition. But suppose it is in another language? Or even that it overlaps partly with what the living poet is himself trying to do. The doctrine of imitation encourages the poet to build on the work of his predecessors, and to do so openly: the reader who knows the original will thereby gain an extra pleasure, the sense that in a living contemporary work the past has been given new life.

This argument assumes resemblance between imitator and imitated, that the power of the new comes from the use of the old. But there can also be differences: the reader who knows the original may see very clearly what you have changed, and so respond instantly to your intention. By this argument, tradition (of which imitation is an extreme form) is not a way of keeping the past alive, but of asserting the identity of the present: when you have a model, your departures from it will be immediately visible, and you will then have a particularly efficient way of showing originality.

We can illustrate both functions of imitation from Pope's poem. Perhaps its most beautiful lines are those describing his own fate (91-100):

> Then learned sir! (to cut the matter short)
> What'er my fate, or well or ill at Court,
> Whether old age, with faint but cheerful ray,
> Attends to gild the evening of my day,
> Or Death's black wing already be displayed,
> To wrap me in the Universal shade . . .

This is a surprisingly lyrical note in the middle of the satire. In the course of telling us that whatever happens to him he will go on writing, he includes four moving and dignified lines on the fact that he may live long or die soon; and the reader who knows his Horace will be aware that much the same happens in the original:

> Ne longum faciam; seu me tranquilla senectus
> Expectat, seu mors atris circumvolat alis;

> To cut the matter short; whether peaceful old age awaits me,
> or whether death with black wings is hovering above me.

Pope added the imagery about old age, we notice, and though the black wing of death was in Horace it was Pope who drew out of it the conceit that that wing itself could be used to wrap him in the universal shade; in Horace the wing is only for flying. But above all, what gives these lines their effect is the change of tone, the lyrical melancholy that contrasts so strongly with the casualness that precedes and follows. The fact that the same change of tone is found in Horace does not make it any less beautiful in Pope; it means that the reader who is also a classical scholar can notice that a recipe which worked before is working again.

In offering this example I have shown that to imitate is also to change; now here is another in which the change is more striking than the resemblance. When Trebatius tells Horace that he ought to stop writing, Horace replies

> Peream male si non
> Optimum erat: verum nequeo dormire

> Strike me dead if that not the best advice,
> but I can't sleep.

Pope has removed the admission that the advice is good; but out of the last three lines he has made:

> Not write? but then I think,
> And for my soul I cannot sleep a wink.
> I nod in company, I wake at night,
> Fools rush into my head, and so I write.

That last couplet is pure Pope: he has taken a hint from Horace in order to be himself. His the uproarious contrast between sleeping in company and waking at night (a good recipe for writing, as he remarked in a letter), his the perfectly controlled speech rhythm, the rapid movement gathering speed over two lines and ending in a shrug of the shoulders on the last few words. Here the effect of knowing the original would above all be to see how Pope had let himself go.

Two concluding remarks about imitation. The first is that I have, in explaining it, exaggerated the extent to which it is a doctrine strange to us. Imitation is not by any means dead in the twentieth century. Ezra Pound and T. S. Eliot deliberately wrote poetry that draws its strength from the past, though often by contrasting past and present: they quote freely and sometimes deliberately misquote, so that we can watch them tampering with the past. Among living poets, Robert Lowell is probably the most distinguished of imitators, keeping his own linguistic genius alive even when drawing most on those he is almost—never quite—translating.

The second is a point that has no doubt already occurred to you, but that ought to be admitted explicitly: that though imitation may offer a lot extra to the reader who knows the original, it takes nothing away from the ignorant. The reader who has never heard of Horace is not handicapped in reading this poem: if it has difficulties, they lie elsewhere, as we shall see. I thought it best to begin by discussing the question of imitation for two reasons. The first is that, as, Pope's title makes clear it is important for the understanding of the kind of poem we have here; the second is that, in another sense, it is not important at all, and the reader who wants to take Pope entirely on his own terms may be glad to have it out of the way. From now on, it will not be necessary to mention Horace again.

> There are (I scarce can think it, but am told)
> There are to whom my Satire seems too bold

In a sense, the poem could begin with the second line: the repetition and the parenthesis add nothing to the meaning. But to remove that first line would be poetically disastrous: for it is precisely that repetition, and that smiling, mock-modest parenthesis, that set the easy conversational tone which is so important in the poem. This is to be an informal poem, we see: it is to have the relaxed air and the easy flow of good conversation. We know these are qualities that Pope valued. In a letter—an ordinary prose letter this time—to his friend Henry Cromwell, Pope describes his intention as

"To make use of that freedom and familiarity of style which we have taken up in our Correspondence, and which is more properly talking upon Paper, than Writing . . ."

This ideal is naturally appropriate to epistolary prose: Pope values and practises it in verse as well, and nowhere better than in his satires. In the most famous of all the satires, the *Epistle to Dr Arbuthnot,* this quality is seen at its most perfect:

> Shut, shut the door, good John! fatigued I said,
> Tie up the knocker, say I'm sick, I'm dead,
> The Dog-star rages! nay tis past a doubt,
> All Bedlam, or Parnassus, is let out:
> Fire in each eye, and papers in each hand,
> They rave, recite and madden round the land.

All that is needed to appreciate the skill of these lines is to read them aloud. The first couplet is metrically perfect, and at the same time has completely captured the rhythm of real speech. The poem is a complaint that he is constantly besieged by the importunities of amateur poets and hack journalists who pester him for help and criticism, and since it is also a letter to one of Pope's closest friends the required tone is one of half-resigned, half-resentful amusement; so in these opening lines the plague of poets is seen as a kind of dance of madmen, or a natural phenomenon appropriate to the hot season ("the Dog-star rages"). The jokes are effortless: "Bedlam" was the hospital for the insane and so the fourth line suggests that the sacred mountain of poetry has now become a kind of lunatic asylum. The last couplet continues the same thought: the stream of importunate callers is seen as a stream of madmen, and the uproarious quality of the vision comes most of all from the use of the three verbs (that could apply to poets *or* lunatics) as verbs of motion.

There are similar effects in *To Mr Fortescue:* the self-deprecating shrug, for instance, with which he suggests that being attacked from both sides is a proof of his good sense:

> In Moderation placing all my glory,
> While Tories call me Whig, and Whigs a Tory.

—or the lines immediately following, which apologize gracefully for his attacks:

> Satire's my weapon, but I'm too discreet
> To run amuck, and tilt at all I meet;
> I only wear it in a land of Hectors,
> Thieves, supercargoes, sharpers and directors.

"Hectors" were a group of dissolute young gentlemen who swaggered round London by night, causing damage to property and assaulting men and women alike. "Supercargoes" were commercial officers on board merchant ships, and the occupation was famed for its wealth. "Sharpers" are no doubt card-sharpers, or perhaps more generally confidence tricksters. In the first couplet, the poet presents himself as a reasonable man and discriminating satirist; in the second he lists the provocations that do draw his indignation. The list is a cunning sneer at contemporary society, for it alternates those who are clearly criminal with respectable members of society, as if they are all equally representative of the world he is obliged to live in. The result is to suggest: I'm a reasonable man and only use my satire on the following categories—who (you will notice) are typical of the times, so of course I have to attack everyone in the end, not because I'm unreasonable but because the world is.

These couplets would be nothing without their ability to capture the speaking voice: the barbed effect, for instance, that can be achieved by a short pause in the last line, before it ends with the devasting politeness of "—and directors". But that ability in turn would be nothing if not matched against the perfection of rhyme and metre: the feeling of completing the line with a kind of inevitability adds enormously to the power of the insult. There will be a discussion of the heroic couplet in the Crabbe essay which follows this one, but one point of general importance can be made now. The rhythm of real speech is naturally irregular: whereas metrical patterns (that is what makes them patterns) are regular. There is a certain formal pleasure in the pure regularity of perfectly metrical lines, in which the stresses fall exactly according to rule

—All Nature mourns, the skies relent in showers—

but its artificiality soon palls; and there is a pleasure in listening to the rhythms of actual speech, but it is not a specifically literary pleasure, and those modern poets who write in pure speech rhythm

> —We finished clearing the last
> Section of trail by noon,
> High on the ridge-side
> Two thousand feet above the creek—

offer us the pleasure of recognizing the genuine but in the end are behaving more like tape-recorders than poets. The complex pleasure of a poet who is a master of ryhthm consists in an interplay between the metrical pattern and the true movement of speech, and these couplets of Pope are a perfect example of this.

The ideal of "talking on paper" is not confined to Pope, and its importance is not simply metrical. Behind it lies a wider set of ideals generally held by the Augustans: the admiration for civilized urbanity, for moderation and good sense, and the corresponding rejection of extreme passions such as avarice and prodigality, fanaticism or tyranny. Almost all Pope's poetry can be seen as praise of these ideals, and in this he is certainly a man representative of his time. His fourth *Moral Essay*, for instance, the *Epistle to Bolingbroke on the Use of Riches,* is really a discussion of the social function of architecture, which makes fun of Timon's villa, where regularity and abstract principle have banished nature:

> Grave nods at grave, each alley has a brother,
> And half the platform just reflects the other.
> The suffering eye inverted Nature sees,
> Trees cut to statues, statues thick as trees;
> With here a fountain, never to be played,
> And there a Summer-house, that knows no shade.

Most of the poem is an exposure of folly, but it does eventually state the positive values that the satire implies, above all in the couplet

> 'Tis use alone that sanctifies expense,
> And splendour borrows all her rays from sense.

Relaxed and reasonable mockery, delivered with moderation in the tone of easy conversation: among the words most frequently used to describe this in the early eighteenth century were "decorum" and "raillery". Decorum (the observing of what is decorous or fitting) was an aesthetic term in the sixteenth century, but by Augustan times its meaning had become partly social: it is the ability to find the right tone, to say only what is suitable to the company you are in, and to say it in a way acceptable to them. Here is the ideal as stated in Pope's early statement of his doctrines, *An Essay on Criticism:*

> 'Tis not enough your counsel still be true;
> Blunt truths more mischief than nice falsehoods do;
> Men must be taught as if you taught them not,
> And things unknown proposed as things forgot.
> Without good breeding, truth is disapproved;
> That only makes superior sense beloved.

This could as easily be advice on how to behave in company as advice on how to write poetry: social and artistic decorum are seen as much the same thing. In the to-and-fro of the discussion with Fortescue, this ideal is never lost sight of, and when (for instance) Pope protests his inability to write heroic verse, celebrating warlike victories in the style of Sir Richard Blackmore, author of *Prince Arthur*

> —Rend with tremendous sound your ears asunder,
> With gun, drum, trumpet, blunderbuss and thunder—

we can even see this as an indirect assertion of his good breeding, and his mastery of the familiar style.

Raillery includes the idea of teasing, or making fun of the person you are addressing, though always with great tact, wrapping up a single criticism in layers of praise. There does not seem to be any teasing of Fortescue in this poem, but there is no doubt about the pride Pope takes in his tact and delicacy. Horace was the appropriate model for this, since he was famed for his delicacy, and often contrasted with the *saeva indignatio,* the fierce indignation of the much more passionate satirist Juvenal, also an eighteenth-century favourite. A play on words was sometimes used to make the contrast, since raillery could be contrasted with "railing", delivering oneself of violent complaints and invective. Pope certainly thought of himself as a follower of Horace not of Juvenal, though there are passages in his work when he rails instead of rallying, as in these powerful lines from the *Epilogue to the Satires:*

In soldier, churchman, patriot, man in pow'r,
'Tis av'rice all, ambition is no more!
See, all our nobles begging to be slaves!
See all our fools aspiring to be knaves!
The wit of cheats, the courage of a w——,
Are what ten thousand envy and adore;
All, all look up, with reverential awe,
At crimes that 'scape, or triumph o'er the law;
While truth, worth, wisdom, daily they decry—
"Nothing is sacred now but villany."

If we compare the list in that first line with "Thieves, super-cargoes, sharpers and directors" we can immediately see the difference. Now there is none of the delicate interplay between two kinds of person: the list is not complex and shifting in its effect, but simply cumulative. When two lines are balanced, as in the second couplet, or two half lines, as in the second line of the first couplet, they repeat and reinforce each other, rather than contrasting. This is more straightforward writing, more eloquent, less subtle. There is no playfulness, though there may be greater power.

They are also much easier to understand on a first reading; and it is time now to mention one strong disadvantage of the conversational style, its particularity. Conversation is usually full of facts and names that are known to the speakers but not to anyone outside their circle: the attempt to make us feel that we are overhearing genuine talk between friends has led to a poem that would have seemed topical and gossipy to Fortescue himself and to their immediate circle, but that may well have puzzled the public, even at the time, and in the twentieth century needs footnotes. Few readers today will know that "Sir Richard" is Sir Richard Blackmore, and fewer still will ever have looked at *Prince Arthur;* no one except an expert will know who Scarsdale, Darty and Ridotta are, or that F— stands for Fox: the elder brother Stephen was an MP at the time of Pope's writing, the younger brother Henry was not yet one. Whether Henry really did frequent the bear-garden of Hockley Hole in Clerkenwell, or whether Pope is passing on malicious gossip, is now virtually impossible to know.

There is no space in this essay to explain all the allusions in the poem, though we can notice in passing that they are of several kinds. There are references to Pope's own poetry: these are perhaps inevitable in a poem that discusses how his earlier satires have been received, and they are of two kinds. "Wise Peter" and "Chartres" (lines 3–4) are real people who were mentioned unkindly in the third of Pope's *Moral Essays*: Peter Walter was a successful financier of doubtful honesty, and Francis Chartres had an evil reputation for gambling, dishonesty and rape. "Timon" and "Balaam" are fictitious characters from the fourth and third *Moral Essays* respectively, and the only knowledge needed to recognize them is a knowledge of Pope's work. The difference between real and fictitious characters is in fact one of the points made by Fortescue:

> Bond is but one, but Harpax is a score.

There is another reference to the third *Moral Essay*. It is dangerous enough to name your victim, Fortescue suggests; it may be even more dangerous to make him fictitious since a score of people can then believe themselves to be the one intended. Then there are references to the writers whom Pope regards as his models and whom the educated reader is likely to know something about, then as well as now—Montaigne (1. 52) whose *Essais* were regarded as a model of the familiar and intimate style, and Boileau and Dryden, the great fathers of Augustan poetry. Next come Pope's friends: St John (1. 127) is Viscount Bolingbroke, one of the most celebrated intellects and politicians of the time, whose influence over Pope was enormous; lines 129–30 refer to the Earl of Peterborough, conqueror of Barcelona and Valencia: and Fortescue himself was a lawyer and leading politician with whom Pope had long been friendly. None of these names need provide us with much difficulty: but the most numerous and the most troublesome are those of Pope's victims, the contemporaries he selects for his attacks, almost all of whom are now forgotten—the Scarsdales and the Dartys.

How much does this matter? Do we need to read the *Imitations of Horace* in an annotated edition, pausing constantly to look up who everyone was? No clear answer is possible, and if we get to know the poem well then curiosity is likely to lead us to want to know more. But the experience of receiving the poem may well be independent of all this knowledge, for the very fact that there are so many names can be seen as an invitation to regard them as mere details thrown out in passing. It is obvious that Pope considered Scarsdale a drunkard and Darty a glutton, as he considered Peter Walker (deliberately mis-spelt as "Waters" in 1. 89) and Chartres a couple of rogues. Even if we knew who they were, it is unlikely that we would ever know enough to be able to judge the truth of these charges. Perhaps it is best simply to regard them as symbolic figures, representing drunkenness and gluttony.

> Slander or poison dread from Delia's rage,
> Hard words or hanging, if your judge be Page.

In the original edition this was printed "if your J—— be P——". The story has it that Sir Francis Page was certain that the reference must be to him, and even sent his clerk to Pope to complain "that no other word will make sense of the passage ', so the use of dashes (most of the names had dashes in the first edition) can have been little more than a token disguise. We cannot know how many readers recognized Mary Howard, Countess of Delorain, under the name "Delia" or Lady Mary Wortley Montague under "Sappho"; but we can certainly regard this gliding from real to false names as a excuse for us to read them all as fictitious.

I have claimed that the conversational style is something characteristically Augustan; but it is also true that this amassing of particular names and references is the very opposite of an Augustan principle. Dr Johnson claimed that the aim of poetry was "just representations of general nature", and the valuing of general principles, if possible universally valid, is central to the ideals of the Enlightenment. Thus Johnson's most famous poem begins

> Let Observation with extended view
> Survey mankind from China to Peru.

The Vanity of Human Wishes is a general moral that can be illustrated from all times and all places: for human nature is the same in China and Peru, in eighteenth-century England and Augustan Rome. As well as being very particular, Pope can be very general, as in the lines quoted above from the Epilogue to the Satires: there has after all never been a time or place in which people did not consider that morality was declining, see avarice and ambition all round them, and claim that "Nothing is sacred now but Villainy."

Something of this tension between the particular and the universal is represented in the practice of imitation. Horace writes about his own times, as (we have seen) does Pope; by basing himself on so distant an original, the modern poet shows that he is making general points even when at his most particular, surveying mankind from modern London to ancient Rome.

Finally, a word on satire: to establish what kind of poem Pope is writing, and what the characteristics, the strengths and dangers of that kind are. We have already encountered some of these questions in considering Raleigh's poem: here the issues are similar, though raised in a different way, by a very different poem.

Pope and his contemporaries were aware of the dangers of satire. Merely to deliver yourself of your dislike of an enemy, merely to abuse those you hate—this (surely) will not lead to poetry. How do we distinguish satire from invective or lampoon?

Pope's answer was a moral one: the true satirist is the guardian of traditional moral values, and his aim is not simply to triumph over his enemies, but to defend virtue against vice. In the *Epilogue to the Satires* he writes:

> Yet think not friendship only prompts my lays;
> I follow Virtue, where she shines, I praise . . .
> To find an honest man I beat about,
> And love him, court him, praise him, in or out.

We have already seen a similar statement of moral purpose in *To Mr Fortescue,* and indeed it provides the whole climax of the poem, culminating in his claim (directly translated from Horace) that he is "to virtue only and her friends a friend". The poet who cannot say this is a mere libeller or lampooner gratifying private revenge, indulging personal spleen like (we are told) Delia or Sappho.

How common it was, before the growth of more sophisticated philosophies of art in our time, for poets to defend what they did in moral terms; and how often it seems to us, looking back, that such defences simply do not account for the excellence of the poetry.

For it is difficult to regard the climax of this poem with the same unqualified admiration as it appears to demand. It begins impressively enough:

> What? armed for Virtue when I point the pen,
> Brand the bold front of shameless guilty men;
> Dash the proud gamester in his gilded car;
> Bare the mean heart that lurks beneath a star. . . .

After Fortescue's worried suggestion that his enemies will beat him up, these ringing lines sound like a proud assertion of the true purpose of satire. The third line seems almost to attribute godlike powers to the satirist, and the fourth has a haunting power because of the rich overtones of "star"—literally, of course, the decoration worn by a nobleman, but suggestive of so much more. The lines are impressive as an account of what satire can do; their weakness lurks in the use of "I". If we think of them as a personal boast, as Alexander

Pope asserting his moral purity, the very quality that made them so impressive turns to smugness. And as we read on, the personal note does grow more marked, and the self-satisfaction more unmistakable.

> Unplaced, unpensioned, no man's heir, or slave?

Again an impressive line if seen as an assertion of poetic independence—and the absence of any personal pronoun perhaps enables us to see it that way. But again, it is a dangerously smug line if seen as a boast by Alexander Pope. And the lines that follow are more difficult to defend:

> I will, or perish in the generous cause . . .

Perhaps it was unwise to put a statement like this in the future: it makes it too like like the boast of a primitive warrior, an altogether inappropriate picture for the morally committed satirist. The most unfortunate touch of all, however, is seen at 1. 133.

> Envy must own, I live among the great . . .

Since it is important for the effect of the earlier lines that they should be read as impersonally as possible, as a statement of the mission of the true satirist, not of the excellence of the speaker himself, the one thing he should not do is praise himself for *other* qualities—such as his friendship with great men, his trustworthiness, or his generosity. To find the very extreme of such self-satisfaction we can turn to the second dialogue of the *Epilogue to the Satires*, where we find the outrageous couplet

> Yes, I am proud; I must be proud to see
> Men not afraid of God, afraid of me . . .

Poetic boasting did not begin (or end) with Pope: he is no more pleased with his achievement than is—for instance—Milton, telling us that he intends to write of "things unattempted yet in prose or rhyme", or painting a picture of the poet "soaring in the high region of his fancies, with his garland and singing robes about him", and hoping that he "might perhaps leave something to aftertimes, as they should not willingly let it die". But there is a difference. Milton, when he writes like this, forgets his individual self. He boasts because he is conscious of the importance of his role: it is the epic poet we are listening to, the man charged by Providence with a high task, not John Milton the man. Now this losing of self in persona is (as we have already seen) not the case with Pope. He takes great pains to remind us that he is Alexander Pope, he tells us about his house at Twickenham and his subterranean grotto, he names his friends, he reminds us of his financial independence, and how he earned it. This autobiographical strain fits the conversational style admirably, but is highly inappropriate to the assertions of virtue.

The moral conception of satire contains in fact a great moral danger. It is traditional for the satirist to talk about himself and to use the first person frequently; and that habit fits very ill with the moral claims we have seen Pope making, for all conviction that one has done right, and all forms of self-satisfaction, are variants of pride, the first and greatest of the sins. If we want a more acceptable account of the power of satire, and what distinguishes it from invective, we should think not of virtue but of control; not of perferring good emotions and worthy purposes to hatred and anger, but of how the emotion is expressed; not in moral but in aesthetic terms. This will enable us to see that some of the polished, dignified statements of how he is serving virtue may be less sensitive, and less powerful, than, for instance

> From furious Sappho scarce a milder fate,
> P-xed by her love, or libelled by her hate.

There is nothing admirable in the purpose of this couplet: it is not sadly conceding that Sappho has failed to live up to some dearly held ideal of virtue. It is an expression of hatred, but its icy measured movement, its unrestrained emotion in such perfectly restrained metre, its one fierce monosyllabic vulgarity in the midst of otherwise dignified language, the mocking symmetry of "love–hate" as a structure to fill with so much venom—all this makes it, in its distasteful way, one of the most brilliant couplets in the poem.

The greatest poets do not require us to choose between artistic power and moral approval. Nor (but for different reasons) does Pope, since when he is approving of himself it is hardest for us to approve of him, and this discrepancy becomes an artistic as well as a moral flaw. What *To Mr Fortescue* does require, I believe, when we reflect on it, is that we should judge the poetry as poetry, not by our approval or disapproval of the satirist himself. If we take such a couplet as

> There St John mingles with my friendly bowl
> The feast of reason and the flow of soul. . . .

simply as a declaration of friendship, we can find it wholly attractive, and memorable for its witty blending of the good conversation with good food and drink. It is only as part of a boast that it is offensive, a boast that hovers uneasily between a claim to virtue and a claim to social success.

The poem really has two endings. The couplet which has the ring of finality is surely lines 137–8.

> To help who want, to forward who excel;
> This, all who know me, know; who love me, tell. . . .

That last line is very skilful, and makes a fine climax to the boasting; but once again it can ring in our ears in a way that makes us doubt. What do we tell to who, of those we love? Their virtues to the world? Well, yes. Their virtues to them? Yes, that too, and once we have thought of this meaning, it is hard to keep it out of the line: it would go so well after a critical line—after say

> Yes, I excel; but know that I excel.

And then comes an untidy coda of eighteen lines, or fifteen if we begin it after "rest my cause". The statement of intention having been rounded off, the poem returns to its unbuttoned, colloquial manner, in which a rather laboured joke is built on Fortescue's legal knowledge. This conclusion is closely based on Horace, but though that may be an explanation it cannot justify it artistically, and it certainly replaces a rather formal, final sounding ending with something much more light-hearted. And perhaps, though it is not memorable and not witty, this is right: for the poem is retreating to the urbane colloquial note on which it began. Solemnity was not an unmixed success, so we shrug it off.

# 9

# Peter Grimes

Old Peter Grimes made fishing his employ,
His wife he cabined with him and his boy,
And seemed that life laborious to enjoy:
To town came quiet Peter with his fish,
And had of all a civil word and wish.
He left his trade upon the sabbath-day,
And took young Peter in his hand to pray:
But soon the stubborn boy from care broke loose,
At first refused, then added his abuse:
His father's love he scorned, his power defied,
But being drunk, wept sorely when he died.
    Yes! then he wept, and to his mind there came
Much of his conduct, and he felt the shame,—
How he had oft the good old man reviled,
And never paid the duty of a child;
How, when the father in his Bible read,
He in contempt and anger left the shed:
"It is the word of life," the parent cried;
—"This is the life itself," the boy replied;
And while old Peter in amazement stood,
Gave the hot spirit to his boiling blood:—
How he, with oath and furious speech, began
To prove his freedom and assert the man;
And when the parent checked his impious rage,
How he had cursed the tyranny of age,—
Nay, once had dealt the sacrilegious blow
On his bare head, and laid his parent low;
The father groaned—"If thou art old," said he,
"And hast a son—thou wilt remember me:
Thy mother left me in a happy time,
Thou killedst not her—Heaven spares the double crime."
    On an inn-settle, in his maudlin grief,
This he revolved, and drank for his relief.
    Now lived the youth in freedom, but debarred
From constant pleasure, and he thought it hard;
Hard that he could not every wish obey,
But must awhile relinquish ale and play;
Hard! that he could not to his cards attend,

But must acquire the money he would spend.
　With greedy eye he looked on all he saw,
He knew not justice, and he laughed at law;
On all he marked he stretched his ready hand;
He fished by water, and he filched by land:
Oft in the night has Peter dropped his oar,
Fled from his boat and sought for prey on shore;
Oft up the hedge-row glided, on his back
Bearing the orchard's produce in a sack,
Or farm-yard load, tugged fiercely from the stack;
And as these wrongs to greater numbers rose,
The more he looked on all men as his foes.

　He built a mud-walled hovel, where he kept
His various wealth, and there he oft-times slept;
But no success could please his cruel soul,
He wished for one to trouble and control;
He wanted some obedient boy to stand
And bear the blow of his outrageous hand;
And hoped to find in some propitious hour
A feeling creature subject to his power.

　Peter had heard there were in London then,—
Still have they being!—workhouse-clearing men,
Who, undisturbed by feelings just or kind,
Would parish-boys to needy tradesmen bind:
They in their want a trifling sum would take,
And toiling slaves of piteous orphans make.

　Such Peter sought, and when a lad was found,
The sum was dealt him, and the slave was bound.
Some few in town observed in Peter's trap
A boy, with jacket blue and woollen cap;
But none inquired how Peter used the rope,
Or what the bruise, that made the stripling stoop;
None could the ridges on his back behold,
None sought him shivering in the winter's cold;
None put the question,—"Peter, dost thou give
The boy his food?—What, man! the lad must live:
Consider, Peter, let the child have bread,
He'll serve thee better if he's stroked and fed."
None reasoned thus—and some, on hearing cries,
Said calmly, "Grimes is at his exercise."

　Pinned, beaten, cold, pinched, threatened, and abused—
His efforts punished and his food refused,—

Awake tormented, —soon aroused from sleep,—
Struck if he wept, and yet compelled to weep,
The trembling boy dropped down and strove to pray,
Received a blow, and trembling turned away,
Or sobbed and hid his piteous face;—while he,
The savage master, grinned in horrid glee:
He'd now the power he ever loved to show,
A feeling being subject to his blow.

   Thus lived the lad, in hunger, peril, pain,
His tears despised, his supplications vain:
Compelled by fear to lie, by need to steal,
His bed uneasy and unblessed his meal,
For three sad years the boy his tortures bore,
And then his pains and trials were no more.

   "How died he, Peter?" when the people said,
He growled—"I found him lifeless in his bed:"
Then tried for softer tone, and sigh'd, "Poor Sam is dead.'
Yet murmurs were there, and some questions asked,—
How he was fed, how punished, and how tasked?
Much they suspected, but they little proved,
And Peter passed untroubled and unmoved.

   Another boy with equal ease was found,
The money granted, and the victim bound;
And what his fate?—One night it chanced he fell
From the boat's mast and perished in her well,
Where fish were living kept, and where the boy
(So reasoned men) could not himself destroy:—
"Yes! so it was," said Peter, "in his play,
(For he was idle both by night and day),
He climbed the main-mast and then fell below:"—
Then showed his corpse and pointed to the blow:
What said the jury?—they were long in doubt,
But sturdy Peter faced the matter out:
So they dismissed him, saying at the time,
"Keep fast your hatchway when you've boys who climb."
This hit the conscience, and he coloured more
Than for the closest questions put before.

   Thus all his fears the verdict set aside,
And at the slave-shop Peter still applied.

   Then came a boy, of manners soft and mild,—
Our seamen's wives with grief beheld the child;
All thought (the poor themselves) that he was one
Of gentle blood, some noble sinner's son,

Who had, belike, deceived some humble maid,
Whom he had first seduced and then betrayed:—
However this, he seemed a gracious lad,
In grief submissive and with patience sad.

Passive he laboured, till his slender frame
Bent with his loads, and he at length was lame:
Strange that a frame so weak could bear so long
The grossest insult and the foulest wrong;
But there were causes—in the town they gave
Fire, food, and comfort, to the gentle slave;
And though stern Peter, with a cruel hand,
And knotted rope, enforced the rude command,
Yet he considered what he'd lately felt,
And his vile blows with selfish pity dealt.

One day such draughts the cruel fisher made,
He could not vend them in his borough-trade,
But sailed for London-mart: the boy was ill,
But ever humbled to his master's will;
And on the river, where they smoothly sailed,
He strove with terror and awhile prevailed;
But new to danger on the angry sea,
He clung affrighten ed to his master's knee:
The boat grew leaky and the wind was strong,
Rough was the passage and the time was long;
His liquor failed, and Peter's wrath arose,—
No more is known—the rest we must suppose,
Or learn of Peter;—Peter says, he 'spied
The stripling's danger and for harbour tried;
"Meantime the fish, and then the apprentice died."

The pitying women raised a clamour round,
And weeping said, "Thou hast thy prentice drowned."

Now the stern man was summoned to the hall,
To tell his tale before the burghers all:
He gave th'account; professed the lad he loved,
And kept his brazen features all unmoved.

The mayor himself with tone severe replied,—
"Henceforth with thee shall never boy abide;
Hire thee a freeman, whom thou durst not beat,
But who, in thy despite, will sleep and eat:
Free thou art now!—again shouldst thou appear,
Thou'lt find thy sentence, like thy soul, severe."

Alas! for Peter, not a helping hand,
So he was hated, could he now command;

Alone he rowed his boat, alone he cast
His nests beside, or made his anchor fast;
To hold a rope or hear a curse was none,—
He toiled and rail'd; he groaned and swore alone.
   Thus by himself compelled to live each day,
To wait for certain hours the tide's delay;
At the same times the same dull views to see,
The bounding marsh-bank and the blighted tree;
The water only, when the tides were high,
When low, the mud half-covered and half-dry;
The sun-burnt tar that blisters on the planks,
And bank-side stakes in their uneven ranks;
Heaps of entangled weeds that slowly float,
As the tide rolls by the impeded boat.
   When tides were neap, and, in the sultry day,
Through the tall bounding mud-banks made their way,
Which on each side rose swelling, and below
The dark warm flood ran silently and slow;
There anchoring, Peter chose from man to hide,
There hang his head, and view the lazy tide
In its hot slimy channel slowly guide;
Where the small eels that left the deeper way
For the warm shore, within the shallows play;
Where gaping mussels, left upon the mud,
Slope their slow passage to the fallen flood;—
Here dull and hopeless he'd lie down and trace
How sidelong crabs had scrawled their crooked race;
Or sadly listen to the tuneless cry
Of fishing gull or clanging golden-eye;
What time the sea-birds to the marsh would come,
And the loud bittern, from the bull-rush home,
Gave from the salt-ditch side the bellowing boom:
He nursed the feelings these dull scenes produce,
And loved to stop beside the opening sluice;
Where the small stream, confined in narrow bound,
Ran with a dull, unvaried, saddening sound;
Where all, presented to the eye or ear,
Oppressed the soul with misery, grief, and fear.
   Besides these objects, there were places three,
Which Peter seemed with certain dread to see;
When he drew near them he would turn from each,
And loudly whistle till he passed the reach.
   A change of scene to him brought no relief;

In town, 'twas plain, men took him for a thief:
The sailors' wives would stop him in the street,
And say, "Now, Peter, thou'st no boy to beat:"
Infants at play, when they perceived him, ran,
Warning each other—"That's the wicked man":
He growled an oath, and in an angry tone
Cursed the whole place and wished to be alone.

    Alone he was, the same dull scenes in view,
And still more gloomy in his sight they grew:
Though man he hated, yet employed alone
At bootless labour, he would swear and groan,
Cursing the shoals that glided by the spot,
And gulls that caught them when his arts could not.

    Cold nervous tremblings shook his sturdy frame,
And strange disease—he couldn't say the name;
Wild were his dreams, and oft he rose in fright,
Waked by his view of horrors in the night,—
Horrors that would the sternest minds amaze,
Horrors that demons might be proud to raise:
And though he felt forsaken, grieved at heart,
To think he lived from all mankind apart;
Yet, if a man approached, in terrors he would start.

    A winter passed since Peter saw the town,
And summer-lodgers were again come down;
These, idly curious, with their glasses spied
The ships in bay as anchored for the tide,—
The river's craft,—the bustle of the quay,—
And sea-port views, which landmen love to see.

    One, up the river, had a man and boat
Seen day by day, now anchored, now afloat;
Fisher he seemed, yet used no net nor hook;
Of sea-fowl swimming by no heed he took,
But on the gliding waves still fixed his lazy look:
At certain stations he would view the stream,
As if he stood bewildered in a dream,
Or that some power had chained him for a time,
To feel a curse or meditate on crime.

    This known, some curious, some in pity went,
And others questioned—"Wretch, dost thou repent?"
He heard, he trembled, and in fear resigned
His boat: new terror filled his restless mind;
Furious he grew, and up the country ran,
And there they seized him—a distempered man:—

Him we received, and to a parish-bed,
Followed and cursed, the groaning man was led.

Here, when they saw him, whom they used to shun,
A lost, lone man, so harassed and undone;
Our gentle females, ever prompt to feel,
Perceived compassion on their anger steal;
His crimes they could not from their memories blot,
But they were grieved, and trembled at his lot.

A priest too came, to whom his words are told;
And all the signs they shuddered to behold.

"Look! look!" they cried; "his limbs with horror shake,
And as he grinds his teeth, what noise they make!
How glare his angry eyes, and yet he's not awake:
See! what cold drops upon his forehead stand,
And how he clenches that broad bony hand."

The priest attending, found he spoke at times
As one alluding to his fears and crimes:
"It was the fall," he muttered, "I can show
The manner how—I never struck a blow:"—
And then aloud—"Unhand me, free my chain;
On oath, he fell—it struck him to the brain:—
Why ask my father?—that old man will swear
Against my life; besides, he wasn't there:—
What, all agreed?—Am I to die to-day?—
My Lord, in mercy, give me time to pray."

Then, as they watched him, calmer he became,
And grew so weak he couldn't move his frame,
But murmuring spake, —while they could see and hear
The start of terror and the groan of fear;
See the large dew-beads on his forehead rise,
And the cold death-drop glaze his sunken eyes;
Nor yet he died, but with unwonted force
Seemed with some fancied being to discourse:
He knew not us, or with accustomed art
He hid the knowledge, yet exposed his heart;
'Twas part confession and the rest defence,
A madman's tale, with gleams of waking sense.

"I'll tell you all," he said, "the very day
When the old man first placed them in my way:
My father's spirit—he who always tried
To give me trouble, when he lived and died—
When he was gone, he could not be content
To see my days in painful labour spent,

But would appoint his meetings, and he made
Me watch at these, and so neglect my trade.
  "'Twas one hot noon, all silent, still, serene,
No living being had I lately seen;
I paddled up and down and dipped my net,
But (such his pleasure) I could nothing get,—
A father's pleasure, when his toil was done,
To plague and torture thus an only son!
And so I sat and looked upon the stream,
How it ran on, and felt as in a dream:
But dream it was not; no!—I fixed my eyes
On the mid stream and saw the spirits rise;
I saw my father on the water stand,
And hold a thin pale boy in either hand;
And there they glided ghastly on the top
Of the salt flood, and never touched a drop:
I would have struck them, but they knew th'intent,
And smiled upon the oar, and down they went.
  "Now, from that day, whenever I began
To dip my net, there stood the hard old man—
He and those boys: I humbled me and prayed
They would be gone;—they heeded not, but stayed:
Nor could I turn, nor would the boat go by,
But gazing on the spirits, there was I:
They bade me leap to death, but I was loth to die:
And every day, as sure as day arose,
Would these three spirits meet me ere the close;
To hear and mark them daily was my doom,
And 'Come,' they said, with weak, sad voices, 'come'.
To row away with all my strength I tried,
But there were they, hard by me in the tide,
The three unbodied forms—and 'Come,' still 'come,' they
    cried.
  "Fathers should pity—but this old man shook
His hoary locks, and froze me by a look:
Thrice, when I struck them, through the water came
A hollow groan, that weakened all my frame:
'Father!' said I, 'have mercy:'—He replied,
I know not what—the angry spirit lied,—
'Didst thou not draw thy knife?' said he:—'Twas true,
But I had pity and my arm withdrew:
He cried for mercy which I kindly gave,
But he has no compassion in his grave.

"There were three places, where they ever rose,—
The whole long river has not such as those,—
Places accursed, where, if a man remain,
He'll see the things which strike him to the brain;
And there they made me on my paddle lean,
And look at them for hours;—accursed scene!
When they would glide to that smooth eddy-space,
Then bid me leap and join them in the place;
And at my groans each little villain sprite
Enjoyed my pains and vanished in delight.
    "In one fierce summer-day, when my poor brain
Was burning hot and cruel was my pain,
Then came this father-foe, and there he stood
With his two boys again upon the flood;
There was more mischief in their eyes, more glee
In their pale faces when they glared at me:
Still did they force me on the oar to rest,
And when they saw me fainting and oppressed,
He, with his hand, the old man, scooped the flood,
And there came flame about him mixed with blood;
He bade me stoop and look upon the place,
Then flung the hot-red liquor in my face;
Burning it blazed, and then I roared for pain,
I thought the demons would have turned my brain.
    "Still there they stood, and forced me to behold
A place of horrors—they cannot be told—
Where the flood opened, there I heard the shriek
Of tortured guilt—no earthly tongue can speak:
'All days alike! for ever!' did they say,
'And unremitted torments every day'—
Yes, so they said:" —But here he ceased and gazed
On all around, affrightened and amazed;
And still he tried to speak, and looked in dread
Of frightened females gathering round his bed;
Then dropped exhausted and appeared at rest,
Till the strong foe the vital powers possessed;
Then with an inward, broken voice he cried,
"Again they come," and muttered as he died.

                                    *George Crabbe*  (*1810*)

Here we have a narrative poem very different in method from the
ballad. The story is told fully and at length covering the whole life

of Peter Grimes. There are only occasional touches of dialogue, and the method is not dramatic but straightfoward narrative. So our commentary can follow the poem, and, to begin with, move through the story from beginning to end. We can divide it roughly into four parts: a short preface, describing Grime's relations with his father and his establishing a way of life; then his treatment of his boys; his solitary life; and finally his own story. Each has a slightly different flavour.

The preface, as I have called it, takes us to line 50. It is the most cursory, and there is no real explanation of the father–son situation, but the poem's ability to surprise us strikes home in the couplet

> His father's love he scorned, his power defied,
> But being drunk, wept sorely when he died.

The first line is so brief as to seem hurried, and does not prepare us at all for the savage comment of the second, whose movement invites us to linger on "wept sorely" in a way that might sound strongly emotional if the harsh announcement of the first three words did not turn it to mockery. The poem has made its announcement that no sentimentality will be tolerated: Peter is to be ruthlessly exposed.

There is a moment in Peter's rebellion against his father at which he might seem to capture our sympathy:

> "It is the word of life," the parent cried;
> —"This is the life itself," the boy replied.

Is this the rebellion of spontaneity against repression, of living against books, of youth against the stiffness of age? We might think so, from this single very effective couplet, but the next few lines soon withdraw any such sympathy, as the "hot spirit" issues mainly in oaths and rage.

When he has to set up life for himself, Peter finds it hard to accept reality, that he "must acquire the money he would spend". The mere balancing of the two verbs in that line shows us the inevitability of the statement: spending presupposes acquiring, and what Peter is rebelling against is quite simply the basic fact of economic life. His thieving, and his withdrawal from human society, result from his own inability to accept necessary reality. He is no romantic rebel, no embodiment of energy, but simply a work-dodger.

Then comes the episodes of the boys and their deaths. It is mere cruelty that drives him to want a boy to exercise mastery on, and a social abuse—the irresponsibility of the "workhouse-clearing men" —gives him his desire. The poem does not mince words in describing the suffering, nor in describing the pleasure felt by the master at having

> A feeling being subject to his blow.

It takes three deaths before Peter is forbidden to keep a boy. Each death, clearly, is caused by him, though in each case the narrative steps back a moment, not telling us in so many words that the boy was murdered. We are told quite explicitly of the starving and the beating, even to such details as the "knotted rope" in line 135, but in each case the climax is simply the mention of the boy's death, and we are left to draw our own conclusions. This puts us in the same position as the community, who knew perfectly well how Peter had treated the boys, but had no direct evidence that he had killed them. It is mainly in this part of the poem that attention widens to include the rest of the community, and we ask if they too are included in its scorn.

> Much they suspected, but they little proved,
> And Peter pass'd untroubled and unmoved.

Are they slow to punish without proof? or slow to protect the victim? These two lines merely tell us what happened, implying no clear value-judgement; but the reaction to the next death is more interesting.

> What said the jury? They were long in doubt,
> But sturdy Peter faced the matter out:
> So they dismissed him, saying at the time,
> "Keep fast your hatchway when you've boys who climb."

Clearly the jury were tempted to condemn this time; and it was partly Peter's own boldness that protected him. This suggests a process of law that faltered at the crucial moment, and perhaps that is what the poem is suggesting, but the sardonic last line, though it shows their evasiveness, also shows their caustic wit: they have not been fooled, and they speak with the voice of the poet himself, for their comment has his insight and his cool irony. Finally, in the voice of the mayor, comes the voice not merely of sarcasm but of decision, and the solemnity of the line.

> Henceforth with thee shall never boy abide . . .

has a quite different kind of power: the voice of morality, not of wit.

And now we come to the third and by far the finest part of the poem. What we have seen so far can be matched from elsewhere in Crabbe. The caustic note we saw in Peter's drunken weeping, and the moral dignity of the judge's pronouncement, were already present in his first serious poem, *The Village,* in which we can find the following description of the parish poorhouse:

> Here too the sick their final doom receive,
> Here brought, amid the scenes of grief, to grieve,
> Where the loud groans from some sad chamber flow,
> Mixt with the clamours of the crowd below;
> Here, sorrowing, they each kindred sorrow scan,
> And the cold charities of man to man.

The control shown in these couplets lends a dignity to the anger. The syntax of the second line, for instance, helps to make the poem's point: the verb "grieve", following so hard upon the noun "grief", suggests the inevitability of the whole process, the way one after another the inmates all go the same way. And there is a savage power in the weighty movement of the last line, the way "charities" draws so much contempt from being joined to "cold". Anyone who knew *The Village* would feel no surprise at reading the first 170 lines of *Peter Grimes*: he would recognize the same dignity, the same moral concern, the same weighty irony. But there is nothing else in Crabbe, indeed hardly anything else in English poetry, quite like the thirty-five lines which follow.

The technique of matching landscape to feeling, of making descriptive poetry functional, is an old one, in painting as well as poetry. Heroic action takes place against dramatic settings of mountain and cloud; melancholy thoughts are placed in darkness in a churchyard. Crabbe's originality lies in the kind of landscape he chooses and the kind of emotion he matches it to. Grimes, left to himself, sinks into melancholia; and as he grows more and more alienated from his fellow-men, day follows day monotonously, with no emotional peaks, no warmth, no colour. What scene would match this? Crabbe was an East Anglian, and so he gives us the flat bleak landscape of the fens, marshy, monotonous, unattractive. Lines 171–

80 set the scene, and attach it to Peter by telling us he was compelled to look at it and nothing else:

> At the same time the same dull views to see.

Everything works to slow down the movement of this line. Monosyllables always tend to slow us down, as does the presence of two separate adjectives, not joined by "and" or "but", in front of the same noun. Here we have a whole line of monosyllables, the repetition of "same", and the two drawn-out words "same dull" in front of "views". Then come a series of visual details each seen with the beady eye of the unresponsive Peter and culminating in the brilliant couplet

> Heaps of entangled weeds that slowly float,
> As the tide rolls by the impeded boat.

The lines move in the same clogged way as the scene they are describing. The first offers the contrast between its one complicated word "entangled"—describing the one complicated idea—and the monotony of "slowly float"; the second begins with the same slow movement, then catches us up in the word "impeded", that impedes *our* movement through an otherwise straightforward line.

The idea of the tides is very important to this whole passage, which is filled with gradual and imperceptible movement—like the movement of time in Peter's monotonous life. It is completely appropriate to choose neap tides—the time of the month at which the difference between high and low tide is least, so that the movement is even more imperceptible. There is a tremendous sense of power in the line

> The dark warm flood ran silently and slow,

where the first four words, particularly, build up the feeling of inevitable movement (again, the monosyllables help). Then, after the tide has been described, we move to details of water creatures, all of them caught on the land in some way, all having difficulty in getting back to their element; and of birds, whose cries all capture the hideous monotony of the scene. Then we move back again to the movement of the water:

> Where the small stream, confined in narrow bound,
> Ran with a dull, unvaried, saddening sound

It is a piece of careful description, memorable and acceptable on the literal level; but it is easy to see it, too, as the lapsing of Peter's own life, which runs with the same unvaried sound. Only now, in line 204, do we move to an explicit statement of the emotions being conveyed, "misery, grief and fear". By itself, this line would have no power or vividness: it is only the power of description building up to it that justifies it poetically.

These lines are worth reading and savouring over and over. Their appropriateness to Peter's situation draws on their power as pure description of a marshy landscape; and the description engaged our attention because of its correspondence to the emotion. Each part of the effect would be much weaker without the other. There is unfortunately nothing so powerful in the rest of the third part, which moves from the landscape to details of Peter's isolation, a description of the horrors that haunted his dreams, and then the account of how he went distracted and was brought to a "parish-bed"—perhaps in the very poorhouse so scathingly described in *The Village*. And this takes me to the last and longest part of the narrative, Peter's confession, in which he goes over his whole life story in his own words. The description of the raving that introduces it shows perhaps the weakest side of the poem:

"Look! look!" they cried; "his limbs with horror shake,
And as he grinds his teeth, what noise they make!
How glare his angry eyes, and yet he's not awake. . . ."

These are stock details of guilt and madness, and the poem here relies on them in a way that sounds merely melodramatic: the language does not respond to the emotion with anything like the same sensitivity we have seen before. Perhaps the same easy and stereotyped effect is seen in the "hollow groan" that weakened all his frame in line 331. But there is none the less a great deal that is very effective in this last part.

The most powerful element in Peter's confession comes from the change in viewpoint. The very same period in his life that had been rendered through a description of the bleak landscape is now narrated by Peter himself: and we discover that his life had not merely been isolated, but haunted. His guilt over his father had not taken the form of repentance—he still feels resentment at him, and describes him as

he who always tried
To give me trouble when he lived and died—

but his fantasy indulges in what in psychoanalytic terminology is called projection. The guilt he is unconsciously aware of, but will not admit to himself, is projected on to the figure of the father (the natural representative of a moral code one feels one has broken); and because of his disordered state of mind his father is not symbolized by some other authority figure, but actually appears as a ghost. By means of this psychic mechanism, he is able to conceal from himself the fact that he feels guilt, but only at a terrible price—eventually the price of his sanity. Crabbe would of course have been surprised to see the story explained in this psychoanalytic language, none of which would have been familiar to him, but it is tempting to think, on the strength of this poem, that he would have understood, and even accepted, the idea of unconscious guilt. And we may be sure that he intended the ghosts to be interpreted not as supernatural apparitions, but as the product of Peter's own fantasy.

Perhaps the most powerful lines in Grimes's own story are 306–13.

> But dream it was not; no!—I fixed my eyes
> On the mid stream and saw the spirits rise;
> I saw my father on the water stand,
> And hold a thin pale boy in either hand;
> And there they glided ghastly on the top
> Of the salt flood, and never touched a drop:
> I would have struck them, but they knew the intent,
> And smiled upon the oar, and down they went.

The fascinated horror of the experience is captured in several details of the language: in the matter-of-fact insistence of the verb (slightly underlined by alliteration) in "saw the spirits rise", subtly reinforced by the (now emphasized) repetition of "saw" in the next line, when attention is turned to the details of the vision. The "thin pale boy" has a double suggestiveness, for the boys can be thin and pale because they are ghosts, or because they pined and wasted under Peter's cruelty, and both interpretations would fit. Like all ghosts they are intangible and cannot be reached by blows; and like so many ghosts they smile in the superiority of their insight and their invincibility. Perhaps the main reason for the power of this passage lies in its sense of quiet. Instead of the crude horror of grinding teeth or hollow groans, we have a silent vision and slow irresistible movement. Those ghosts take their identity from Peter's imaginings, but much of their quality from the tides and the landscape.

In the end, the quiet horror turns to violence; and Peter's guilt turns to a vision of hell. The transition from ghost to devil, from bleak landscape to place of torment, grows quite explicit in the episode that begins at line 348. The day is hot, and his brain seems to be burning: we can see that a subjective explanation of it all is possible. But to Peter the vision was horribly real, and the blending of water and fire gives a grotesque and shocking climax:

> He, with his hand, the old man, scooped the flood,
> And there came flame about him mixed with blood;
> He bade me stoop and look upon the place,
> Then flung the hot-red liquor in my face.

That single gesture marks the final collapse of Grimes. The spirit is no longer mockingly aloof, but taunts him actively: his inner defences are no longer able to keep it at bay, and the final line, with the strong emphatic verb "flung", seems to reach out and impose the terrible climax on us. After that, there is nothing left for Peter but to die.

George Crabbe was born in 1754, and died in 1832. In 1754 the first great generation of Augustan writers, Pope, Swift and Addison, were all dead; Dr Johnson was forty-five, Gray thirty-eight, Goldsmith twenty-six. Crabbe belongs to a later generation than all of them, and by the time he began writing the conventions of eighteenth-century poetry were long established and even old-fashioned. On the other hand, he was older than the great Romantics, for Wordsworth was not born until sixteen years later, Coleridge eighteen, Byron thirty-four and Shelley thirty-eight. The usual picture of English poetry and its history sees the Romantic movement as the great rebellion against the conventions of eighteenth-century poetry, and Crabbe seems chronologically placed to be the last survivor of an outmoded poetic tradition. Certainly the Romantic poets regarded him as old-fashioned, and Wordsworth, Coleridge and Keats all spoke slightingly of him; the only Romantics who admired him, Scott and Byron, are those who were most strongly in sympathy with the eighteenth century. The particular complaints made by Wordsworth and Coleridge, that his pictures are "mere matters of fact" and that he had "an absolute defect of high imagination," show that they found him wanting in the central Romantic quality of imagination. In this respect *Peter Grimes* is not typical of Crabbe's work. Most of his tales stick more closely to the realistic surface of social life, and contain none of the visions of horror and suggestions of the supernatural that seem to relate this poem more closely than usual to the kind of story that attracted the Romantics. Yet if we put Grimes next to some of the great Romantic solitaries—Byron's Manfred, say, or Shelley's Alastor, or Coleridge's Ancient Mariner—we must be struck by the profound differences. The mysterious adventures of the Ancient Mariner lead him into encounters with the supernatural that arouse awe as much as horror, that suggest a world of spiritual creatures watching over nature, rather than simply the dreams of a bad conscience.

> The upper air burst into life;
> And a hundred fire-flags sheen;
> To and fro they were hurried about!
> And to and fro, and in and out,
> The wan stars danced between.

It can remind us of the fire that Grimes "sees" on the water in his final madness, but how different. Coleridge's verse quickens with some of the excitement of the vision itself: for him it is not evidence of someone's breakdown, but a glimpse into the mysterious world that the imagination explores.

Even the solitude of Grimes is not altogether a Romantic solitude: there is no suggestion that his imagination is enriched through lonely contact with Nature (as with Wordsworth's Wanderer), nor that a restless quest for knowledge separates him from the common herd (as with Byron's Manfred, or his prototype Faust): Crabbe assumes a social ethic, and shows us the collapse of a spirit that refuses the responsibilities of society. Aristotle believed that the man who fled from human society must be either a beast or a god. Romantic poetry is full of solitaries striving to be gods, but for Crabbe Grimes is sinking below the human.

So it is not surprising to learn that as Romantic taste prevailed in England, Crabbe sank out of fashion. Crabbe's early poems, published in the 1780s, were successful, his *Tales of the Hall* (1819) even more successful, but during the last ten years of his life Crabbe was no longer popular. The common reader's rejection of eighteenth-century taste was belated but firm.

If then we are going to look at Crabbe historically, it seems natural to treat him as the last Augustan. Literary history is not the main purpose of this book, though I have tried to see every poem with an awareness of its place in a tradition; but there are good reasons for being more explicitly historical in our approach to Crabbe. For he both is and is not an Augustan poet; and by comparing his couplets with the standard model we can learn a good deal about what the poetry is doing.

The fact that he wrote almost exclusively in couplets is the first and most obvious Augustan feature of Crabbe's poetry; for the heroic couplet, as we have seen in discussing Pope, is the standard Augustan form, embodying so much of the ideology of the age. It is true that the Romantics also used couplets, but how differently.

> A haunting music, sole perhaps and lone
> Supportress of the fairy-roof, made moan
> Throughout, as fearful the whole charm might fade.
> Fresh-carved cedar, mimicking a glade
> Of palm and plantain, met from either side,
> High in the midst, in honour of the bride:
> Two palms and then two plantains, and so on,
> From either side their stems branch'd one to one
> All down the aisléd place; and beneath all
> There ran a stream of lamps straight on from wall to wall.

This description of the magic palace from Keats's *Lamia* is rich in everything that is missing from Augustan poetry. The very subject shows a fascination with legend, fairy-tale and the supernatural that is rare in the eighteenth century, and the vocabulary is deliberately exotic to match the scene: it seems written with a feeling that unusual words, like unusual things, are more interesting than the ordinary. So the pillars are of cedar, and pretend to be like palm and plaintain trees; and the weird suggestion that the roof is held up only by music is conveyed in the odd word "supportress", just as the plan of the palace is conveyed in words like "aisléd", and the series of lamps (blurring no doubt in the brightness) is a "stream". These points of subject-matter and vocabulary are what is most striking in the passage, but we can match them with metrical points as well. First and most obviously, Keats's couplets are not all end-stopped. He is always willing to allow the sense to carry over without pause from one line to the next: there is no pause after "lone" or "moan" or "glade", and only a minimal one after "all". The result of this is that the rhymes are not used with any great emphasis to mark out the structure of the verse; and indeed, Keats does not seem very interested in rhyme, as we see from the casualness with which he uses the trivial phrase "and so on", matching it against the false rhyme of "one". The long line on which this passage ends (six stressed syllables instead of five) is called an Alexandrine, and its use is not unknown in Augustan poetry, usually to mark a break in the sense, or to reaffirm a previous point with extra emphasis; Keats, however, uses it more frequently, and often simply to add variety to the movement, for he clearly does not regard regularity and firm discipline as poetic virtues.

To Pope they sometimes seem the supreme virtues, and his couplets maintain a perfect and ordered balance. Let us recall some of the concluding couplets in the first Imitation of Horace:

> Envy must own, I live among the great,
> No pimp of pleasure, and no spy of state,
> With eyes that pry not, tongue that ne'er repeats,
> Fond to spread friendships, but to cover heats,
> To help who want, to forward who excel;
> This, all who know me, know; who love me, tell.

These are not among the best lines in the poem, for they bear little sign of the speech rhythm that elsewhere is so brilliantly played against the metrical norm; but in their weighty gravity they are probably the most typically Augustan. The central principle of the heroic couplet is balance and contrast. It falls naturally into two contrasting halves, underlined by the rhymes; and each line is normally spoken with a pause in the middle, known as the caesura. Since the line has ten syllables, the natural place for the caesura to fall is after the fourth, fifth or sixth syllables, though sometimes to make a special point it may come earlier or later. In Pope the commonest position is after the fourth syllable, and it is very unusual to have it after (for instance) the second or the eighth: in the lines above you can tell by counting that it comes in the following positions: fourth, fifth, fifth, sixth, fourth, sixth. Keats on the other hand is much freer in variation and his positions are fourth, eighth, second, fourth, fourth, fourth, eighth, ?, sixth, ? In both the lines I have queried there seems to be no caesura, and the last one in particular ought doubtless to be read without pause, to show how the eye is led on unchecked by the "stream of lamps".

But symmetry goes even further in Pope: for each half of the line is itself divided into two. One of the five beats usually falls on a comparatively unimportant word, on which in the reading there will be only a weak stress, as is that on "among" in the first line, or on "and" in the second; so that there are really four stressed syllables that correspond to the four important units of meaning in the line, arranged in parallel or contrasting pairs—and the whole line contrasted with the other half of the couplet. This is the perfect form for making balanced, considered assertions, in which virtue is set against vice, appearance against reality, or duty against its fulfilment:

With eyes/that pry not,//tongue/that ne'er repeats,
Fond/to spread friendships,//but to cover/heats . . .

"Eyes" is matched with "tongue" and each followed by the debased function that it avoids; "fond" (retaining some of its older meaning of "foolish") is matched with "friendships"—the alliteration providing an extra signpost, to tell us that that is the only kind of folly he indulges in. In the hand of a master like Pope, the form offers a rigid logical structure under a surface of apparently casual ease (the one dispensable stress makes possible an easy colloquial movement that clothes without hiding the underlying balance).

If we turn now to Crabbe, there is no doubt where he belongs.

> Thus lived the lad, in hunger, peril, pain,
> His tears despised, his supplications vain:
> Compelled by fear to lie, by need to steal,
> His bed uneasy and unblessed his meal,
> For three sad years the boy his tortures bore,
> And then his pains and trials were no more.

Though there is nearly eighty years between Pope's lines and these, and less than ten between them and those of Keats, we have here completely orthodox Augustan couplets, with exactly the same reduction of the units of meaning to balanced pairs.

> Compelled//by fear/to lie,//by need/to steal,
> His bed/uneasy//and unbless'd/his meal. . .

The first line makes use of all five stresses, but since "compelled" applies to the whole of the rest of the line, we have our two balanced pairs in the remaining eight syllables—a balance of parallelism rather than contrast in this case. In the second line "bed" contrasts with "uneasy" in a way exactly parallel to the contrast between "meal" and "unblessed".

Not every line has a single central ceasura. In the Pope, the one exception was

> This,/all who know me,/know;//who love me/tell . . .

where there are extra pauses—as many as three, if the line is read deliberately—and a sense of complicated movement that results from the syntax. The line is saying something logically involved, and its movement is due to that, whereas such complications in a Keats

line would reflect emotion or action rather than logic. In the Crabbe
we have a simpler departure from symmetry in

>  Thus lived the lad in hunger, peril, pain,

where balance gives place to a list; and even more in line 79:

>  Pinned, beaten, cold, pinched, threatened and abused,

where the whole line is a list, and we are required to give more than
five stresses—the result being a sense of there being more causes for
our anger and compassion than a single line can hold. Immediately
after that line, the norm of balance is reasserted, and the next line
has four contrasting units of meaning again:

>  His éfforts/púnished//and his fóod/refúsed.

Crabbe, like Pope, has an essentially logical mind, and his verse
corresponds to the way he makes his points. What then is the sense
in which Crabbe is not an Augustan? To answer this we ought to
start from something more ordinary than the *Imitations of Horace*.

>  Go, gentle gales, and bear my sighs along!
>  For her, the feathered quires reflect their song:
>  For her, the limes their pleasing shades deny;
>  For her, the lilies hang their heads and die——
>  Go, gentle gales, and bear my sighs away!
>  Cursed be the fields that cause my Delia's stay;
>  Fade every blossom, wither every tree,
>  Die every flower, and perish all, but she.

Here we have the young Pope (it is from the third of his *Pastorals*,
written when he was in his teens) writing an elegant, complimentary
and wholly artificial love poem, using the balance of his already
polished couplets to match nature to his feelings by pretending that
summer is over because his lady has gone away. Nature is described
in the ornate language suited to poetry in cultivated circles: the
birds are "the feathered quires", the details are wholly general, and
each carries its correct adjective like a label—"pleasing shades",
"gentle gales". Such graceful and passionless verse, we may feel,
never sees the countryside, and it is against this that Crabbe reacted
in anger. Because he felt there had been too much of this elegant

trifling, he announced in *The Village* that he was going to write about

> The poor laborious natives of the place,

and describe the real sufferings of the poor, not the pretended love-sickness of the poet with a private income:

> Then shall I dare these real ills to hide
> In tinsel trappings of poetic pride?

So much for Pope's *Pastorals*. In the *Imitations of Horace* we can find a good deal of the realism that Crabbe demanded, and this more mature and down-to-earth Pope is clearly a greater poet than the Pope of the *Pastorals*: he has more or less abandoned poetic diction in favour of a vigorous, colloquial style. Yet he has not really done what Crabbe is asking, for the realism is personal not social. Pope talks about himself with casual frankness, but he does not show the social reality around him in its ugly matter-of-factness, that reality which we have seen Crabbe offering in such passages as the description of the village poorhouse already quoted, or in the glimpses of local gossip in *Peter Grimes*. But there is one place in which we can find Crabbe's programme, stated in words he would certainly have understood and responded to.

"Humble and rustic life was generally chosen, because, in that condition, the essential passions of the heart find a better soil in which they can attain their maturity, are less under restraint, and speak a plainer and more emphatic language. . . . The language too, of these men has been adopted . . . because from their rank in society and the sameness and narrow circle of their intercourse, being less under the influence of social vanity, they convey their feelings and notions in simple and unelaborate expressions. Accordingly, such a language, arising out of repeated experience and regular feelings, is a more permanent, and a far more philosophical language, than that which is frequently substituted for it by Poets . . . in order to furnish food for fickle tastes, and fickle appetites, of their own creation."

Not quite Crabbe's programme, perhaps: there is more admiration here for the virtues of the poor, and perhaps less indignation at their sufferings, but there is the same dismissal of "tinsel trappings", the same appeal to truth and directness. The passage comes from Wordsworth's famous *Preface* to the second edition of *Lyrical Ballads*, and it announces not the Wordsworth we shall be discussing in the next chapter, but the narrative Wordsworth, the author of such poems as *Michael, The Thorn* or *The Ruined Cottage* (this last to become Book I of *The Excursion*). There is far more to say about the differences and similarities between Wordsworth and Crabbe than space allows, but we can at least point out that *Peter Grimes* would serve very well as a specimen of the sort of narrative that the famous *Preface* is here calling for.

We have seen what Wordsworth thought of Crabbe: though, ironically, Wordsworth himself was accused of being too prosaic, sometimes in language very similar to that he used in his complaint. What he disliked in Crabbe can clearly not have been the absence of poetic elaboration, for Crabbe as we have seen has nothing in common with the Pope of the *Pastorals*; but what he had in common with the Pope of the *Imitations* may well have been what Wordsworth disliked, and to a reader who found the clear savage logic of invective unsympathetic, could have led to accusations that Crabbe lacked imagination. Let us take one final look at the verse of *Peter Grimes*:

> With greedy eye he looked on all he saw,
> He knew not justice, and he laughed at law;
> On all he marked, he stretched his ready hand;
> He fished by water and he filched by land. . . .

In form these are perfect Augustan couplets; but one cannot quite imagine Pope writing them. Partly, it is the bluntness of the last line, which balances its contrast on the close resemblance in sound between the down-to-earth verb "fished" (unpoetic enough by Augustan standards) and the more outrageous colloquialism of "filched": the language is going out of its way to be coarse, and by doing so it makes a point. Also the point is social: what matters is not just that something is wrong with Peter's character, but that it led to a particular way of getting his living. The same social point had already been made in the line we have looked at, describing what Peter found hard:

> Hard! that he could not to his cards attend,
> But must acquire the money he would spend.

The line states a simple fact of economic life; and states it, we can now add, with the force of a typically Augustan line. There are only three units of meaning this time: the noun "money" and the two verbs that are attached to it symmetrically in order to show that it cannot have the one without the other. This is not the sort of point Augustan poetry was used to making.

Who then is the revolutionary, Wordsworth or Crabbe? The question is worth asking, but not because there is really an answer; for it should show us that there are different ways to be revolutionary. In terms of the history of English poetry, Crabbe marks a dead end: for in him there is none of the sensibility that Wordsworth, Shelley and Keats brought into the language. In political terms, too, he was a conservative, as Wordsworth later became. But in terms of the infusion of social meaning into existing poetic forms he achieves something that Wordsworth often failed to do. Perhaps we can end on an image, and say that Crabbe poured new wine into old bottles; the Romantics set out to remake the bottles.

# 10

# Elegiac Stanzas suggested by a picture of Peele Castle, in a storm, painted by Sir George Beaumont

I was thy neighbour once, thou rugged Pile!
Four summer weeks I dwelt in sight of thee:
I saw thee every day; and all the while
Thy Form was sleeping on a glassy sea.

So pure the sky, so quiet was the air!
So like, so very like, was day to day!
Whene'er I looked, thy Image still was there;
It trembled, but it never passed away.

How perfect was the calm! it seemed no sleep;
No mood, which season takes away, or brings:
I could have fancied that the mighty Deep
Was even the gentlest of all gentle Things.

Ah! then, if mine had been the Painter's hand,
To express what then I saw; and add the gleam,
The light that never was, on sea or land,
The consecration, and the Poet's dream;

I would have planted thee, thou hoary Pile
Amid a world how different from this!
Beside a sea that could not cease to smile;
On tranquil land, beneath a sky of bliss.

Thou shouldst have seemed a treasure-house divine
Of peaceful years; a chronicle of heaven;—
Of all the sunbeams that did ever shine
The very sweetest had to thee been given.

A Picture had it been of lasting ease,
Elysian quiet, without toil or strife;
No motion but the moving tide, a breeze,
Or merely silent Nature's breathing life.

Such, in the fond illusion of my heart,
Such Picture would I at that time have made:
And seen the soul of truth in every part,
A steadfast peace that might not be betrayed.

So once it would have been,—'tis so no more;
I have submitted to a new control:
A power is gone, which nothing can restore;
A deep distress hath humanised my Soul.

Not for a moment could I now behold
A smiling sea, and be what I have been:
The feeling of my loss will ne'er be old;
This, which I know, I speak with mind serene.

Then, Beaumont, Friend! who would have been the Friend,
If he had lived, of Him whom I deplore,
This work of thine I blame not, but commend;
This sea in anger, and that dismal shore.

O 'tis a passionate Work!—yet wide and well,
Well chosen is the spirit that is here;
That Hulk which labours in the deadly swell,
This rueful sky, this pageantry of fear!

And this huge Castle, standing here sublime,
I love to see the look with which it braves,
Cased in the unfeeling armour of old time,
The lightning, the fierce wind, and trampling waves.

Farewell, farewell the heart that lives alone,
Housed in a dream, at distance from the Kind!
Such happiness, wherever it be known,
Is to be pitied; for 'tis surely blind.

But welcome fortitude, and patient cheer,
And frequent sights of what is to be borne!
Such sights, or words, as are before me here—
Not without hope we suffer and we mourn.

*William Wordsworth*  (*1805*)

The long circumstantial title of this poem points to its origin in the
events of Wordsworth's life; so perhaps we should follow its indication, and begin with the facts. Peele Castle is a ruin on the coast of
North Lancashire, on a promontory near Rampside. Wordsworth
stayed there during the summer of 1794, when he was twenty-four;
the time stayed in his memory as an idyllic, eventless dream.

Sir George Beaumont was a cultured gentleman and patron of the
arts, seventeen years older than Wordsworth, who knew and helped
many of the poets and painters of the age, often inviting them to his

country home, Coleorton Hall in Leicestershire. He spent much of his life helping the arts: he was largely responsible for founding the National Gallery, and spent much time improving his estate at Coleorton—at one time calling in the advice of Wordsworth, who collaborated with the gardener in designing a garden that would "move the affections" and give the impression of contact with "the holiness of Nature". Sir George was a painter himself, though his work is now forgotten, and he painted his picture of Peele Castle in a storm about 1783; Wordsworth, however, did not see it until he was staying with the Beaumonts in London in 1806, twelve years after his own visit to Peele Castle. As the poem makes clear, a "deep distress" has in the meantime intervened, which makes the picture seem right to him. If he could have painted the scene in 1794, he would have tried to recapture the unearthly calm that then hung upon it (and that his memory has perhaps exaggerated); but now he finds himself responsive to the bold and melodramatic effect of stormy sky and sea, swirling clouds, ship in distress and the broken outlines of the huge ruin. Sir George's picture is a characteristic piece of eighteenth-century sublime, full of space and light and movement.

The deep distress that had intervened was the death of Wordsworth's brother. John Wordsworth was a sailor and captain of the *Earl of Abergavenny*, on which he had made two trips to the East Indies; on 5 February 1805 his ship was wrecked off Portland Bill and he was drowned. The news was a terrible blow to William and his sister Dorothy: the ties of affection between them had been very strong, and John had looked forward to retiring from the sea and settling with them in the Lakes. When the shock had worn off, William began to write poems about his brother's death—two in June of 1805, and one the following year. They are printed together in his works.

The first one to be written was *Elegiac Verses in Memory of my Brother, John Wordsworth*. It starts from a detail of rural scenery:

> The Sheep-boy whistled loud, and lo!
> That instant, startled by the shock,
> The Buzzard mounted from the rock
> Deliberate and slow:
> Lord of the air, he took his flight;
> Oh! could he on that woeful night
> Have lent his wing, my Brother dear,
> For one poor moment's space to Thee,
> And all who struggled with the Sea,
> When safety was so near.

It then goes on to recall walks he had taken at that spot, New Gras-
mere, with his brother, and how John's hopes of retiring from the
sea to live there had been thwarted:

> All vanished in a single word,
> A breath, a sound, and scarcely heard.
> Sea—Ship—drowned—Shipwreck—so it
>     came,
> The meek, the brave, the good, was gone;
> He who had been our living John
> Was nothing but a name.

Returning to the rural scene, he finds comfort in a humble plant (a
note tells us it is the Moss Campion) which

> Is in its beauty ministrant
> To comfort and to peace . . .

and he reflects how much his brother would have loved its "modest
grace".

Shortly after this Wordsworth wrote *To the Daisy,* which begins
from the dead brother's love for flowers, and also uses a plant as
symbol for comfort and peace. It tells how when John went ashore on
the Isle of Wight, before setting off on a voyage,

> he sought
> The tender peace of rural thought:
> In more than happy mood
> To your abodes, bright daisy Flowers!
> He then would steal at leisure hours,
> And loved you glittering in your bowers,
> A starry multitude.

He then sailed off, but on this third voyage

> sorrow was at hand
> For him and for his crew.

We are given an account of the "ghastly shock", the "last death-
shriek", and the fact that the "brave Commander" went down with
the ship and lay undersea for six weeks until his body was found and
buried near the sea he loved.

> The birds shall sing and ocean make
> A mournful murmur for *his* sake;
> And then, sweet Flower, shalt sleep and wake
> Upon his senseless grave.

When we turn from these two poems to the *Elegiac Stanzas* (written the following year) we are in another world; there is no trace in them of the depth of thought and magical atmosphere with which Peele Castle is described. Why should Wordsworth have written two conventional, rather pedestrian poems on his brother's death, and one masterpiece? We can't answer, of course—questions like that can never be definitively answered—but we can at least indicate how different the strategy is which he has used in the one really successful poem. None of the poems start with the true subject. *To the Daisy* begins in a characteristically Wordsworthian way, with its invocation to the "sweet flower", and then moves to John Wordsworth by recalling his love for daisies. The *Elegiac Verses* also begin with a typical Wordsworthian scene, the sheep-boy's whistle and the buzzard, vivid and actual, then turns by a kind of poetical flourish to the memory of the shipwreck: "Oh! could he" seems to turn a poem of sharp immediacy into a rather fulsome and elaborated lament. In both cases Wordsworth has used a rather mechanical association of ideas (he loved daisies; the bird would have been useful to him) to turn from the kind of poem he is used to writing to something more uplifting, more "poetical". And we can hardly fail to notice that poetical treatments of bad news are not what he is gifted in:

> "Silence!" the brave Commander cried . . .

> Sea—Ship—drowned—Shipwreck—so it came . . .

Cliché and melodrama have replaced simple directness.

These two poems seem to suggest that the explicit treatment of the disaster and the bad news have failed to engage with Wordsworth's true talents; so it is not surprising to notice that in the *Elegiac Stanzas* we are not even told what his grief is. In one sense, this poem is not about John Wordsworth's death at all: anyone who read it in ignorance of the circumstances (as most readers probably do read it, at any rate for the first time) would have to realize that some great sorrow had come to the poet, but he would not know what it was, and would not need to, in order to understand the poem's structure. That structure hinges on the contrast between the mood of the "four summer weeks" and the new mood which finds Beaumont's picture so appropriate. It is time now to drop the biographical origins of the poem, and to turn to this contrast, so marvellously conveyed and so central, as it happens, to Wordsworth's poetical development.

What Wordsworth has learned, clearly, is the reality of suffering. The "steadfast peace that might not be betrayed" is the youthful and over-confident vision of the man whom grief has not yet humanized. "Humanized": it is a strong word to use. The young man is not yet fully human, because he has not suffered. That detail must make it clear to anyone familiar with Wordsworth's life that he is not just writing about his brother's death: for he had suffered a good deal before 1805. In fact, he had suffered a good deal before 1794, as a result of his disillusionment with the French Revolution, and had spent some time in a more or less neurotic state of paralysis of the will (we are told of this in *The Prelude*). The contrast of the *Elegiac Stanzas* probably cannot be too closely tied to biographical details, but it is none the less a crucial contrast in Wordsworth's picture of his own development.

In *Tintern Abbey* Wordsworth contrasts the intensity of his youthful delight in nature

> when like a roe
> I bounded o'er the mountains, more like a man
> Flying from something that he dreads, than one
> Who sought the thing he loved—

with a calmer acceptance that has come to him as a result of living in towns, looking back on his early experiences and drawing on them for spiritual comfort in moods of depression:

> I have owed to them
> In hours of weariness, sensations sweet,
> Felt in the blood, and felt along the heart;
> And passing even into my purer mind,
> With tranquil restoration.

And so he is now able to revisit the banks of the Wye, after an absence of five years, and feel that although he has lost the intensity of the time when nature was all in all to him

> —That time is past,
> And all its acting joys are now no more,
> And all its dizzy raptures—

he has learnt a new, mature, sober love of nature, in which he no longer figures as the isolated, intensely subjective young man, but as a man among men:

> For I have learned
> To look on nature, not as in the hour
> Of thoughtless youth; but hearing oftentimes
> The still sad music of humanity,
> Nor harsh nor grating, though of ample power
> To chasten and subdue.

A deep distress has humanized his soul: in this poem too, awareness of humanity is awareness of suffering, and the contrast is with the "fond illusion" of an earlier phase.

The same contrast provides the structure of the *Immortality Ode*. Here the earlier phase belongs in childhood

> There was a time when meadow, grove, and stream,
> The earth, and every common sight,
>     To me did seem
>   Apparelled in celestial light,
> The glory and the freshness of a dream.
> It is not now as it hath been of yore;—
>     Turn wheresoe'er I may,
>       By night or day,
>     The things which I have seen I now can see no more.

This time Wordsworth is less anxious to describe the early vision as illusion: it is a transfiguring light that he longs for, and its loss means

> That there hath passed away a glory from the earth.

The first part of the *Ode* culminates in lines of puzzled distress, deeply moving in their sad bewilderment:

> Whither is fled the visionary gleam?
> Where is it now, the glory and the dream?

None the less, the poem goes on to a reassurance that a new strength comes with maturity:

> We will grieve not, rather find
> Strength in what remains behind;
> In the primal sympathy
> Which having been must ever be;
> In the soothing thoughts that spring
> Out of human suffering;
> In the faith that looks through death,
> In years that bring the philosophic mind.

Once again, maturity is associated with suffering. It is given a hint of Christianity here ("In the faith that looks through death") but no more than a hint. Though Wordsworth had probably become an orthodox Christian by the time he wrote the *Elegiac Stanzas,* his poetry did not become explicitly Christian until his later years, when his talent was almost exhausted. The contrast we are here concerned with is between a youthful state that is outgrown, and a stoic acceptance of suffering.

Certainly stoic acceptance is the mood of the last part of the *Elegiac Stanzas.*

> The feeling of my loss will ne'er be old;
> This, which I know, I speak with mind serene.

There is a calm assurance about the rhythm of that last line which conveys the confidence that the poem is here trying to express. The castle is now seen as a symbol of courage and endurance: "cased in the unfeeling armour of old time", it resists the storm that as well as being (obviously) a reminder of the shipwreck is now a symbol of the passions that the mature heart is proof against. And so the poem concludes on an explicitly stoical stanza.

> But welcome fortitude and patient cheer.

Reducing one's expectations from life is sometimes regarded as a sign of maturity: and certainly the poem ends not only with a statement that suffering is inevitable, but with a kind of acceptance, even glad acceptance, of this reduced state. The last line takes on a Miltonic movement, as Wordsworth's verse so often does when he writes of the acceptance of suffering. Even in the very different mood of the *Elegiac Verses* there are three lines that make the same point with much the same central terms:

> With calmness suffer and believe,
> And grieve, and know that I must grieve,
> Not cheerless, though forlorn.

The *Elegiac Stanzas,* then, absorb the death of John Wordsworth into a theme that is quite as central to Wordsworth's poetry as the simple nature description with which the other two elegies begin; and a theme which can more successfully be integrated with the fact of the death, since what we now have is not a clumsy transition from the one subject to the other, but its use as an almost invisible pivot (generalized to "a deep distress") on which the poem's argument turns.

By saying this we have indicated how the strategy of this poem differs from that of the other two; we have stated its argument and shown how Wordsworthian it is; but we have not yet approached the most elusive but most important point of all, its poetic quality. For the power of this poem is in direct opposition to its theme. It owes its immortality not to the dignified stoicism of the close, but to the "fond illusion" of its youthful vision.

To what do we attribute the magic of the seven marvellous stanzas with which the poem begins? All we can do is suggest. The regular movement of its classical stanzas, with their iambic penta-meters in alternating rhymes (the metre of Gray's *Elegy*), is wholly appropriate to the calm mood, and also to the presence of the poet himself: "So like, so very like, was day to day" is not a voice from memory but the voice of the poet now recalling and describing what he remembers. But the regular stanza is much less obviously appro-priate to the sense of wonder, the almost magical light, that trans-figures his memory; and here the relationship between emotion and form is one of counterpoint. The poem gives a sense of calm control that was wholly absent from the original vision, but that does perhaps correspond to the steady voice with which it is now being described.

There are other examples of tension in this description, such as the two lines about the sea:

> I could have fancied that the mighty Deep
> Was even the gentlest of all gentle Things.

Wordsworth had previously tried to capture the mingling of power and gentleness in our picture of the ocean, in his sonnet on Calais beach "It is a beauteous evening, calm and free":

> The gentleness of heaven broods o'er the sea.
> Listen, the mighty Being is awake,
> And doth with his eternal motion make
> A sound like thunder, everlastingly.

Imagery and rhythm correspond perfectly to the sense of slow movement and enormous power that can be absorbed into a mood of awe; and once again the regularity of the verse expresses one aspect of the scene, and is played against another.

All the first seven stanzas are imbued with a sense of awe, of the strange, slightly unreal beauty of the memory. As with so much of Wordsworth's best poetry, the writing is so close to the ordinary that it is almost impossible to say wherein the power consists. Two words we can point to, since they are certainly important, are "form" and "image". Both are favourite words of Wordsworth, and both have a significant range of meaning. They can be contrasted with the process of ordinary perception: the image of a castle could be its reflection, or a painting of it, even a mirage or a memory; its form could be an abstraction, the outline of its shape, or even the Platonic Form. Now in both cases Wordsworth is using the word to mean "what he actually saw", but the choice of terms, and especially the way they are led up to in a hushed movement, suggests some of these other meanings (and "image" certainly looks at first as if it means "reflection", until we realize it is trembling in the warm air, not in the sea). The result of this surely is to give the impression that the castle he is seeing is unreal, is a version of it somehow different from ordinary perception; and so to add to the sense of wonder.

But the most intensely compelling stanza of all is certainly the fourth, in which the awe comes to a climax in two of the most famous lines Wordsworth ever wrote:

> The light that never was, on sea or land,
> The consecration, and the Poet's dream . . .

It comes as a shock to many readers to realize that these two haunting lines, which they may have known without being aware what poem they came from, are part of the "fond illusion": they describe what Wordsworth is rejecting. It is a shock, too, to realize that Wordsworth considered changing them. When the poem was published for the third time in the 1820 edition of Wordsworth's poems, the lines ran

> and add a gleam
> Of lustre, known to neither sea nor land
> But borrowed from the youthful Poet's dream.

The changes are small, but vital. The sense of wonder conveyed by "The light that never was" has given place to a sober assertion of how far-fetched it is. "Borrowed" reminds us that the light is unreal; "youthful" anticipates the rejection of the poet's dream later in the poem. Even the change of article is important: *a* gleam is something regarded from the outside, and will be easier to reject than the sense of familiarity assumed in "the gleam", as if there is one well-known irresistible impact that poetry makes. Wordsworth may have felt this immediately, for in the *Errata* to the 1820 volume he restored "the gleam, the lustre" (still keeping however the more ponderous, less compelling "lustre", instead of the straightforward "light"); and in 1832 he restored the original reading of the lines. It is clear what he was up to: he wanted to attach the lines more firmly to the argument of the poem, indicating more clearly that they describe a "fond illusion"—and he did this successfully, but at the cost of all their poetic power. There is a clash, in the *Elegiac Stanzas,* between poetry and coherence of argument: a clash that no poet can ever be certain of avoiding, for it is a sad truth that no poet can control how well the various parts of a poem are written. It is gratifying to find that Wordsworth, realizing how much damage he had done, preferred poetry to coherence.

And the same point can be made—often is made—about the two poems we have used as parallels. It is less clear in *Tintern Abbey*, for there is a moving sense of conviction about its vision of maturity, culminating in the much-quoted and (indeed) haunting line,

> The still sad music of humanity.

Two passages in particular enlist the poetic power of *Tintern Abbey* on the side of its argument. One is the account of the

> Presence that disturbs me with the joy
> Of elevated thoughts,

which really forms its climax: probably the most famous statement of Wordsworth's pantheism:

> a sense sublime
> Whose dwelling is the light of setting suns,
> And the round ocean and the living air,
> And the blue sky, and in the mind of man;
> A motion and a spirit, that impels
> All thinking things, all objects of all thought,
> And rolls through all things.

This passage too has become detached from its poem in the minds of many readers; but to put it back in context is not, this time, to be surprised, for its eloquent assertion is in no way denied by the movement of the poem as a whole. On the contrary, everything is meant to lead up to it. The other passage is the account of the trance-like state of inner vision which used to come to him during his moods of depression in the city:

> that blessed mood
> In which the burthen of the mystery,
> In which the heavy and the weary weight
> Of all this unintelligible world,
> Is lightened:—that serene and blessed mood,
> In which the affections gently lead us on,—
> Until, the breath of this corporeal frame
> And even the motion of our human blood
> Almost suspended, we are laid asleep
> In body, and become a living soul:
> While with an eye made quiet by the power
> Of harmony, and the deep power of joy,
> We see into the life of things.

These lines relate the deepest emotional experiences not to the external stimuli received from "bounding o'er the mountains", but to the rising up of memory when we are in a state of depression and an environment that offers little stimulation. They are among those passages in which we can see Wordsworth as an anticipator of Proust, the other great poet of memory. For Proust too it is when we are in a state of deprivation that we are most deeply moved by experiences of fulfilment—usually called up in us by some trivial external stimulus, such as the tap of a woman's heels on the pavement outside while we lie in bed, far from the countryside that feeds our spirit. In Wordsworth there may be no external stimulus at all— "the affections gently lead us on"—and the resulting state is almost one of communion with the world. The lines surely make it clear— and powerfully clear—that to live through suffering and deprivation is to open up the possibility of deeper and richer experience.

*Tintern Abbey* is an almost completely successful poem. By "successful" I mean that the author has managed to control how well the various parts are written, and to enlist his greatest power when it is most needed. Almost completely successful: but perhaps not quite. First of all, the climax. It is a fine climax, and an eloquent statement of Wordsworth's philosophy of nature. To say this is praise, certainly, but is it not limited praise? Those cumulative phrases, joined by a series of "ands", leading up to their culmination in "the mind of man", seem perhaps too much designed to impress; they do impress, but not with the sudden shock of imaginative surprise. Perhaps what has made this the most famous passage in the poem is not exactly that it is the finest poetry, but that it is a certain kind of poetry. I called it eloquent, and eloquence suggests something memorable, but it doesn't suggest personal immediacy, the shock of direct emotion. And elsewhere in *Tintern Abbey* we can find just this shock:

> the sounding cataract
> Haunted me like a passion: the tall rock,
> The mountain, and the deep and gloomy wood,
> Their colours and their forms, were then to me
> An appetite; a feeling and a love,
> That had no need of a remoter charm,
> By thought supplied.

These lines do not reverberate with philosophic significance, but they have the blunt power that comes from writing that is very close to remembered emotion: they are not eloquent, but they are urgent. And so one could understand a reader who maintained that the poem is not as satisfied as it claims with the movement from youth to maturity.

It is a debatable question with *Tintern Abbey;* but there can be little doubt about the *Immortality Ode*. Its opening stanzas, for all their dignity and formality, are heavy with nostalgia, and they enact a struggle between responsiveness to the stimulus of spring that urges cheerfulness, and the longing for the glory that has passed away. So when Wordsworth writes "I hear, I hear, with joy I hear" he is not being crassly over-insistent, he is assuring himself that he does respond to nature still. Immediately after that line he continues

> —But there's a Tree, of many, one,
> A single Field which I have looked upon,
> Both of them speak of something that is gone:
> The Pansy at my feet
> Doth the same tale repeat:
> Whither is fled the visionary gleam?
> Where is it now, the glory and the dream?

The poem was begun in 1802, and broken off there; two years later

Wordsworth returned to it, and the next section begins with the famous statement of the doctrine of pre-existence.

> Our birth is but a sleep and a forgetting:
> The Soul that rises with us, our life's Star,
>     Hath had elsewhere its setting,
>         And cometh from afar:
>     Not in entire forgetfulness,
>     And not in utter nakedness,
> But trailing clouds of glory do we come.

Surely the difference between these two passages is something like that between the climax of *Tintern Abbey* and the account of the aching joys. The assertion of pre-existence is memorable and dignified: it has the Wordsworthian eloquence. The rhythm is deliberately slow: there is the weightiness of philosophic assertion (carefully not carried away by enthusiasm) in the way the emphasis falls on "entire" in the fifth line, "utter" in the sixth. The earlier lines, in contrast, have a puzzled air. The line

> But there's a Tree, of many, one . . .

is brilliantly clumsy. Its aim is to establish the individuality of the particular tree (like the individuality of the rock and the cataract). Other nineteenth-century poets might have done this by vivid particularity of description, earlier poets by attributing a symbolic significance to the tree; Wordsworth tells us nothing about it, but he dramatizes the act of thinking about it, of picking it out and assuring us, I mean *that* tree, by the way the syntax moves. And so the questions on which the passage ends capture the puzzlement and the loss that fill the opening of the poem. It seems appropriate that Wordsworth had to break off after these questions, and that when he started again his touch was more confident but less urgent. And it is not surprising that the conclusion of the poem, which asserts confidently that the mature vision is ample compensation for the loss of childhood glory, should sound at times little better than doggerel:

> We will grieve not, rather find
> Strength in what remains behind.

These three poems are not alone in Wordsworth's work: we could have derived much the same point from the eighth book of *The*

*Prelude,* or (in a rather different form) from *The Excursion.* In each case, we find a contrast between a compelling youthful vision, and the more sober outlook of maturity: the latter is preferred, but the intensity of the poetry sometimes betrays how much stronger is the grip of the former.

Wordsworth's development followed a reverse movement to the development of English poetry. Trusting the imagination, trusting the youthful vision, preferring an intensity of sensibility to sober maturity, valuing the beauty of strangeness—all these are the characteristics of the Romantic movement that in English literature we associate with Wordsworth as much as with anyone. The stoicism with which Wordsworth replaced it as he grew older (until he grew older still and wrote with failed inspiration as an orthodox Christian) seems to belong more to the eighteenth century, and it is striking that the stoic Wordsworth often uses the style and phrasing of the Augustans—in the *Ode to Duty* for instance, or in the later parts of the *Elegiac Stanzas,* where we find eighteenth-century descriptive lines

—This rueful sky, this pageantry of fear—

or such touches of sober Augustan judiciousness as

This work of thine I blame not, but commend.

If we glance across the channel we can see a kind of parallel in Chateaubriand, whose two short novels *Atala* and *René* (1801 and 1802) owed their enormous popularity to their setting in the vast forests of North America, their sense of the strange beauty of the New World, and their melancholic, passionate heroes, though in both books passion and melancholy are explicitly rebuked as self-centred, and traditional moral codes are affirmed. Chateaubriand is a Romantic who was read for his new sensibility, while his own moral judgements were largely ignored.

The growth to maturity recorded in the *Elegiac Stanzas* then, is a renunciation of the true source of Wordsworth's poetic genius. English poetry did not share the renunciation, and while the imprint of neo-classicism on his work became clearer (though never completely stifling his genius), those poems which we see as the work of the truly Romantic Wordsworth strengthened their hold on the hearts of his readers.

# 11

# Stanzas written in Dejection, near Naples

The sun is warm, the sky is clear,
The waves are dancing fast and bright,
Blue isles and snowy mountains wear
The purple noon's transparent might,
The breath of the moist earth is light,
Around its unexpanded buds;
Like many a voice of one delight,
The winds, the birds, the ocean floods,
The City's voice itself, is soft like Solitude's.

I see the Deep's untrampled floor
With green and purple seaweeds strown;
I see the waves upon the shore,
Like light dissolved in star-showers, thrown;
I sit upon the sands alone,—
The lightning of the noontide ocean
Is flashing round me, and a tone
Arises from its measured motion,
How sweet! did any heart now share in my emotion.

Alas! I have nor hope nor health,
Nor peace within nor calm around,
Nor that content surpassing wealth
The sage in meditation found,
And walked with inward glory crowned—
Nor fame, nor power, nor love, nor leisure.
Others I see whom these surround—
Smiling they live, and call life pleasure;—
To me that cup has been dealt in another measure.

Yet now despair itself is mild,
Even as the winds and waters are;
I could lie down like a tired child,
And weep away the life of care
Which I have borne and yet must bear,
Till death like sleep might steal on me,
And I might feel in the warm air
My cheek grow cold, and hear the sea
Breathe o'er my dying brain its last monotony.

Some might lament that I were cold,
As I, when this sweet day is gone,
Which my lost heart, too soon grown old,
Insults with this untimely moan;
They might lament—for I am one
Whom men love not, —and yet regret,
Unlike this day, which, when the sun
Shall on its stainless glory set,
Will linger, though enjoyed, like joy in memory yet.

*Percy Bysshe Shelley   (1818)*

This is certainly the most lyrical poem in the book, and also the simplest, so simple that it communicates immediately, even (surely) on a single reading: the sunlit scene, the calm sea, the surrounding peace, and the dejection of the poet—all these are given in a series of effortless stanzas. And it is a pure lyric: its aim is the direct expression of personal emotion. Lyrical poetry (the word is derived from "lyre") originally had some connection with music, and though few modern lyrics are designed to be sung, a poem that has retained a purely lyric quality is one that could be turned into a song, as this one certainly could.

How does a lyric poet convey his emotion? Most obviously, by statement: "Alas," he says, "I have nor hope nor health." Or he tells us that he feels "a grief without a pang, void, dark or drear", or that he "prayed aloud in anguish and in agony". Most lyric verse includes such direct statement somewhere, but that alone is not enough to make it into a poem: for poetry does not just describe or name an emotion, it *expresses* it, that is, the language is felt in some way to contain, to be charged with the emotion. Imagery and rhythm will suggest the emotion: they may suggest it so powerfully that it will not even be necessary to state it. Here for instance are some other stanzas written in dejection by Shelley:

A widow bird sat mourning for her love
Upon a wintry bough;
The frozen wind crept on above,
The freezing stream below.

There was no leaf upon the forest bare,
No flower upon the ground,
And little motion in the air
Except the mill wheel's sound.

These marvellous lines express a very similar emotion to the stanzas written near Naples—despondency, grief, a feeling of rejection. But the poet does not enter in his own person, and the word "I" is never used, for the emotion is conveyed by presenting an objective situation that corresponds to it. Since the bird is said to be "mourning" you may feel that the emotion is, in effect, named; but the really powerful effect created by the poem does not come from that first line, but from the sense of failing life in the winter landscape —from the way "frozen" is half-echoed by "freezing" to give the impression that all movement is beginning to cease, or from the flatness of the second stanza. "No leaf . . . no flower" is taken up by "*little* motion" in a way that forms a kind of logical parallel to "frozen . . . freezing": everything is coming to a standstill, and the only motion is inanimate. The flatness of the scene is echoed by the flatness of rhythm, and the bareness of the statement (there are no adjectives in the second stanza, except "little", which is not descriptive at all). Here is emotion perfectly expressed, not by statement but in the qualities of the language: not directly, we may say, but obliquely, in the way appropriate to poetry.

What then are the oblique methods used to express emotion in the *Stanzas written in Dejection near Naples*—what gives it a poetic identity? There are several devices central to the poem that we can point out. First, the setting, which occupies virtually the whole of the first two stanzas. For the most part, these stanzas are plain and unelaborated, in descriptive language that is almost that of prose: "the sun is warm, the sky is clear". But as they proceed, we find touches of highly distinctive writing, the first being "the purple noon's transparent might", where the abstract noun "might", coming when we might expect something concrete like "air", invites us to think outwards from the immediate scene, to imagine it as part of some larger process. The next striking effect, though different, is also achieved by using abstract where concrete might be expected: this is the simile that ends the stanza, where all the voices are "soft like Solitude's". As it happens, this is a favourite technique of Shelley's: he loves to explain the familiar by the unusual (dead leaves before the wind "are driven, like ghosts from an enchanter fleeing"). The effect here of course is to prepare us for the introduction of the poet himself: the voices sound like solitude's because the listener is so conscious of his own solitude.

The second stanza also begins quite straightforwardly; and its description becomes highly distinctive with the vividly accurate image of the waves "Like light dissolved in star-showers". Then comes the first explicit mention of the poet who, we are immediately told, is sitting alone; then another mention of the voice of the ocean, and we can assume that the tone which "arises from its measured motion" is also soft like solitude's. And then we move from the setting to the poet.

It is clear that the use of the setting here is exactly the opposite to that in "A widow bird". Here setting and emotion contrast: landscape and weather suggest calm joy, and seem appropriate to a poem of happy oneness with nature. The only hints of what is to come are the references to his solitude, both explicit and in the feeling he gets from surrounding nature; and though these certainly prepare us for the later stanzas, it is very unlikely, if we stopped reading after stanza two, that we would realize that it was a poem of dejection. Instead, therefore, of corresponding to the feeling, the setting exists in a kind of tension with it: the result is less inevitable than the impact of "A widow bird", less appropriate perhaps, but in a way more poignant.

As well as the setting, there is the rhythm: and here again there is a kind of tension. The rhythm of these gracefully moving stanzas is smooth, even melodious, suited completely to the attractiveness of the weather. There is, if we think about it, a kind of inappropriateness in lines like

> Alas! I have nor hope nor health,
> Nor peace within nor calm around,
> Nor that content surpassing wealth
> The sage in meditation found . . .

They move so gracefully that they suggest peace, calm, content—all the things they are denying: so much so that it is easy to imagine them running

> And peace within and calm around,
> And that content surpassing wealth . . .

The only moment when the dejection is seen to break up the smooth movement comes at the end of this stanza:

> Others I see whom these surround—
> Smiling they live and call life pleasure;—
> To me that cup has been dealt in another measure.

To make that last line scan it is necessary to read it so unnaturally (stressing "been" and "in" instead of "dealt") that we must conclude that it is meant to sound as if the rhythmic movement has been arrested so that we may feel the limping tread of the poet's own wretchedness instead. It would have been possible to build such effects much more prominently into the poem, but Shelley has chosen not to: for the most part the calm rhythm insists on the calm scene, not on the poet who does not fit.

And in the fourth stanza we see why: for in this (surely by far the most moving stanza of all) we are made to feel that the dejection *does* in a way belong to the sunlight, the calm and the soothing ocean. Despair is mild because it is the despair not of protest but of resignation: his longing is to belong to the nature that lulls him, even if this means losing his identity, even if it means being assimilated to the extent of ceasing to exist. The stanza culminates in the act of dying, or rather imagining oneself dying, as an act of supreme peace.

Dying as supreme peace: as something longed for. We can find other examples of this longing, and put them next to Shelley's poem.

Whereto answering, the sea,
Delaying not, hurrying not,
Whisper'd me through the night, and very plainly before daybreak,
Lisp'd to me the low and delicious word death,
And again death, death, death, death,
Hissing melodious, neither like the bird nor like my arous'd child's
      heart,
But edging near as privately for me rustling at my feet,
Creeping thence steadily up to my ears and laving me softly all over,
Death, death, death, death, death.

This is the climax of Walt Whitman's long moving childhood reminiscence, "Out of the cradle endlessly rocking". Its emotional effect is almost identical with Shelley's *Stanzas*. The fact that Whitman's whole poem is presented as a memory of childhood shows us how important is Shelley's simile "I could lie down like a tired child": this peaceful dying is seen as a return to infancy, a loss of the too painfully individual consciousness of the adult. And Whitman, like Shelley, finds himself near the sea, and hears the call to oblivion in the sound of the waves, so that they suggest a kind of painless drowning. And Whitman too has an insistent, lulling rhythm, all the more marked for being in free verse, that seems to subdue all individuality, reducing consciousness to a mere awareness of the sea's "last monotony".

I suggested that this is felt as a kind of painless drowning: here now are some lines in which the drowning is quite explicit.

> But me, they'll lash me in hammock, drop me deep
> Fathoms down, fathoms down, how I'll dream fast asleep.
> I feel it stealing now. Sentry, are you there?
> Just ease these darbies at the wrist,
> And roll me over fair.
> I am sleepy, and the oozy weeds about me twist.

Here the situation is different. These are the last lines of Herman Melville's *Billy in the Darbies,* a dramatic monologue supposedly spoken by Billy Budd, the innocent young sailor who committed a murder, on the night before his execution ("darbies" are the irons he is secured in). Here then we have someone who is actually waiting to die: yet his soliloquy culminates in a lulling movement, a fascination with the peacefulness of death by drowning, that has much of the lyric quality of Shelley's poem and Whitman's And this may give us a clue towards a psychological interpretation of the death-wish.

Why should we long to die? True, in extreme depression death may seem the only refuge because life is unbearable; but to say that does not, somehow, seem appropriate to any of these three poems, for in them death is made to seem attractive. It is made to seem like sleep: Billy, as his poem ends, is not clear on the difference between the two. The wonderfully suggestive confusion of the last line conveys this; and so in a different way does the insistent rhythm of Whitman, the "last monotony" of Shelley's ocean. Why should it seem attractive to think about death, and to confuse it with sleep? Once we ask the question that way, the answer is obvious: if sleep is like death, then death is like sleep. If as we fall asleep we wish to imagine we are dying, then we are telling ourselves that as we die it will be like something familiar, of which we are not afraid. The death-wish is a protection against the fear of death: it is a way of saying surreptitiously "Dying is no worse than falling asleep."

After the moving simplicity of this death-wish, there is little for the last stanza to do. It admits explicitly the point I have already made about the contrast between emotion and setting, by saying that his heart "insults" the sweet day; and it finishes on another contrast, that between the regret with which—perhaps—men will regard his memory, and the continuing joy with which this day will be remembered. By turning from himself to the beauty of the day as he ends the poem, Shelley brings it full circle, leaving us with the renewed feeling that his dejection does not, after all, belong to the setting.

That is certainly what the final stanza is saying, but we ought to notice that it is not altogether clear. "Some might lament that I were cold," it begins, "as I—" as he what? Two subordinate clauses, beginning with "when" and "which" intervene, and we would then expect the verb, most probably "as I . . . shall lament it", but we get a semi-colon, and then a new sentence begins. It is as if the poet has forgotten how he began the sentence, and feeling that it has said what it was meant to say, he ends it. We have, surely, to attribute this to carelessness, and this seems the more plausible since the poem (like so many of Shelley's lyrics) was never published in his lifetime, but found among his papers and brought out by his widow in a volume of *Posthumous Poems* in 1824 (Shelley died in 1822). In her preface Mary Shelley remarks that many of the poems in his manuscript books were "written on the spur of the occasion and never retouched", and this seems sufficient explanation of the faulty syntax.

Such carelessness may seem surprising in a poem so carefully polished, and certainly it teaches us something very interesting about Shelley's way of writing. He must have found rhyme and metre so effortless that he was able to write perfect stanzas (for this last is metrically as perfect as the others) more easily than correct syntax, as if he did not naturally think in sentences, since his poems followed the movement of the feeling, but did think in rhyme and metre. From so intensely personal a poet, it is a clear sign of how natural such forms can become.

Our discussion might end here, if it was only concerned with the impact of the poem itself; but I shall continue by adding an historical and a theoretical point. The historical point concerns Romantic poetry, of which this poem is so typical an example. I have already indicated how widespread in lyric poetry is the kind of dejection that can issue in a death-wish, but I should really have said "in nineteenth-century lyric poetry". It would have been much harder to find examples from earlier periods and also harder to find quite this note of swooning luxury in twentieth-century poetry, but it is a thoroughly characteristic Romantic note. No work is more characteristic of its time, and more central to the Romantic sensibility, than Senancour's *Obermann* (1804). In this series of melancholy meditations in the form of a novel in letters, in which there is hardly any action, the writer describes, at enormous length, his despair, his weariness of life, the sensitivity that makes all effort unbearable, and his inability to find a purpose in living. Obermann insists constantly that his trouble is not particular sorrows that could be cured or outlived or set against contrasting benefits, but a sense of general futility, all the more depressing because felt in youth, which should be the age of happiness. He can feel only despair as he contemplates *cet espace desénchanté où vont se trainer les restes de ma jeunesse et de ma vie,* the disenchanted space through which the remnants of his youth and all his life will drag themselves. This concentration on an emotion that has neither cause nor cure, but permeates everything, gives the work a lyric quality, and the very things that make *Obermann* tedious as a novel make parts of it as moving a lyric by Shelley, and sometimes in the same way: he contrasts the mild climate, the beautiful scenes, a splendid and expressive nature with himself, lonely and ill at ease in the world. The helplessness of the crushed will, the ineluctable melancholy of the sensitive man, is remorselessly spread over a whole lifetime and four hundred pages of melodious French.

So extreme an expression of lyric melancholy must lead many of its readers to cry "enough"; to reject angrily, even contemptuously, such crippling introspection. Having made the historical point that such dejection is typical of Romantic poetry, we can now make a critical point, and ask, is that not so much the worse for Romanticism? We can point out the lurking disapproval in some of the terms I have already used (as when I spoke of "swooning luxury"), and we can introduce a term that I have carefully not used so far, and describe the emotion as one of self-pity. We can even call it an adolescent feeling.

Is there much self-pity in Romantic poetry, and is there anything wrong with it if there is? And the *Stanzas written in Dejection*: should they rather be called the stanzas written in self-pity? This is not just a question of terminology, but of understanding our attitude towards the poetry, and our judgement of its value. Let us now introduce a whole lyric poem for comparison, and let us take it from a Romantic poet who certainly suffered from melancholia and depression, which he displayed in his poetry.

### The Pains of Sleep

Ere on my bed my limbs I lay,
It hath not been my use to pray
With moving lips or bended knees;
But silently, by slow degrees,
My spirit I to Love compose,
In humble trust mine eye-lids close,
With reverential resignation,
No wish conceived, no thought exprest,
Only a sense of supplication;
A sense o'er all my soul imprest
That I am weak, yet not unblest,

Since in me, round me, every where
Eternal Strength and Widsom are.

But yesternight I prayed aloud
In anguish and in agony,
Up-starting from the fiendish crowd
Of shapes and thoughts that tortured me:
A lurid light, a trampling throng,
Sense of intolerable wrong,
And whom I scorned, those only strong!

Thirst of revenge, the powerless will
Still baffled, and yet burning still!
Desire with loathing strangely mixed
On wild or hateful objects fixed.
Fantastic passions! maddening brawl!
And shame and terror over all!
Deeds to be hid which were not hid,
Which all confused I could not know
Whether I suffered, or I did:
For all seemed guilt, remorse or woe,
My own or others still the same
Life-stifling fear, soul-stifling shame.

So two nights passed: the night's dismay
Saddened and stunned the coming day.
Sleep, the wide blessing, seemed to me
Distemper's worst calamity.
The third night, when my own loud scream
Had waked me from the fiendish dream,
O'ercome with sufferings strange and wild,
I wept as I had been a child;
And having thus by tears subdued
My anguish to a milder mood,
Such punishments, I said, were due
To natures deepliest stained with sin,—
For aye entempesting anew
The unfathomable hell within,
The horror of their deeds to view,
To know and loathe, yet wish and do!

Such griefs with such men well agree,
But wherefore, wherefore fall on me?
To be beloved is all I need,
And whom I love, I love indeed.

Coleridge wrote this poem in 1803 but did not publish it till 1816: he may have considered it too personal. If this is not a poem of self-pity then the term has no meaning. A preliminary section on the calm with which he normally goes to sleep; a violent account of the terrifying experience of "yesternight"; and then a third section that can only be described as whining, complaining that it's not fair, and why did all this not happen to those who deserve it more, to the "natures deepliest died with sin":

> Such griefs with such men well agree,
> But wherefore, wherefore fall on me?

Of course this poem is very different from the *Stanzas:* it has nothing of its contrasting setting in sunny nature. It is more urgent, more nakedly self-centred, and perhaps, in its middle section, more powerful. But let us for the moment concentrate on what the two have in common, which is (surely) what links them to Senancour, the picture of the poet as a special person, marked by suffering and so distinguished from the common herd of men. Is this not mere egoism? But then is not all lyric poetry egoistic, since it is the poet's expression of his own emotions?

The problem is tricky, and important: and I suggest we should ask ourselves whether, when we censure someone for self-pity, we are making a moral or an aesthetic complaint. In real life, it would no doubt be a moral complaint: we would be telling him that he ought not to give in to a feeling so harmful to human relationships; that he ought to blame himself and be sorry for others, instead of blaming others and feeling sorry for himself. That refers to real life: but what have such moral judgements to do with lyric poetry? If the lyric is the direct expression of emotions why should it not express *any* emotion? Our emotional life is not confined to those emotions we approve of, and there are powerful lyrics which express much worse emotions than self-pity—hatred (as in some satire, including that of Pope) or cruelty and aggression (as in some "Into battle" poems) or disdain (as in some of Donne's lyrics about women). These can be genuine poetry; and we may even feel that to respond to the expression of our own more dangerous or deplorable emotions may help us to come to terms with ourselves.

If self-pity produces bad poetry it must be because it is poetically bad—that is, because it impedes the act of expression. It must be because it is self-regarding in a way that muddles the language, that prevents us from coming properly to terms with anything. It was ambiguous to say that all lyric poetry is egoistic. It is true if it means that the poet accepts his own feelings without pausing to judge or improve them; but there is a difference between attending to one's emotion and attending to oneself, and if the poet is so busy thinking about himself that he cannot allow the emotion to speak clearly or to inform the language, then he is being egoistic in a damaging way. This distinction can be seen very clearly if we contrast the second and the third sections of *The Pains of Sleep*. The second section makes so strong an impact because it lets the feelings speak: "Desire with loathing strangely mixed" is so powerful a line because it is at the same time restless with the agony it speaks of, and able to step back and be puzzled, offering us a touch of objectivity in that very effective "strangely". The poet enters in his own person, but as the object of his own puzzlement: "I could not know Whether I suffered or I did." Once again, the restlessness is there, but so is the objectivity. It is a glimpse of the wonderful clinical note that makes Coleridge's famous Dejection Ode so great a poem.

The third section opens with much of the same power; but its last ten lines turn into a self-justifying whine that is poetically as well as morally objectionable, culminating in the almost petulant repetition of the long-drawn out "wherefore, wherefore", as if plain honest "why" was not an important enought word for his indignation, and in the earnest self-defence of the last anxious couplet.

And now if we turn back to the *Stanzas written in Dejection*, we must surely pronounce them almost entirely free of this artistically crippling self-pity. Shelley's picture of himself as in tension with the beauty of the day has in no way damaged the description, so that the contrast between weather and mood is allowed to speak for itself; and the expression of the mildness of the despair that longs to weep away life never falters in its fidelity to the emotion. It does not matter how we put this point, as long as we are clear on the distinction. We can say that Shelley's poem expresses dejection and not self-pity; or we can say that it expresses self-pity in a way that does no damage poetically.

No damage? Well, in the very last stanza a false note begins to sound. Perhaps it was anticipated in the third, when he sees himself as contrasting with "others" who are able to call life pleasure— contrasting with them and perhaps, in his sensitivity, superior to them? It is only a tremor; in the last stanza it becomes something more: "for I am one Whom men love not." Here the dangerous note of self-pity begins to sound; here he seems to be attending not to his emotions but to himself. Yet compared with Coleridge— or with Obermann—or with some of Shelley's inferior lyrics—it is still, really, only a tremor. The *Stanzas* retain their pure lyric note almost to the end.

Both Coleridge and Shelley were men of enormous learning and intellectual power: in representing them by such overwhelmingly personal poems, have I not given a thoroughly lop-sided picture of their poetical genius? To represent Shelley by his translations from Greek or Italian or Spanish, or by his *Prometheus Unbound*, or by the historical sweep of the *Ode to Liberty*, would have shown us Shelley indeed. Yet in a way this very lopsidedness is necessary to the picture, and shows us how central the lyrical note, and in particular the introspective lyric of dejection, is to Romantic poetry. Even these intellectual giants felt they were writing their truest poetry when they laid their souls bare in all simplicity.

# 12

# Johannes Agricola in Meditation

There's heaven above, and night by night,
  I look right through its gorgeous roof;
No suns and moons tho' e'er so bright
  Avail to stop me; splendour-proof
I keep the broods of stars aloof:
For I intend to get to God,
  For 'tis to God I speed so fast,
For in God's breast, my own abode,
  Those shoals of dazzling glory, pass'd,
I lay my spirit down at last.
I lie where I have always lain,
  God smiles as He has always smiled;
Ere suns and moons could wax and wane,
  Ere stars were thundergirt, or piled
The heavens, God thought on me his child;
Ordained a life for me, array'd
  Its circumstances, every one
To the minutest; aye, God said
  This head this hand should rest upon
Thus, ere He fashion'd star or sun.
And having thus created me,
  Thus rooted me, He bade me grow,
Guiltless for ever, like a tree
  That buds and blooms, nor seeks to know
  The law by which it prospers so:
But sure that thought and word and deed
  All go to swell his love for me,
Me, made because that love had need
  Of something irreversibly
Pledged solely its content to be.
Yes, yes, a tree which must ascend,
  No poison-gourd foredoom'd to stoop!
I have God's warrant, could I blend
  All hideous sins, as in a cup,
To drink the mingled venoms up,
Secure my nature will convert
  The draught to blossoming gladness fast,
While sweet dews turn to the gourd's hurt,

And bloat, and while they bloat it, blast,
As from the first its lot was cast.
For as I lie, smiled on, full fed
  By unexhausted power to bless,
I gaze below on Hell's fierce bed,
  And those its waves of flame oppress,
Swarming in ghastly wretchedness;
Whose life on earth aspired to be
  One altar-smoke, so pure!—to win
If not love like God's love for me,
  At least to keep his anger in;
And all their striving turn'd to sin.
  Priest, doctor, hermit, monk grown white
With prayer, the broken-hearted nun,
  The martyr, the wan acolyte,
The incense-swinging child,—undone
Before God fashioned star or sun!
God, whom I praise; how could I praise,
  If such as I might understand,
Make out and reckon on His ways,
  And bargain for his love, and stand,
Paying a price, at his right hand?

                         *Robert Browning*   (1836)

St Paul's Epistle to the Romans is the most famous statement in the New Testament of the doctrine of justification by faith alone. Because men are sinful, they cannot obey the moral law:

"I delight in the law of God after the inward man: but I see another law in my members, worrying against the law in my mind, and bringing one into captivity to the law of sin which is in my members. O wretched man that I am! who shall deliver me from the body of this death?"  (*VII. 23–4*)

The way out of this despair is provided by the gospel of Jesus Christ. All men being sinners, our righteousness cannot save us; but we are "justified freely by [God's] grace through the redemption that is in Christ Jesus."  (*III. 24*)

Not only does this grace save us, it has been arranged from all eternity that it should be so, for God has predestined the salvation of his elect:

"Whom he did predestinate them also he called: and whom he called, them he also justified: and whom he justified, them he also glorified."  (*VIII. 30*)

The redemption brought by the Gospel, then, is based not upon any righteousness in us, but entirely upon our faith in Jesus Christ, who has atoned for our sins, something we are incapable of doing. It is by this faith that we receive the grace of God.

"And if by grace, then is it no more of works: otherwise grace is no more grace. But if it be of works, then is it no more grace." (*XI. 6*) Here is one of the most important doctrines in the history of Christianity, a doctrine that 1500 years later roused the passions of men with what might seem to us unbelievable intensity. If the Reformation was about any one thing, it was about this. Out of Paul's Epistle Luther drew his famous doctrine of justification by Faith alone—that human nature was so depraved by sin that only God's grace could redeem us, not our own righteousness; and it was precisely this doctrine that the Council of Trent rejected when it asserted that salvation comes through faith *and works,* thus making clear the central theological difference between Catholic and Protestant. For the Roman Catholic the whole life of a man, lived within the framework of the church, is what counts. For the Protestant, the central experience of religious conversion, an experience which the individual soul receives direct from God, is so important that nothing else really matters.

Calvin too believed in the supreme importance of grace; and he laid particular stress on the idea of election—the belief that a small number of chosen souls were the fortunate recipients of God's grace. With cruel logic, he argued that if we are depraved by sin we can do nothing to ensure our salvation; that since salvation is bestowed wholly by God, it must seem to us to be artitrarily bestowed. Who the elect are, who the damned are, has been predestined from all eternity.

In practice, this savage belief inspired men to moral earnestness and fierce effort. It is a strange paradox that such rigid determinism, instead of sapping the will, should have strengthened it. A Calvinist can never know that he is one of the elect, but many Calvinists behaved as if they did know, and drew a corresponding strength from the conviction. But the doctrine had its bizarre and dangerous forms too, as is hardly surprising. For instance, if your deeds can have no influence on your salvation, then perhaps the redeemed ought to lie or steal or fornicate simply to show that they can do this without losing their inner purity. The Gospel has freed us from the shackles of the law. This statement, which meant so much to the men of the sixteenth and seventeenth centuries, can be taken on two levels. Historically, the New Testament has superseded the Old, and the gospel of Jesus has replaced the Mosaic law. And morally, in the heart of each believer, the spirit of Jesus has replaced the moral rules. It is easy to see what a liberating experience such a belief could be: but it is easy to see too how it can be turned into a licence to do anything.

St Paul was careful to guard against this conclusion: "What then? shall we sin, because we are not under the law, but under grace? God forbid." (*VI. 15*)
But there were sects who did exactly this; and—more important for our purposes—there were theologians who maintained that Christians were entirely free from the Mosaic law. To this doctrine Luther gave the name Antinomianism, and though we can see that it is a possible corollary of his own doctrine, he attacked it bitterly. The man he accused of Antinomianism was his former friend Johannes Agricola of Eisleben, with whom he had a bitter controversy at Wittenberg in the 1630s. Here is an account of Antinomianism, taken from *The Dictionary of All Religions* (1704):
"Antinomianism, so denominated for rejecting the law as a thing of no use under the gospel dispensation: they say that good works do not further, nor evil works hinder salvation; that the child of God cannot sin, that God never chastiseth him, that murder, drunkenness, etc., are sins in the wicked but not in him, that the child of grace, being once assured of salvation, afterwards never doubteth . . . that God doth not love any man for his holiness, that sanctification is no evidence of justification, etc."
I doubt if Browning expects us to know much about Johannes Agricola himself. It is interesting, no doubt, to read that he and Luther had been fellow-students, to follow his career as one of the leading Protestant reformers, and to learn that when he left Wittenburg as a result of the dispute with Luther he bacame court preacher and general superintendent at the court of Brandenburg in Berlin, where he had a long and busy career till he died in 1566. This is interesting, but quite unnecessary for the appreciation of the poem. What we need to know about is not Agricola's life but his belief—that he was an Antinomian and a believer in predestination.

Predestination seems an ugly doctrine to us nowadays. A God who quite arbitrarily condemns the majority of mankind to everlasting perdition is surely a particularly hideous God. It seems to argue a kind of moral perversion in the mind of sixteenth-century Europe that men could then worship such a God and call him the God of love. We may even feel relieved that in all the horrors of the twentieth century we have, at any rate, outgrown *that*. Browning was a Christian, but he was not that kind of Christian; and this poem, published in 1836, stands far nearer to us than it does to *Johannes Agricola* itself.

It is the work of a man who finds predestination astonishing: and who has responded by trying to understand it. Can the doctrine be presented in its full ruthlessness, and at the same time be made to sound like a doctrine which men really believed, and believed with enthusiasm? Can we be shocked by its horror, but also shocked into accepting it? Well, perhaps not accepting it ourselves, but realizing how it could commend itself to men, even inspire them.

This is the starting-point for the poem. If we begin it (as most readers surely do begin it) with no idea of who Johannes Agricola was—even whether he really existed or was invented by Browning— the first thing to strike us will surely be the strangeness, and also the intensity, of his beliefs. Protestantism, I have suggested, believes in the supreme importance of direct contact with God, without an intermediary: hence Luther's doctrine of the priesthood of all believers. A true believer needs no priest for he receives God's grace immediately. And just as Luther impatiently brushed aside all human institutions, so Agricola brushes nature aside: it may be God's work but it can be seen as an interference, keeping us from God.

In John Donne's *Second Anniversary,* a highly personal but basically orthodox religious meditation (prompted by or at any rate attached to the death of Elizabeth Drury, his patron's daughter, it includes the results of a lifetime's tortured speculation), there is a passage on the release of the soul from the body by death:

> Think thy shell broke, think thy Soule hatch'd but now.
> And think this slow-pac'd soule, which late did cleave
> To'a body, and went but by the body's leave,
> Twenty, perchance, or thirty mile a day,
> Dispatches in a minute all the way
> Twixt heaven, and earth; she stays not in the air,
> To look what Meteors there themselves prepare.

Then comes a list of the astronomic and scientific points the soul won't have leisure to stop and investigate. All curiosity will be extinguished in her hurry to get to God:

> She baits not at the Moon, nor cares to try
> Whether in that new world, men live and die.

She will not pause to find out whether there is a ring of fire (the lightest element) above the air, nor how Venus

> Can (being one star) Hesper and Vesper be;

—and so on, and so on: detail after detail of what the soul will ignore, fascinating problems all, but—

> But ere she can consider how she went,
> At once is at, and through the Firmament.

The comparison with *Johannes Agricola* is illuminating. Both poets tell us how the soul journeys through the firmament, impatient to arrive at its goal. But Donne is writing with the intensity of a lifetime's scientific curiosity. How much we could learn about the universe, if we could only take a trip to the upper regions above the air! (Now that we've taken such trips, we know that almost all the problems Donne lists are not problems, for he assumes a medieval world picture that we have now quite rejected—but this fact too would fascinate him.) Telling us that the soul will no longer care about such things, he none-the-less pauses to list them and linger on them: the result is a tension that increases the sense of hurry—the poem does precisely what the soul doesn't do, and thus leads us to realize more fully what she is rejecting.

Agricola, in contrast, practises what he preaches. If he finds the roof of heaven gorgeous, he only tells us so in the very act of looking right through it. The speed of his mystical journey does not emerge, like that of Donne's more literal journey, by contrast, but in the way he brushes the splendour of the stars aside. And so his poem contains a blunt, almost monosyllabic, almost brutally crude line:

> For I intend to get to God.

There is nothing in Donne like that naked assertion of the will: what Donne strives towards, Browning simply states. Even the metre seems to help, for the shorter, four-beat line can more easily sound blunt than the pentameter.

When Agricola has found his way to God there will be no change: once there, "I lie as I have always lain". That is the theme of the middle section of the poem, that God has always loved him, for his election was predestined. Predestination means so much to Agricola because it shows God as above time, and God's interest in man as preceding the creation of the universe

> aye, God said
> This head this hand should rest upon
> Thus, ere he fashioned star or sun.

"There's a special providence in the fall of a sparrow." If you believe in a special providence governing every detail then you can see yourself in the very moment of having the thought, you can see even the way you are sitting, head on hand, as the result of God's particular intention—an intention dating back to the beginning of time. Egoism carried to such an extreme—is it mad, or sublime? The conviction that the way you are sitting matters more to God than the whole universe is a mark of how carefully God is looking after you.

He looks after you because you are elected; and in a way he looks after the reprobate as well, but in reverse. This is the point of the image of the tree and the gourd. The tree is so created that whatever nourishment it takes (however poisonous) will help it to grow upward; the poison-gourd is "foredoomed to stoop" and everthing, even "sweet dew" only helps it to grow downward. The point made in this image is also made explicitly. Agricola states his Antinomianism quite clearly when he asserts that

> could I blend
> All hideous sins, as in a cup,
> To drink the mingled venoms up . . .

it would all contribute to his redemption. And then he goes on to draw the full and cruel consequence of predestination. All that God does is good, because God does it. If he chooses to condemn the reprobate to hell fire, the blessed should not only accept but rejoice in this. The acceptance of hell was for many centuries so central a point of Christian belief that we cannot find Agricola exceptional here. When the mildest of men believed that God would condemn (indeed, had already condemned) the majority of mankind to everlasting perdition, Agricola is doing what thousands did when he pictures himself gazing below on hell's fierce bed, contemplating (enjoying?) the "ghastly wretchedness" of the damned.

Dramatic poetry is easy to define: it is poetry in which our awareness of the speaker is part of our response. This is quite clear in the case of a play: remove the indications of who says what, and it would cease to be a play.

> Put up your bright swords or the dew will rust them

is a marvellously haunting and dignified line, and it might stay in the memory of someone who heard it in isolation; but when we read or see *Othello*, we hear that line as something that Othello says, and its force includes what it is telling us about his dignity, quiet authority and imagination.

Work on, my medicine, work: thus credulous fools are caught

is an insidiously rhythmic line, whose lilt is both gripping and sinister and it too would have great power in isolation; but once again, in our experience of the play, that line is something Iago says, and its meaning includes what it tells us about his delight in the artistry of evil and his power over Othello.

The fact that different characters speak to each other naturally forces us to be constantly aware of the identity of who is speaking; but there is no reason in principle why this awareness can only come to us in a play. Suppose the text of *Othello* was lost, but one of Iago's speeches had survived, say by being quoted in a playgoer's diary; we would know that it came from a play, we might guess something of the action, and we would form a fair idea of what sort of man Iago was. All this would form part of our awareness as we read the speech, for it would be quite clear that this was dramatic poetry.

What we would then have in fact would be a dramatic monologue: that is, a poem which offers awareness of the dramatic without using other speakers. The art of writing dramatic monologues requires two gifts in particular. The first is more or less technical: the insertion of clues about the situation, information on who is speaking to whom, where and when, into the speech itself. The second, which is much more fundamental, is the dramatic awareness itself.

For an example of the first we can look at the opening lines of *Fra Lippo Lippi*:

> I am poor brother Lippo, by your leave!
> You need not clap your torches to my face.
> Zooks, what's to blame? you think you see a monk!
> What, 'tis past midnight, and you go the rounds,
> And here you catch me at an alley's end
> Where sportive ladies leave their doors ajar!
> The Carmine's my cloister; hunt it up,
> Do—harry out, if you must show your zeal,
> Whatever rat, there, haps on his wrong hole,
> And nip each softling of a wee white mouse,
> *Weke, weke,* that's crept to keep him company!
> Aha, you know your betters? Then, you'll take
> Your hand away that's fiddling on my throat,
> And please to know me likewise.

These lines do a great deal. They give us the character of Fra Lippo vividly enough—impulsive, hot-tempered, amused, enjoying his own eloquence, not altogether serious when he stands on his dignity. It is the character that underlies his contribution to painting, and for Browning it is an essential part of the movement from the other-worldliness of medieval art to the vivid awareness of this world in Renaissance art. But as well as—even before—doing this, they do something more practical. They tell us where we are and what's going on. Lippi has slipped out of his convent on some unmonkish pleasure escapade, and the watch have caught him. We are even told, with the greatest naturalness, how late at night it is, and what his convent is called. This is skill of a fairly mechanical kind, but skill none the less.

It is not necessary that time, place and circumstances should be so specific, though they often are in Browning. The speaker may be writing a letter, or sitting talking to himself. We may even forget the time and place as the poem proceeds. It is not, after all, very plausible that Lippi should tell the whole story of his life in the street at mid-night to a set of strangers. Perhaps he doesn't—perhaps Browning intends us to forget the particularity of the opening as we read on, absorbed in the revelation of Lippi's life and character. There is no great harm in departing from the technical scene-setting, but the poem must not, of course, depart from the dramatic mode.

Browning is both the greatest and most prolific writer of dramatic monologues in English, on both counts. It is strange that he had no talent for writing plays. His marvellous sense of the dramatic took him to the point of complete awareness of the speaker, and an implication of who else is present, or listening, or talked about; but it did not extend to creating more than one speaker simultaneously, and showing their interaction. Readers of Browning grow so familiar with his gift, that they cease to notice how surprising it is that he went so far and no further, that he knew his own talent so perfectly, and found a mode of writing so exactly suited to it.

What is the value of the dramatic? The value of the lyrical is obvious—a poet strives to express his own sensibility to the fullest. The dramatized speaker may have lyrical gifts—as in their different ways have both Othello and Iago—but the poet will only allow him to use these in so far as they are dramatically appropriate. This implies an element of holding back, a deliberate cramping and limiting of poetic reach, and so it can lead to—for instance—objections like this:

"If a poet is endeavoring to communicate his own best understanding of a human situation, that is one thing. If he is endeavoring to communicate approximately a plausible misunderstanding of a situation on the part of an imaginary character much less intelligent than himself, that is quite another. He can only guess at the correct measure of stupidity which may be proper to such a character in a given situation."

Yvor Winters here rejects the very idea of the dramatic with a ruthlessness seldom found in critics. It is for him an example of "the fallacy of imitative form: the procedure by which the poet surrenders the form of his statement to the formlessness of his subject-matter." If we accept Winter's criterion, then the value of dramatic verse will depend very closely on the insight available to the speaker: and in fact Winters continues, in this essay ("Problems for the Modern Critic of Literature"), by explaining that *Macbeth* ("the greatest play with which I am acquainted") is damaged by the fact that Macbeth in the opening scenes "is uneducated by his sin", so that Shakespeare is not able to give to his speeches "the best poetry of which he is capable".

It's an unusual view of Macbeth: I have quoted it here because it leads us to see that there are two kinds of argument for dramatic poetry, according to whether or not the insight and ability of the speaker matters. Most of the speakers of Browning's dramatic mono- logues are very intelligent; so that when he shows them struggling to overcome some limitation in their outlook (as he likes to do for instance with the intelligent pagan on the verge of discovering Christianity, as in *Creon,* or *An Epistle . . . of Karshish the Arab Physician*) the struggle has genuine interest. Even when the speaker is not intelligent, as with the Caliban of *Caliban on Setebos,* he is given a kind of brilliant madness, or divine inarticulateness, from which we have much to learn. One reply to Winters, then, is to point out how often the dramatic poet chooses a speaker who does not have to be given inferior or limited poetry.

But there is another and more radical reply which would claim that *any* speaker is worth using: that the very act of dramatic writing has a value. This view can be defended on two different—indeed, opposite—grounds. The first is irony. A limited outlook by the speaker may be transcended by the poet, who silently signals to us, inviting awareness of the limitations of what we hear. There is plenty of such irony in Browning, who might invite us to distance ourselves from simple-mindedness (*Up at a Villa—down in the City*), the misguided ingenuities of hatred (*Soliloquy in a Spanish Cloister*), or the ruthlessness of a pride based on exquisite taste (*My Last Duchess*). Yet even at his most ironic, Browning never (or never when at his best) writes without a deep respect, perhaps despite himself, for his speakers. And so to the second reason, for which we need a very general and potentially sentimental phrase like human solidarity. To enter into the sensibility of anyone is to make the kind of assertion that the person was worth knowing. And in the end, I believe Yvor Winters is wrong because he betrays contempt for his fellow men, because he is too readily sure that most sensibilities are crude, many minds stupid. To believe in human variety enlarges the imagination more than to believe in human stupidity.

We have taken it for granted so far that the poem is dramatic, and not a statement of Browning's own views. Can we be sure that he was not himself an Antinomian, writing directly from his own convictions?

We can be quite sure of this from external evidence. Not only the title of the poem, not only the fact that Browning was a regular writer of dramatic monologues, but also the circumstances of the poem's publication make this clear. It first appeared in 1836, in a periodical called the *Monthly Repository*, along with a companion piece in the same metre, *Porphyria's Lover*; and it was preceded by a note on Antinomianism from the *Dictionary of all Religions* (1704), which has already been quoted, in fact: it is the passage beginning "Antinomians, so denominated . . .". Six years later Browning reprinted both poems together in his book *Bells and Pomegranates* under the common heading "Madhouse Cells" (though he later separated them). So it is quite clear not only that he regarded Antinomianism as an unusual and fascinating historical phenomenon, but also that he regarded Agricola as mad.

Since *Porphyria's Lover* was intended as a comparison piece, we had better read it:

### Porphyria's Lover

The rain set early in tonight
   The sullen wind was soon awake,
It tore the elm-tops down for spite,
   And did its worst to vex the lake,
I listened with heart fit to break;
When glided in Porphyria: straight
   She shut the cold out and the storm,
And kneeled and made the cheerless grate
   Blaze up, and all the cottage warm;
Which done, she rose, and from her form
Withdrew the dripping cloak and shawl,
   And laid her soiled gloves by, untied
Her hat and let the damp hair fall,
   And last, she sate down by my side

And called me. When no voice replied,
She put my arm about her waist,
  And made her smooth white
                      shoulder bare,
And all her yellow hair displaced,
  And, stooping, made my cheek
                      lie there,
And spread o'er all her yellow hair,
Murmuring how she loved me; she
  Too weak, for all her heart's endeavour,
To set its struggling passion free
  From pride, and vainer ties dissever,
And give herself to me for ever:
But passion sometimes would prevail,
  Nor could tonight's gay feast restrain
A sudden thought of one so pale
  For love of her, and all in vain:
So, she was come through wind and rain.
Be sure I looked up at her eyes
  Proud, very proud; at last I knew
Porphyria worshipped me; surprise
  Made my heart swell, and still it grew
While I debated what to do.
That moment she was mine, mine, fair,
  Perfectly pure and good: I found
A thing to do, and all her hair
  In one long yellow string I wound
Three times her little throat around,
And strangled her. No pain felt she;
  I am quite sure she felt no pain.
As a shut bud that holds a bee
  I warily oped her lids; again
Laughed the blue eyes without a stain.
And I untightened next the tress
  About her neck; her cheek once more
Blushed bright beneath my burning kiss:
  I propped her head up as before,
Only, this time *my* shoulder bore
Her head, which droops upon it still:
  The smiling rosy little head,
So glad it has its utmost will,
  That all it scorned at once is fled,
And I, its love, am gained instead!

> Porphyria's love: she guessed not how
> > Her darling one wish would be heard.
> And thus we sit together now,
> > And all night long we have not stirred,
> And yet God has not said a word!

Psychologically, this is most interesting—even more interesting, perhaps, than Browning would easily have admitted. The narrator murdered Porphyria in order to preserve for all time a moment of perfect love. It is clear their love had been imperfect and disturbed: we are not told why (was Porphyria married? Did her parents object to the narrator as her suitor?), and it does not matter. The interest lies not in the facts of their situation but in the strange perverted wish to immortalize the perfect moment by killing her. The modern reader is likely to see this in sexual terms, to regard the murder as a sexual surrogate—and the fact that there is no overt sexuality between them makes this more plausible still.

Yes, Porphyria's lover is a pathological case, and a madhouse cell is where he belongs. Yet he does not speak like a madman. The poem is so quiet, so meticulous, so lucid, that we can be forgiven for feeling, as we read, that the whole thing was understandable, even natural. The link between sex and death is very old, and underlies much love poetry; and no doubt the psychological connection (like most psychopathology) is in some milder sense present to all of us. The suicide pact has always been linked with romantic love, and though this is murder not suicide it was based on a strange almost mystical (if twisted) respect for Porphyria's feelings. Browning has painted not violence or hysteria but a terrible calm. Only in the last line do we hear the first giggle of terror, and even that can be spoken with a quiet assurance—mad, doubtless, but horribly plausible.

Mad, yes, but in a way that makes him sound sane: just as Agricola, whose theological position was widespread and even respected is also, in a sense, mad. It is true, certainly, that Agricola's logic is self-defeating: for if his God is careful to damn those who think they're saved, will he not damn Agricola? Yet if that is madness, many brilliant and apparently sane men have been mad, perhaps even Calvin.

The effect of reading these two poems as a pair is to make us question the obvious distinction between madness and sanity. We see how a terrible lucidity and a remorseless logic can present a vision in which the highest egoism and the deepest humility are indistinguishable. Porphyria's lover acted as if he was above all human law; yet there is a kind of humble passiveness in his urge to preserve a moment when to his astonished delight Porphyria gave herself to him. And Agricola, looking for an explanation of God's mysterious arbitrariness, of the incomprehensible fact of his own election, finds it in an extreme of humility—how could one worship a God one could understand? Both poems are written in a quiet tone in which utter egoism becomes indistinguishable from utter self-forgetfulness.

Hence the strange power of the end of *Agricola*. It should be read, surely, in a tone of astonished awe. Astonishment combines with a sense of absolute fitness as he realizes that God's glory requires incomprehensibility.

> how could I praise,
> If such as *I* might understand . . .

A lingering stress on that second "I" will convey the gesture that combines delighted worship with self-abnegation. If he could understand, God's glory would be less; for by understanding it we would too easily turn it into a bargain, something to be reckoned. Is this the extreme of humility, or the extreme of insane egoism? It is impossible to say.

There are discoveries to be made about ourselves as well as others, if we have the patience to submit ourselves to another personality. The final answer to Yvor Winters is not simply that the dramatic teaches us not to dismiss our fellow men; but also that it enables us to understand connections and complex emotions that might have remained beyond the understanding of the poet who tries to express only his own personality.

# 13

# The Ruined Maid

"O 'Melia, my dear, this does everything crown!
Who could have supposed I should meet you in Town?
And whence such fair garments, such prosperi–ty?"—
"O didn't you know I'd been ruined?" said she.

—"You left us in tatters, without shoes or socks,
Tired of digging potatoes, and spudding up docks;
And now you've gay bracelets and bright feathers three!"—
"Yes: that's how we dress when we're ruined," said she.

—"At home in the barton you said 'thee' and 'thou',
And 'thik oon', and 'theäs oon,' and 't'other'; but now
Your talking quite fits 'ee for high compa–ny!"—
"Some polish is gained with one's ruin," said she.

—"Your hands were like paws then, your face blue and bleak
But now I'm bewitched by your delicate cheek,
And your little gloves fit as on any la–dy!"—
"We never do work when we're ruined," said she.

—"You used to call home-life a hag ridden dream,
And you'd sigh, and you'd sock; but at present you seem
To know not of megrims or melancho–ly!"—
"True. One's pretty lively when ruined," said she.

—"I wish I had feathers, a fine sweeping gown,
And a delicate face, and could strut about Town!"—
"My dear—a raw country girl such as you be,
Cannot quite expect that. You ain't ruined," said she.

*Thomas Hardy* (1866)

Another ballad: very different from *Clerk Saunders* in its effect, but
using many of the same techniques. It describes a single episode:
a young country girl comes up to town, and there to her surprise she
meets "'Melia," whom she'd known on the farm. Amelia is now
finely dressed, and clearly doing very well because, as she explains,
she's been "ruined". The story is told entirely in dialogue, the two
girls being the only speakers: the poet says nothing. It uses a refrain,
though flexibly: the last line of each stanza keeps the same basic
pattern, culminating in the all important "ruined", to produce an

effect of parallelism, but each time it is adapted to produce a reply to the stanza that goes before. The rhythm is regular and striking:

> × / × × / × × / × × /
> Your hands were like paws then, your face blue and bleak
> × / × × / × × / × × /
> But now I'm bewitched by your delicate cheek.

Four stresses in each line, all of them except the first preceded by two unstressed syllables. There is a name for the unit, or foot, out of which the lines are built(× × / ): it is called an anapaest, and the effect of an anapaestic line is a tripping movement, rapid and often gay, well suited to a music-hall song. The language and form of the poem clearly relate it to popular and not learned tradition, as fits the speakers: its effect is succinct and at the same time forceful, not subtle or complex.

A ballad, yes, but not a ballad in the same tradition as *Clerk Saunders,* which as we saw was Scottish and rural, probably transmitted orally for centuries, tragic, tight-lipped, with touches of the supernatural. *The Ruined Maid* looks to another and newer tradition, though an equally popular one: that of the broadside ballad. A broadside is a crudely printed sheet of paper sold in markets and fairs and on street corners, and broadside ballads, often in crude doggerel, were written on recent public events, or on the exploits of famous criminals, or on popular stories. Autolycus, the pedlar in Shakespeare's *The Winter's Tale,* sells ribbons and ornaments and also ballads: "He hath songs for man or woman of all sizes . . . he has the prettiest love songs for maids", and he sings in praise of his own wares "as they were gods or goddesses: you would think a smock were a she-angel, he so chants to the sleevehand." So we hear him singing a delightful advertising jingle:

> Lawn as white as driven snow,
> Cypress black as e'er was crow;
> Gloves as sweet as damask roses,
> Masks for faces and for noses. . . .
> Come buy of me, come, come buy, come buy,

—and describing the ballads he has for sale:
"Here's one to a very doleful tune, how a usurer's wife was brought to bed of twenty money-bags at a burden, and how she longed to eat adders' heads and toads carbonadoed. . . . This is a passing merry one, and goes to the tune of 'Two maids wooing a man'. There's scarce a maid westward but she sings it." (*The Winter's Tale, IV. 4*) We can see from this that the broadside or printed ballad has a long history, perhaps almost as old as the traditional oral ballads: it was

familiar enough to Shakespeare's audience for him to make fun of it on the stage. As time passed the two traditions naturally separated into town and country, and broadside ballads tended to be associated with the urban, even the industrial world. Here are the first two stanzas of *The Oldham Weaver*, a Lancashire song, as it is recorded by Elizabeth Gaskell in her novel of life in Manchester, *Mary Barton* (1848):

> Oi'm a poor cotton weyver, as mony a one knoowas,
> Oi've nowt for t' yeat, an' oi've worn eawt my clooas,
> Yo'ad hardly gi' tuppence for aw as oi've on,
> My clogs are both brosten, an' stuckings oi've none,
>> Yo'd think it wur hard
>> To be browt into th'warld,
> To be—clemmed, an' do th' best as yo con.
>
> Owd Dicky o' Billy's kept telling me lung,
> Wee s'd ha' better toimes if I'd but howd my tung,
> Oi've howden my tung, till oi've near stopped my breath,
> Oi think i' my heart oi'se soon clem to deeath,
>> Owd Dicky's weel crammed,
>> He never wur clemmed,
> An' he ne'er picked ower i' his loife.

("clem" is to starve with hunger, to "pick over" is to throw the shuttle in hand-loom weaving.) The people's voice can be heard in this song about working conditions: the poor cotton-weaver tells of his sufferings with complete matter-of-factness—a touch of pathos, and a touch of protest. The second stanza hovers on the edge of politics: Dicky has told him not to complain and things will get better, and his reply to this is a reminder that Dicky (who perhaps is a foreman) has never known the same poverty and exploitation that he has. This is a common reply from the poor when told to accept their lot: to ask whoever is telling them just how much privation he has known.

The sufferings of the poor then, sometimes accompanied by a blunt social criticism, is a familiar theme of the popular urban ballad. Here are two more stanzas from *The Oldham Weaver*:

> Owd Billy o' Dans sent th' baileys one day,
> Fur a shop deebt oi eawd him, as oi could na pay,
> But he wur too lat, fur owd Billy o' th' Bent
> Had sowd th' tit and cart, an' ta'en goods for th' rent,
>> We'd neawt left bo' th' owd stoo',
>> That wur seats fur two,
> An' on it ceawred Marget an' me.

Then t' baileys leuked reawnd as sloy as a meawse,
When they seed as aw t' goods were ta'en eawt o' t' heawse,
Says one chap to th' other, 'Aws gone, theaw may see;'
Says oi, "Ne'er freet, mon, yeaur welcome ta' me."
> They made no moor ado,
> But whopped up th'eawd stoo',
An' we booath leet, whack—upo' t' flags!

("sowd the tit and cart": sold the donkey and cart; "creawred". sat)
Poverty brings debt, debt brings the bailiffs, and taking away their
last stool leaves them sitting on the floor; and in the following stanzas
the weaver remarks to his wife "We's never be lower in this world,
oi'm sure." Without losing sight of the suffering, we have here reached
the comic; and it is worth quoting Mrs Gaskell's comment on the
poem:
"The air to which this is sung is a kind of droning recitative, depend-
ing much on expression and feeling. To read it, it may, perhaps, seem
humorous; but it is that humour which is near akin to pathos, and
to those who have seen the distress it describes it is a powerfully
pathetic song."
In the novel, *Mary Barton*, the heroine, hears the song sung during a
time of depression by a sallow, unhealthy young working woman
called Margaret, who "seemed to become more and more absorbed
in realizing to herself the woe she had been describing," and is able
to translate her own emotion into her singing. After she has finished
the ballad she is lost in thought for a while, then
"Suddenly she burst forth with all the power of her magnificent
voice, as if a prayer from her very heart for all who were in distress,
in the grand supplication, 'Lord, remember David.' Mary held her
breath, unwilling to lose a note, it was so clear, so perfect, so
imploring."
Here we have the popular ballad in its setting: sung by ordinary
people as a record of their own woes and their own grief, mingling
the pathetic and the comic in an effect whose genuineness and power
makes up for the lack of poetic polish. Sometimes the social protest
is more direct than that of *The Oldham Weaver;* sometimes we
have appeals to the powerful, instead of protest. *The Red Wig* describes a self-made overseer called little Charly, who makes shoddy
goods and exploits the workmen:

By pinching his workmen and his runners likewise,
He has brought them to poverty and gained himself a prize,
By cheating the country with his one-thread lace,
He has ruined the trade and brought the town disgrace.

*My Master and I* has a speaker who has just joined a trade union, and is trying to tell his master that it is his right as an Englishman to do this

> —And tho' I respect you, remember I'm free,
> No master in England shall trample on me—

while at the same time reassuring him that there is no need for labour relations to be based on conflict:

> And tho' likely enough we shall ask for more wage
> I can promise you we shall not get first in a rage.

The clumsy rhythm and awkward wording of that last line reminds us what a hit-or-miss thing, poetically, the broadside ballad often is. Perhape we can even wonder if the clumsiness reveals a certain embarrassment at making such approaches to the master. Sometimes the social protest issues in a comic anecdote, as in *The Coal-owner and the Pitman's Wife*, in which the pitman's wife comes back from hell, explaining that the poor folk are all being turned out to make room for the rich:

> And the coal-owners is the next on command
> To arrive in hell, as I understand,
> For I heard the old devil say as I came out,
> The coal-owners had all received their rout.

In the later part of the poem this sardonic note changes into a peaceful attempt at compromise: the woman urges the owner to pay his men better.

> If you be a coal-owner, sir, take my advice,
> Agree with your men and give them a full price.
> For if and you do not, I know very well,
> You'll be in great danger of going to hell.
>     Derry down, down, down derry down.

> For all you coal-owners great fortunes has made,
> By these jovial men that works in the coal trade.
> Now, how can you think for to prosper and thrive
> By wanting to starve your poor workmen alive?
>     Derry down, down, down, derry down.

And the coal owner promises to go home and agree with his men.

Such an ending blunts the force of the joke, by the very fact of striking a more constructive note. The most helpful attitudes in the real world may be out of place artistically in a poem of sardonic protest.

Work conditions and politics are not of course the only or even the commonest subject of the popular ballad. There are large numbers of love-songs, and large numbers of stories about the consequences of seduction. These latter are of special interest to us here.

The commonest situation in a seduction ballad involves a rich man and the poor girl he betrays: in such a story, class exploitation and sexual exploitation go together, and the poor girl is doubly a victim. This has always been a favourite situation for pathos, not only in ballads but in popular drama and the novel; and it was a favourite with Thomas Hardy. In the earliest of his mature novels, *Far from the Madding Crowd,* the poor girl Fanny Robin, seduced and abandoned by her handsome soldier lover, dies in the workhouse after giving birth to her child. It is a ballad situation (even the girl's name suggests a ballad), and Hardy treats it as a story of timeless suffering. The journey of the dying girl to Casterbridge, in chapter 40, dragging her burden on foot along the weary miles, is one of the most powerful incidents in the book. Fanny becomes a figure of suffering humanity, and the origin of her trouble is forgotten in the intensity of concentration on her struggle. It is only an episode in *Far from the Madding Crowd,* important in its consequences for the main plot, but Fanny is a minor character. In his greatest novel, *Tess of the D'Urbervilles,* Hardy returned to the seduction theme for the centre of the action, and this time the social gap between Alex the seducer and Tess the victim is greater and more significant. There is a good deal in *Tess* that is timeless, an attempt to show the inevitable suffering in the human condition, but there is a good deal too that deals with the particularities of the social situation. This is shown by the fact that Tess is a country girl who has lost her reputation, and the complications that follow when she marries an intellectual of progressive views who turns out not to be progressive enough to tolerate a woman's offence against the sexual code. It is a subtle exploration of how some prejudices turn out stronger than others, at the expense of the innocent girl whom society turns into a victim.

Two novels and several stories; and also a number of ballads. Hardy has left us a range of tragic seduction-stories, and some of the poems are very moving in their rendering of the pathos of the situation. Here is a straightforward narrative, written towards the end of his life:

### The Ballad of Love's Skeleton

"Come, let's to Culliford Hill and Wood,
    And watch the squirrels climb.
And look in sunny places there
    For shepherds' thyme."

—"Can I have heart for Culliford Wood,
    And hill and bank and tree,
Who know and ponder over all
    Things done by me!"

—"Then, Dear, don hat, and come along:
    We'll strut the Royal strand;
King George has just arrived, his Court,
    His guards, and band."

—"You are a Baron of the king's Court
    From Hanover lately come,
And can forget in song and dance
    What chills me numb.

"Well be the royal scenes for you,
    And band beyond compare,
But how is she who hates her crime
    To frolic there?

"O why did you so urge and say
    'Twould soil your noble name!—
I should have prized a little child,
    And faced the shame.

"I see the child—*that should have been
    But was not*, born alive;
With such a deed in a woman's life
    A year seems five.

"I asked not for the wifely rank,
    Nor maiden honour saved;
To call a nestling thing my own
    Was all I craved.

"For what's the hurt of shame to one
  Of no more note than me?
Can littlest life beneath the sun
  More littled be?"

—"Nay, never grieve. The day is bright,
  Just as it was ere then;
In the Assembly Room tonight
  Let's joy again!

"The new Quick-step is the sweetest dance
  For lively toes and heels;
And when we tire of that we'll prance
  Bewitching reels.

"Dear, never grieve! As once we whirled
  So let us whirl tonight,
Forgetting all things save ourselves
  Till dawning light.

"The King and Queen, Princesses three,
  Have promised to meet there
The mayor and townsfolk. I've my card
  And One to spare.

"The Court will dance at the upper end;
  Only a cord between
Them and the burgher-throng below;
  A brilliant scene!"

—"I'll go. You've still my heart in thrall:
  Save you, all's dark to me.
And God knows what, when love is all,
  The end will be."

This time the woman has not been abandoned, though there is a hint in the last stanza that this might happen. Her sorrow is that she was compelled to sacrifice her child: no doubt she found herself pregnant, and had an abortion (a far more traumatic experience then than in our more permissive age). Her lover is clearly above her in social station, and because he is still attached to her, he refused to allow her to have the baby: "'Twould soil your noble name!" She agreed, perhaps because like so many mistresses she was in his power economically; but also, and more compellingly, because she is in love with him and can refuse him nothing. That is the situation, which

the brilliant ambiguity of the title refers to. Love's skeleton is the
foetus who was never born; at the same time it can have a metaphoric
meaning, the skeleton of their love which has now turned into something deadly, since it was allowed to sweep all other moral consider-
ations aside:

> And God knows what, when love is all,
>     The end will be.

In commenting, I have picked out the woman's remarks, since it is
these that tell us the story and reveal its pathos; but this gives a very
misleading picture of the surface of the poem, since so much of it is
spoken by the man. He is intent only on the pleasures they can share
together, walking on the hill, watching the king arrive, going to the
ball; and he lingers on the details of these in a way that reveals his
part in their relationship. He seems fond of her, and wants her to
enjoy herself; but he is at the same time unaware of the depth of her
sorrow. The contrast between his superficiality and her grief is the
central structuring device of the poem, and reminds us yet again how
effective is the dramatic mode of the ballad, that allows clashing
dialogue to reveal a situation without comment by the poet.

And now we have the two elements that must be put together to see
the exact nature of what Hardy has done in *The Ruined Maid*. On the
one hand, the situation: that of the seduced girl, the subject of
pathos, since she is the victim for whom only sorrow and disgrace
are left. But in this ballad Hardy has rejected pathos for comedy: so
on the other hand we need to look at the tradition of sardonic
comment that is found in the satiric ballad.

There are plenty of comic ballads about sex, in which the girl
manages to turn the situation to her advantage. There is, for instance,
*The Lass of Islington*, which tells how the lass meets a vintner, who
tastes her pears (the whole poem is based on sexual inuendos) and
asks to lie all night with her. She asks five pounds, and when he
refuses to pay she goes to a justice to complain. The complaint is all
based on a sexual pun:

> She said she had a cellar let out
>     To a vintner in the town;
> And how that he did then agree
>     Five pound to pay her down

> But now, quoth she, the case is thus,
>   No rent that he will pay;
> Therefore your worship I beseech,
>   To send for him this day.

The vintner claims that he put nothing into the cellar "but one poor pipe of wine"; but

> This fair maid being ripe of wit,
>   She straight replied again,
> There were two butts more at the door,
>   Why did you not roll them in.

The justice then settles in favour of the maid, telling the vintner

> If he a tenant be
> He must expect to pay the same
> For he could not sit rent-free . . .

and the ballad ends on a note of delight that he has been outwitted by a country girl.

The effect of *The Lass of Islington* depends both on a sexual and on a social point. It uses everyday language with a sexually suggestive meaning in exactly the same way as obscene jokes, and our amusement derives from the way in which verbal ingenuity entitles us to say things we are normally expected to keep silent about. At the same time, it compares sex to a commercial transaction, and suggests that if a girl is to succeed she must handle her sexual availability with the same level-headed good sense that a businessman shows when he has premises to let. The pathos that usually attaches to seduction depends on the belief that loss of virginity is a disaster for a girl; and it is true that the high regard for female chastity that has been traditional in our society has often resulted in social ruin for the girl who is seen to lose it. But the comedy that underlies this poem depends on the existence of a counter-tradition: a willingness by men to treat the sexual availability of girls as a saleable commodity. To join the ranks of the prostitutes is a disaster, but at the same time an opportunity: men like to think of it as a disaster for women whom they esteem, but the shrewd girl will see the opportunities. One wonders if *The Lass of Islington* was written by a woman.

Here we are closer than we have yet come to *The Ruined Maid*, and at the same time to an understanding of the social basis of comedy. There is a kind of comedy, of which Bernard Shaw is the most celebrated practitioner, that depends for its effect on the confrontation of convention with reality. Most drama, according to Shaw, is derived from other drama, and if you trace a dramatic convention back, through play after play,

"you finally come to its origin in the inventive imagination of some original dramatist. Now a fact as invented by a dramatist differs widely from the fact of the same name as it exists or occurs objectively in real life. . . . . . Consequently to a man who derives all his knowledge of life from witnessing plays, nothing appears more unreal than objective life. A dramatic critic is generally such a man; and the more exactly I reproduce objective life for him on the stage, the more certain he is to call my play an extravaganza."

What shocks the critic, according to Shaw, may delight the public; and the effect of his comedies, according to him, is due to the simple fact that instead of behaving as a character in such a play is supposed to behave, his persons behave as such a man would in real life. Thus Blüntschli, the professional soldier in *Arms and the Man*, instead of carrying bullets in his cartridge belt, carries chocolate, "the cheapest, most portable and most easily purchased" form of food; and in a dozen other ways he does what real soldiers, in their memoirs, tell us they have done, not what derivative playwrights have made soldiers do on the stage. "I am well aware," said Shaw,

"that if I choose to be guided by men grossly ignorant of dramatic criticism, whose sole qualification is that they have seen cavalry charges on stricken fields, I must take the consequences. Happily, as between myself and the public, the consequences have not been unpleasant." (*A Dramatic Realist to his Critics*)

It is not only playwrights who devise conventions that conceal the truth. In almost every sphere of life, society devises systems of evasions and idealizations whose purpose is to pretend that things are not as they are. We ought not to despise such systems: sometimes they may be essential for social life. We may aim with more confidence at some desirable ideal if we believe it to be more prevalent than it really is. We may only be able to get on with some necessary task if we turn our eyes from social abuses that would reduce us to misery, frustration or inactivity. But though they may sometimes be necessary, such evasions are often pernicious; and we ought to be grateful that they open the door to the kind of comedy Shaw so enjoyed writing.

The evasion that lies behind *The Ruined Maid*, as we have seen, concerns the consequences of seduction. To tell a girl that the loss of her virginity will be disastrous is clearly to imply that she is better off now than she will be then: that is why the two speakers are so important. The raw country girl who has come to town for the day is in the position Amelia used to be in, and it is clear that it was not one to be envied. Perhaps Amelia was particularly unsuited to farm life, perhaps she chafed more than her friend now does, but it is clear that the catalogue of the burdens of labour is objectively true:

> You left us in tatters, without shoes or socks,
> Tired of digging potatoes, and spudding up docks.

If that was her life, then the implied acceptance contained in the injunction to keep her virtue is likely to make a lively girl sceptical.

> Your hands were like paws then, your face blue and bleak
> But now I'm bewitched by your delicate cheek.

Perhaps the speaker is herself beginning to wonder: seeing that the warnings she has (no doubt) been given have turned out so far from the truth, she too may develop doubts about digging potatoes. That we cannot know; but we do know that Amelia has feathers and a fine sweeping gown.

For an example of the kind of injunction that these girls will have been given, we can turn to Samuel Richardson's *Pamela*. In this novel about a servant girl who does *not* lose her virtue and then—improbably—marries the master who had tried to seduce her, we can see the orthodox view set forth with a smugness that seems begging for its Shaw. Pamela is warned by her parents that nothing matters so much as preserving her virtue:
"Everbody talks how you have come on, and what a genteel girl you are; and some say you are very pretty. . . . But what avails all this, if you are to be ruined and undone? My dear Pamela, we begin to be in great fear for you; for what signify all the riches in the world, with a bad conscience, and to be dishonest? We are, it is true, very poor, and find it hard enough to live. . . . But we would sooner live upon the water, and, if possible, the clay of the ditches I dig, than live better at the price of our child's ruin."
In this world, Amelia is the Blüntschli who has determined to follow good sense rather than exhortations to virtue. The fact that these exhortations come from the poor does not disprove the view that they are part of a system of social control intended to keep poor country girls in a place of due subordination; it could simply show how completely the system is accepted, even by those whom it keeps in place. At this point we are on the edge of a political divide. The radical will claim that subordination should be overthrown and

(consequently) the ethical imperatives questioned. The conservative will claim one of two things. If he is a conservative because he believes in a hierarchical society, he will defend the subordination as valuable in itself; if he believes in order and stability, he will resist the questioning of ethical imperatives, though he may be willing to see the subordination gradually modified.

But comedy is not political: it is concerned to show the inconsistencies and evasions of social and moral judgements, not to suggest how society should be changed. It may have political implications, though it will always be difficult to know what these are: both radical and conservative are likely to enjoy it, for different reasons. Within the work of comedy it will always be a mistake to suggest remedies, as we saw when the sardonic joke of *The Coal-owner and the Pitman's Wife* was turned into an appeal for reconciliation, admirable morally but disastrous artistically. So what matters in *The Ruined Maid* is the skill with which it exploits a discrepancy between morality and desire: the morality of Pamela's parents, the quite natural desire not to live on water and the clay of ditches.

This discrepancy is concentrated into a single word, which as it happens Pamela's parents also use: ruined. For centuries it was the commonest of all euphemisms to describe the girl who had lost her virginity without gaining a husband, and it was clearly felt to have a double appropriateness—on the one hand it says that the loss of virginity is itself ruinous, on the other it says that it leads to social ruin. And along comes Amelia and separates the meanings. The first she is not interested in; the second she regards as plainly false. Each line of the refrain draws a slightly different irony from the same basic discrepancy. "O didn't you know I'd been ruined" is splendidly unexpected: its tone of polite curiosity is exactly the tone of "Didn't you know I was married", and the joke comes from the complete lack of embarrassment with which Amelia gives the information (Blüntschli was not embarrassed either about his behaviour on the battlefield). Then the tone changes to condescension: "That's how we dress when we're ruined" is a gracious explanation, for a raw country girl who can hardly be expected to know, of the customs of this new social world. Since these customs are in so many ways superior, a touch of modesty is appropriate in mentioning the advantages: "some polish is gained with one's ruin" has the slightly embarrassed smile of someone anxious not to show off—there is no embarrassment over the ruin itself. And so on, through each stanza: the rustic astonishment of the country girl is constantly countered by the superior grace of Amelia, convinced of her superiority, not needing (though she yields slightly to the temptation at the very end) to rub it in. She never used pronouns like "one", nor self-deprecating adverbs like "pretty" when she was on the farm: "One's pretty lively" is the sophisticated throwaway language of her new life. And each of her lines culminates in the key word whose inappropriateness sums up the irony of the situation.

Is there one point on which the parallel between Amelia and Blüntschli breaks down? Shaw makes it clear that he had drawn on the normal behaviour of soldiers for his effect: Blüntschli is a professional, and he did what others do. The dramatic critic, or the heroine on stage, who is shocked, is merely revealing ignorance. Are we to think the same of Amelia? That she did what all girls do, that only self-deceivers really value chastity? This would make the poem more shocking, and yet there is a hint that it is true—or at any rate that Amelia thinks it. The detail which most clearly conveys this is her use of "we". She seems so at home in the thought that she now belongs to a new culture, and is simply doing what anyone in her position would do, that we are invited to see her case as typical. "We never do work when we're ruined": it is like a boy explaining to the parents visiting him at boarding school what the customs are. They are customs completely taken for granted, and Amelia takes her new culture for granted. It does not include all girls, not even (perhaps) all sensible girls, but it's an established culture that is conscious of itself as a way of life.

Finally, a word on the voices of the poem. The contrast in experience and sophistication must clearly be rendered by a contrast in accent: whereas the country girl will speak in broad Dorset, Amelia's speech has grown refined. Perhaps the refinement should not be too perfect: a touch of country speech might show through now and then, best of all perhaps in making "ru-in" into two syllables, even into "rew-in". And this in turn can lead us to wonder how long her good fortune will last: is she too confident, is she in her turn going to be a victim? But such a thought can exist only at the edge of the poem. If we see Amelia as victim, we turn comedy back to pathos, and the poem becomes more conventional; the central irony depends on the fact that she is right.

*The Ruined Maid* is not a difficult poem: it can be enjoyed and understood on a single reading. The commentary in this chapter therefore has been concerned to show how its central point draws on conflicting social attitudes; and how without the discrepancies in sexual morals the comedy it represents would not be possible. It belongs to a ballad tradition, and draws on popular poetic effects, but its social point is made with a succinctness and irony that few popular ballads can match. This combination of comic insight and ballad liveliness gives it its power.

It will follow from this that if the society changes the artistic materials will change too. We live in an age when female chastity is no longer seen as essential, even sacred; and if the force of official morality is less strong, the comic effect of defying it will be less strong too. It is always hard to assess the strength, even the reality, of such changes; and so the final question is one you can ask yourself. How do you react to the morality of Pamela's parents? And do you feel that as a member of the twentieth century you hold a different code from earlier ages? If so, you should still be able to appreciate *The Ruined Maid;* but your appreciation will be less violently personal, and will depend more on an act of historical imagination.

# 14

# To an Old Philosopher in Rome

On the threshold of heaven, the figures in the street
Become the figures of heaven, the majestic movement
Of men growing small in the distances of space,
Singing, with smaller and still smaller sound,
Unintelligible absolution and an end—

The threshold, Rome, and that more merciful Rome
Beyond, the two alike in the make of the mind.
It is as if in a human dignity
Two parallels become one, a perspective, of which
Men are part both in the inch and in the mile.

How easily the blown banners change to wings. . . .
Things dark on the horizons of perception,
Become accompaniments of fortune, but
Of the fortune of the spirit, beyond the eye,
Not of its sphere, and yet not far beyond,

The human end in the spirit's greatest reach,
The extreme of the known in the presence of the extreme
Of the unknown. The newsboys' muttering
Becomes another murmuring, the smell
Of medicine, a fragrantness not to be spoiled. . . .

The bed, the books, the chair, the moving nuns,
The candle as it evades the sight, these are
The sources of happiness in the shape of Rome,
A shape within the ancient circles of shapes,
And these beneath the shadow of a shape

In a confusion on bed and books, a portent
On the chair, a moving transparence on the nuns,
A light on the candle tearing against the wick
To join a hovering excellence, to escape
From fire and be part only of that of which

Fire is the symbol: the celestial possible.
Speak to your pillow as if it was yourself.
Be orator but with an accurate tongue
And without eloquence, O, half-asleep,
Of the pity that is the memorial of this room.

So that we feel, in this illumined large,
The veritable small, so that each of us
Beholds himself in you, and hears his voice
In yours, master and commiserable man,
Intent on your particles of nether-do,

Your dozing in the depths of wakefulness,
In the warmth of your bed, at the edge of your chair, alive
Yet living in two worlds, impenitent
As to one, and, as to one, most penitent,
Impatient for the grandeur that you need

In so much misery; and yet finding it
Only in misery, the afflatus of ruin,
Profound poetry of the poor and of the dead,
As in the last drop of the deepest blood,
As it falls from the heart and lies there to be seen,

Even as the blood of an empire, it might be,
For a citizen of heaven though still of Rome,
It is poverty's speech that seeks us out the most.
It is older than the oldest speech of Rome.
This is the tragic accent of the scene.

And you—it is you that speak it, without speech,
The loftiest syllables among loftiest things,
The one invulnerable man among
Crude captains, the naked majesty, if you like,
Of bird-nest arches and of rain-stained-vaults.

The sounds drift in. The buildings are remembered.
The life of the city never lets go, nor do you
Ever want it to. It is part of the life in your room.
Its domes are the architecture of your bed.
The bells keep on repeating solemn names

In choruses and choirs of choruses,
Unwilling that mercy should be a mystery
Of silence, that any solitude of sense
Should give you more than their peculiar chords
And reverberations clinging to whisper still.

It is a kind of total grandeur at the end,
With every visible thing enlarged and yet
No more than a bed, a chair and moving nuns,
The immensest theatre, the pillared porch,
The book and candle in your ambered room,

Total grandeur of a total edifice,
Chosen by an inquisitor of structures
For himself. He stops upon this threshold,
As if the design of all his words takes form
And frame from thinking and is realized.

*Wallace Stevens  (1954)*

This is certainly the most difficult poem in this book. It is difficult
in the particular and tantalizing way peculiar to Wallace Stevens.
A good deal of modern poetry is obscure, and has to be treated almost
like a puzzle: ambiguity and puns, irony and extreme concentration
of meaning, learned allusions, deliberately broken syntax—these are
the verbal devices which make the poems of Eliot, Pound, Hart
Crane or Allen Tate so difficult, and their use is defended in T.S.
Eliot's famous essay on the Metaphysical Poets:
"Our civilization comprehends great variety and complexity, and
this variety and complexity, playing upon a refined sensibility, must
produce various and complex results. The poet must become more
and more comprehensive, more allusive, more indirect, in order to
force, to dislocate if necessary, language into his meaning."

Now although Wallace Stevens is a modernist to his fingertips,
and his poetry could near have been written without the symbolist
revolution that Eliot introduced into English poetry, he is not
modern in this way. His poetry is not wrenched apart by a sense of
strain that comes to it from the strains of our civilization; it is on the
contrary slow-moving, thoughtful and impressive, with a magnificent steadiness in its rhythm. It is difficult because it never quite
seems to be saying what it means; because of its eccentric vocabulary,
in which key terms are somehow impressive but not what the reader
expects; because of its air of assuming that we know what it is saying.
A number of obscure sentences in a Stevens poem may add up to a
whole that somehow communicates its meaning. The same poem
may seem crystal clear one day, and quite opaque (though still
impressive) the next. The difficulty of Stevens is not helped by
detailed commentary in the same way as that of Eliot or Empson;
his poems must be allowed to unfold and grow in the mind. More
even than with most poems in this book, it is necessary simply to
read the poem, over and over, before beginning to worry at it.

Can we none the less offer some preliminary help to the reader
who wants to find his way into an understanding? We can, for

instance, ask who the old philosopher is, and this turns out to be an easy question. When Stevens was a student at Harvard he had known George Santayana, then a young teacher there, and he remained interested in Santayana's work. Santayana died in Rome in 1952, after spending the last eleven years of his life in a nrsing home run by the convent of the Blue Sisters. Several of Stevens's letters refer to him, and there is no doubt that he is the old philosopher of this poem. In a letter of 3 May 1949, for instance (when Stevens must have been thinking about this poem) he remarks that he had known Santayana quite well at Harvard, and adds: "That was almost fifty years ago, when he was quite a different person from the decrepit old philosopher now living in a convent in Rome." He then quotes a sentence from a letter Santayana had recently written to a friend of his, "I have always bowed, however sadly, to expediency or fate." "For the last week or two", remarks Stevens, "I have been repeating that sentence".

Of particular interest is a remark in his essay "Imagination as Value", in which Stevens suggests that the idea of imagination can be used to organize our thoughts on life as well as on literature ."Most men's lives are thrust upon them": nevertheless there can be lives which are organized as carefully as a poem might be organized, and that we can think about aesthetically:

"To use a single illustration: it may be assumed that the life of Professor Santayana is a life in which the function of the imagination has had a function similar to its function in any deliberate work of art or letters. We have only to think of this phase of it, in which in his old age he dwells in the head of the world, in the company of devoted women, in their convent, and in the company of familiar saints, whose presence does so much to make any convent an appropriate refuge for a generous and human philosopher."

Does this information help us to understand the poem? It is perhaps clear from the text as we get to know it, that the old philosopher is an invalid, probably bed-ridden, and looked after by nuns (who are mentioned in the sixth stanza); and it is clear too that we are being invited to think about the end of this individual life in the setting of Rome the Eternal City. The fact that he is in a convent leads to reflection upon Roman Catholicism, and the Rome of this poem is the Rome of Popes and Churches: Santayana, though a materialist and an agnostic, insisted that his philosophy did not exclude religion, which he described as "the inevitable reaction of the imagination when confronted by the difficulties of a truculent world". This aspect of Rome is pointed to in stanza sixteen: the church bells that "keep on repeating solemn names" are

> Unwilling that mercy should be a mystery
> Of silence, that any solitude of sense
> Should give you more than their peculiar chords . . .

While the old philosopher lies dying, wrapped in his own thoughts, making his peace with his own life, he is surrounded by a noisy insistence on ritual, by bells that feel, perhaps, that it is too much like Protestantism for the beloved old man to draw his comfort only from his own thoughts. And the old man is at home in all this:

> The life of the city never lets go, nor do you
> Ever want it to.

It is useful then to know something of the end of Santayana's life, and in particular its special relationship to religion; and though the poem itself tells us what we need to know, its style is so allusive that such external information may be very helpful. Equally helpful is the idea of Santayana's life as organized and controlled by the imagination, and here we can quote a remark by Santayana himself, made on his death bed:

"What comes before or after does not matter, and this is especially so when one is dying. It is so easy for one now to see things under the form of eternity—and in particular that little fragment called my life."

It is natural for a man on the verge of death to think of his life "under the form of eternity". If he is a Christian, he will think about survival after death; this remark of Santayana's suggests that he is doing that *kind* of thinking, but what comes before or after does not matter. He is using the imagination to give a setting and a meaning to his individual life, but in his case it does not issue in religious belief, which should perhaps be thought of only as one of the possible reactions of the imagination. This is a point that takes us to the heart of Stevens's poem.

For the poem is about a man "on the threshold of heaven", and it continually contrasts two levels of being, two forms of existence, "two parallels" that "become one". Read through the poem and see how many variants there are on this theme. There are two Romes; things perceived with difficulty change the mode in which we perceive them, till they are

> beyond the eye,
> Not of its sphere, and yet not far beyond . . . .

Examples follow of some sort of transformation taking place in what we perceive:

> The newsboys' muttering
> Becomes another murmuring . . .

It is this transformation of experience that is the portent, the moving transparence of stanza six, the light of the candle that seems struggling to escape into another realm of being, "the celestial possible". In stanza eight this perception of another realm of being is described as feeling "in this illumined large, The veritable small"; in the next two stanzas it is a contrast between grandeur and misery; in stanza eleven the philosopher, poised between the two realms, is "a citizen of heaven though still of Rome". It is no exaggeration to say that this contrast is at the very centre of the poem. What is it a contrast between?

The philosopher is a very old man whose eyesight is failing: perception is difficult for him (Santayana was in fact almost blind in his last years). Hence the confusion on bed and books, hence the dozing in the depths of wakefulness, hence above all the beautiful third stanza, where the things he has difficulty in seeing have become "dark on the horizons of perception", so that luck is needed in order to make them out. This turns them into "accompaniments of fortune", and then we are taken to the essential contrast: the difficulty of seeing takes us from the world of eye to that of spirit, as if what we are seeing is not altogether of this world, for on it is a "portent" or "moving transparence". That is a theoretical statement of what is described with great immediacy in the wonderful opening line of the stanza:

> How easily the blown banners change to wings. . . .

The exclamation is ambiguous: how easy it is to see things wrong when you are old and half-blind; or, how easy, in Rome, to regard the earthly as a symbol of the eternal, to give a religious significance to everyday objects. And that in turn could be the delighted exclamation of the Christian, or the wry comment of the agnostic.

It is natural, in a poem about an old man dying, to see the central contrast as that between heaven and earth, between the soul which is about to escape into a new life and the body which is about to die in this world. And perhaps a devout reader could read this poem without finding anything disturbing in it. But Stevens has taken great trouble to describe the contrast in a way that need not imply any such belief. His terminology is scrupulously general; eye and spirit, known or unknown, and above all the fifth stanza, where everyday objects are

> The sources of happiness in the shape of Rome,
> A shape within the ancient circles of shapes,
> And these beneath the shadow of a shape . . .

This presumably means that the shape of the actual scene around the philosopher exists within the larger whole of Rome that is full of famous old domes and arches ("Its domes are the architecture of your bed"); and that over it all hovers a sense of another realm of being, the shadow of "the celestial possible". The lines are so general that they disintegrate into a kind of conundrum, and the poem at this point seems to be playing tricks on us; but although they may not be very successful poetically we can see what led the poet to such elusive wording.

Santayana's view of religion, then, as an activity of the imagination is an invaluable clue to the understanding of this poem; though since Stevens's poetry is deeply agnostic from first to last, we could as easily have approached the point by looking at some of his other poems, either the elegantly mocking *A High-toned old Christian Woman,* or *Of Heaven considered as a Tomb,* or *Sunday Morning,* Stevens's greatest and most famous poem, or the following beautiful section from *Le monocle de mon oncle:*

> The mules that angels ride come slowly down
> The blazing passes, from beyond the sun.
> Descensions of their tinkling bells arrive.
> These muleteers are dainty of their way.
> Meantime, centurions guffaw and beat
> Their shrilling tankards on the table-boards.
> This parable, in sense, amounts to this:
> The honey of heaven may or may not come,
> But that of earth both comes and goes at once.
> Suppose these couriers brought amid their train
> A damsel heightened by eternal bloom.

Angels descend from heaven to earth—as they might in a medieval vision—in a splendid stately rhythm. But Stevens's angels ride on the most earthly of beasts; they come slowly and, apparently, without enthusiasm ("dainty of their way"). Meanwhile the living are enjoying themselves, crudely and vigorously. The contrast is between the "honey of heaven" which may not exist but must be eternal if it does, and the honey of earth which certainly exists but does not last. It is clearly an agnostic poem which understands that religion is "the inevitable reaction of the imagination", and the stanza ends with a carefully noncommittal suggestion of what heaven might offer us— might but (surely) won't, for if the damsel is to exist on earth her bloom cannot be eternal, and if she truly comes from heaven we would not recognize it as bloom. "The trouble with the idea of heaven", wrote Stevens, commenting on these lines, "is that it is merely an idea of the earth."

The two realms of being in *To an Old Philosopher*, then, are carefully not given a Christian interpretation, despite the insistence of the bells, despite the presence of the nuns. It is equally important to notice how intimately they are fused together; so that although the realm of spirit is constantly contrasted with that of the eye (let us use that terminology for convenience), it cannot really be detached from it: it is "not of its sphere, and yet not far beyond". This is clearest in the ninth and tenth stanzas, which assert the closeness of the two worlds in which the old philosopher lives.

> Impatient for the grandeur that you need
>
> In so much misery,

could describe the believer longing to be freed from the body so that his soul may go to heaven, or the philosopher who needs imagination to rescue him from the "difficulties of a truculent world". The ambiguity is preserved in the next remark: "and yet finding it Only in misery". The believer finds it only in misery through his belief in the Incarnation, in a God who entered into this world, and the philosopher finds it only in misery by seeing the activity of the imagination not as escapist but as a way of illuminating our actual experiences. Here we can find a parallel in another of Stevens's finest poems, *Esthetique du Mal*, whose third section runs as follows:

> His firm stanzas hang like hives in hell
> Or what hell was, since now both heaven and hell
> Are one, and here, O terra infidel.
>
> The fault lies with an over-human god,
> Who by sympathy has made himself a man
> And it is not to be distinguished, when we cry

Because we suffer, our oldest parent, peer
Of the populace of the heart, the reddest lord,
Who has gone before us in experience.

If only he would not pity us so much,
Weaken our fate, relieve us of woe both great
And small, a constant fellow of destiny,

A too, too human god, self-pity's kin
And uncourageous genesis . . . . It seems
As if the health of the world might be enough.

It seems as if the honey of common summer
Might be enough, as if the golden combs
Were part of a sustenance itself enough,

As if hell, so modified, had disappeared,
As if pain, no longer satanic mimicry,
Could be borne, as if we were sure to find our way.

Heaven and hell, we now realize, are ways of talking about this world which has become *terra infidel,* the earth without faith; and the religious poet, whoever he is, who once wrote about hell turns out to have written about earth. Our problem on earth, when we reflect on pain and evil (the whole poem, an aesthetic of evil, is a reflection on just that) comes from Christianity, for the over-human god who became man, who has "gone before us in experience" and so knows our suffering from within, prevents us from accepting our lot with the necessary stoicism, encourages us to expect pity and look outside this world for strength.

It seems
As if the health of the world might be enough.

Stevens is a tantalizing poet when we look for the logic of what his poems are saying, and there is no clear indication of whether this seems to be the case as a result of Christianity, or of whether it seems as if it might be so if it were *not* for the over-human god. The latter reading is certainly the one that fits better into Stevens's work as a whole, and suggests that the view of our fate that we ought to take, freeing ourselves from Christianity, is one that finds this world enough, one in which hell has disappeared and we are "sure to find our way". And that is certainly compatible with *To an Old Philosopher,* in which the grandeur we long for can only be found in the misery of living. On our terra infidel, pain is no longer "satanic mimicry", on longer explained in religious terms, and the most moving poetry is the "profound poetry of the poor and of the dead".

The next stanza is an assertion of the power of simple, direct speech, speech that confronts the misery of life, "poverty's speech". This too is a theme Stevens had previously written about a great deal. There is an alternation in much of his writing between a trust in what he called the "essential gaudiness" of poetry, a taste for baroque elaboration and highly decorative, eccentric and even obscure description; and a simplicity and directness wholly free from ornament. It corresponds to a philosophic tension in his work as he alternates between the belief that we create the world that we write about, and the insistence that we must learn how to see things as they are, that we must try to render the significance of *An ordinary evening in New Haven* (the title of one of his long difficult philosophic poems). The gaudiness produces such poems as *Sea Surface full of Clouds*, of which the opening lines run:

> In that November off Tehuantepec,
> The slopping of the sea grew still one night
> And in the morning summer hued the deck
> And made one think of rosy chocolate
> And gilt umbrellas. Paradisal green
> Gave suavity to the perplexed machine
>
> Of ocean, which like limpid water lay.

The poet's talent here is more concerned to make something out of the scene than to render it with humble accuracy; but in a poem like *The House was Quiet and the World was Calm* we have a complete contrast in both style and thought. Here is the poem complete.

> The house was quiet and the world was calm,
> The reader became the book; and summer night
>
> Was like the conscious being of the book.
> The house was quiet and the world was calm.
>
> The words were spoken as if there was no book,
> Except that the reader leaned above the page,
>
> Wanted to lean, wanted much most to be
> The scholar to whom his book is true, to whom
>
> The summer night is like a perfection of thought.
> The house was quiet because it had to be.

> The quiet was part of the meaning, part of the mind:
> The access of perfection to the page.
>
> And the world was calm. The truth in a calm world,
> In which there is no other meaning, itself
>
> Is calm, itself is summer and night, itself
> Is the reader leaning late and reading there.

Here there is no descriptive extravagance, merely an attempt to put down the scene as it is and to tell us, with a lingering, loving repetitiveness, that spiritual meaning and physical existence are identical, that the only truth is an absorption in ordinary existence. The celestial possible exists in the actual: the extreme of the unknown can be found only in the extreme of the known: the summer night is like a perfection of thought. Starting from an experience of harmony and happiness, this little poem offers the same view of the world as *To an Old Philosopher,* starting from the experience of old age and dying.

And they are the same in style too. A poem which tells us that to find the grandeur you must look in the misery that you want to be rescued from, is sure to prefer simplicity to gaudiness; and the setting of Rome, with all its splendours, will lead to a kind of rejection, a claim that poverty's speech is somehow finer, is "older than the oldest speech of Rome": no monument goes as deep as the fact of human suffering. *This,* this simplicity, poverty's speech, and not the ancient circles of shape, not the reverberations of the bells, is "the tragic accent of the scene". Hence the earlier injunction to the philosopher to

> Be orator but with an accurate tongue
> And without eloquence.

Finally, we come to the old philosopher himself. "And you," the twelfth stanza begins, shifting our attention to "the one invulnerable man among Crude captains". The clue to this account of Santayana himself can be found either in the essay already quoted, or in the final stanza of the poem; but once again the strange evasiveness of Stevens's poetry means that the prose passage provides a useful clue. We are dealing here with a man who planned his own life like a work of art, in which the final phase forms a culmination, a total grandeur. The "total edifice" of the last stanza is Santayana's life. This last phase was not thrust upon him, it was chosen; chosen by "an inquisitor of structures", a phrase which might describe either a philosopher, inquiring into the structure of reality, or an artist, probing and testing the best way of giving structure to a life. So at the end of his life the philosopher stops just before death, as if the life planned by the imagination, the life which was the design of all his writing and thinking, has truly been realized. This is the most emphatic account of his life as the product of the imagination, but there were earlier references in the poem, in stanza eight for instance. The old philosopher is both our master and commiserable (deserving of pity): the first because of the perfection of his life, the second because of his feebleness in old age. The "crude captains" of stanza twelve are presumably the men of action whose life is thrust upon them; and the philosopher, whose life is planned, is invulnerable.

It seems appropriate that this poem was written in Stevens's old age. His last volume has little of the earlier gaudiness, but prefers to assert the need for the acceptance of suffering, and the feeling of being at home in the world, in "poverty's speech." It is not easy to say how successful the result is. Some lovers of Stevens prefer him in his richer vein, even in the vein of extravagance that led him to write what seem gay, incomprehensible nonsense verses; others find his simple, direct poetry enormously moving. It may seem odd to speak of so difficult a poem as simple and direct, yet it is full of individual lines that can be detached from their elusive context and that turn out to have great simplicity and power—such lines as "Profound poetry of the poor and of the dead", or "It is older than the oldest speech of Rome." Perhaps the best way to get to know this poem is to think about these lines, if necessary out of context, or to read over and over those single stanzas that impress us even before they come quite clear—the third stanza, or the tenth, or the last. Then it is possible to reread the whole with a few landmarks which will give meaning and force to the rest.

In one respect, at least, neither this nor any other of Stevens's best poems is "without eloquence". The stylistic contrast I have drawn is very vivid when it comes to imagery, but almost non-existent when it comes to rhythm. Almost all Stevens's poetry is written in a sonorous, slow-moving blank verse of great beauty. The "majestic movement" mentioned in the opening stanza of *To an Old Philosopher* is also the movement of the poem itself, never hurrying, never completely departing from the metrical norm but always supple and varied in movement. Look at the first two lines: the repetition that gathers one word from each of the two phrases of the first line to make the phrase "the figures of heaven" not only ties the second line to the first, it forces us to give a slight emphasis to "Become" and to follow it with a pause, slowing down the line, giving it just a touch of ponderousness appropriate to such an opening announcement. Or look at the opening of the fifth stanza. The first line moves quickly, as we reel off the list of objects perceived, but the adjective in "moving nuns"—not a descriptive elaboration, merely a perceived detail—slows us down somewhat; then we slow down more on the candle, where we are asked to pause and savour a touch of exact description. Then, to gather the list together, there are two monosyllables at the end of the line, forcing us to linger on "these", as if to give due weight to the list of particularities before we move into a line that states the significance of the list. In each case we never lose the music of the line, but it has an individual movement that is tied to the meaning.

For so modern a poet, Stevens is deeply traditional. Wordsworth, Keats and Tennyson are present in the rhythm of his verse. We can even try a little trick:

> Is there no change of death in paradise?
> Does ripe fruit never fall? or do the boughs
> Hang always heavy in that perfect sky?
> Ah happy, happy boughs! that cannot shed
> Your leaves, nor ever bid the spring adieu.

It could be from one poem, though you have perhaps realized that the first three lines are by Stevens (from *Sunday Morning*) and the last two by Keats (from *Ode on a Grecian Urn*). This should not surprise us, for literary revolutions are often made by writers who are deeply in touch with the past: not perhaps the immediate past, not perhaps those qualities their contemporaries had most easily seen, but some element in the past of poetry that can quicken and enhance their use of language. In Stevens's case it is his rhythm that is traditional, and his cavalier attitude to making his train of thought clear that is modern. For that reason he is an excellent example of a poet who can move us to an awareness of the beauty of his verse before we have mastered the argument, a poet who (in Eliot's famous wording) can communicate before he is understood. We should accept such communication and build on it; and as I have tried to show, understanding will follow.

# 15

# City without Walls

... "Those fantastic forms, fang-sharp,
bone-bare, that in Byzantine painting
were a short-hand for the Unbounded
beyond the Pale, unpoliced spaces
where dragons dwelt and demons roamed,

"colonised only by ex-worldlings,
penitent sophists and sodomites,
are visual facts in the foreground now,
real structures of steel and glass:
hermits, perforce, are all today,

"with numbered caves in enormous jails,
hotels designed to deteriorate
their glum already-corrupted guests,
factories in which the functional
Hobbesian Man is mass-produced.

"A key to the street each convict has,
but the Asphalt Lands are lawless marches
where gangs clash and cops turn
robber-barons: reckless he
who walks after dark in that wilderness.

"But electric lamps allow nightly
cell-meetings where sub-cultures
may hold palaver, like-minded,
their tongues tattooed by the tribal jargon
of the vice or business that brothers them;

"and mean cafes to remain open,
where in bad air belly-talkers,
weedy-looking, work-shy,
may spout unreason, some ruthless creed
to a dozen dupes till dawn break.

"Every work-day Eve fares
forth to the stores her foods to pluck,
while Adam hunts an easy dollar:
unperspiring at eventide
both eat their bread in boredom of spirit.

"The week-end comes that once was holy,
free still, but a feast no longer,
just time out, idiorhythmic,
when no one cares what his neighbour does:
now newsprint and network are needed most.

"What they view may be vulgar rubbish
what they listen to witless noise,
but it gives shelter, shields them from
Sunday's Bane, the basilisking
glare of Nothing, our pernicious foe.

"For what to Nothing shall nobodies answer?
Still super-physiques are socially there,
frequently photographed, feel at home,
but ordinary flesh is unwanted:
engines do better what biceps did.

"Quite soon computers may expel from the world
all but the top intelligent few,
the egos they leisure be left to dig
value and virtue from an invisible realm
of hobbies, sex, consumption, vague

"tussles with ghosts. Against Whom
shall the Sons band to rebel there,
where Troll-Father, Tusked-Mother,
are dream-monsters like dinosaurs
with a built-in obsolescence?

"A Gadgeted Age, but as unworldly
as when the faint light filtered down
on the first men in Mirkwood,
waiting their turn at the water-hole
with the magic beasts who made the paths.

"Small marvel, then, if many adopt
cancer as the only offered career
worth while, if wards are full of
gents who believe they are Jesus Christ
or guilty of the Unforgiveable Sin:

"if arcadian lawns where classic shoulders,
baroque bottoms, make *beaux gestes,*
is too tame a dream for the dislocated,
if their lewd fancies are of flesh debased
by damage, indignities, dirty words:

"if few now applaud a play that ends
with warmth and pardon the word to all,
as, blessed, unbamboozled, the bridal pairs,
rustic and oppidan, in a ring-dance,
image the stars at their stately bransels:

"if all has gone phut in the future we paint,
where, vast and vacant, venomous areas
surround the small sporadic patches
of fen or forest that give food and shelter,
such home as they have, to a human remnant,

"stunted in stature, strangely deformed,
numbering by fives, with no zero,
worshipping a ju-ju *General Mo*,
in groups ruled by grandmothers,
hirsute witches who on winter nights

"fable them stories of fair-haired Elves
whose magic made the mountain dam,
of Dwarves, cunning in craft, who smithied
the treasure-hoards of tin-cans
they flatten out for their hut roofs,

"nor choice they have nor change know,
their fate ordained by fore-elders,
the Oldest Ones, the wise spirits
who through the mouths' of masked wizards
blessing give or blood demand.

"Still monied, immune, stands Megalopolis:
happy he who hopes for better,
what awaits Her may well be worse . . . ."

Thus I was thinking at three a.m.
in Mid-Manhattan till interrupted,
cut short by a sharp voice:

"What fun and games you find it to play
Jeremiah-cum-Juvenal:
Shame on you for your *Schadenfreude*."

"My!", I blustered, "How moral we're getting.
A pococurante? Suppose I were,
So what, if my words are true."

Thereupon, bored, a third voice:
"Go to sleep now for God's sake!
You both will feel better by breakfast time."

*W. H. Auden*    (*1969*)

This is clearly a meditation on modern urban life; and we can take the title quite literally, as meaning the city of our age, no longer surrounded by a medieval wall. The purpose of a wall was of course to protect, that is, to keep enemies out, and the title may therefore remind us that the modern city is defenceless; but the effect of a city wall was also to set a limit, to confine the city within its own area, and so it may also remind us of urban sprawl, of the fact that the modern city encroaches more and more on the countryside, and that urban living threatens to be the universal pattern.

The solitude of modern urban life is well known: so we start with the city dweller as hermit. In Byzantine and early Italian painting hermits are depicted in gnarled rocky landscapes, sitting at the mouth of a cave shaped like a tooth, often accompanied by grotesque devils thrusting temptations at them. New York may not look much like this painting, but the poem starts by telling us that in our isolation we inhabit those "unpolicied spaces" (i.e. unadministered or ungoverned spaces: not the only archaic word we shall meet in the poem), living in hotels as if in "numbered caves in enormous jails". Equally well known is urban violence, so that the streets can be compared with a primitive wilderness.

Stanzas five and six mention some of the meetings that take place after dark: meetings of criminals or plotters whom we are invited to look on with dislike and contempt, "their tongues tattooed by tribal jargon". The café talkers appear to be revolutionaries: what they say is dismissed as "unreason", they are all dupes of their nasty oversimplified creed, and the conservative vision of the poem emerges quite clearly from the fact that they are called "work-shy". The great conservative novelist Joseph Conrad sums up his brilliantly contemptuous picture of the revolutionaries in *The Secret Agent* by describing them all as "a lazy lot"—"the majority of revolutionaries are the enemies of discipline and fatigue mostly"—and that note of disdain is clearly what is found here.

Then we turn to the ordinary citizens, called, naturally enough, Adam and Eve. Their lives are empty, without the satisfaction of physical work ("unperspiring") and without the transfigurations of the sacred. "Super physiques" have a certain lurid social prestige ("frequently photographed") but ordinary bodies are being replaced by engines. And so to a glimpse of the future, that future we are so often told about, in admiration or dread, when computers will have taken over many of our functions, and the traditional tensions of being human, such as the son's revolt against the parents, will have disappeared. Stanzas fourteen to sixteen continue to reflect on the emptiness of our gadgeted age, with its illness and psychosis and the decline of so much culture. The world of aristocratic grace—the world, for instance of the pictures of Watteau—is too tame for us now; and traditional comedy, ending in marriage and the bridal dance, has lost its appeal.

Then to another and longer glimpse of the future—this time a future where "all has gone phut", and the poem enters the world of science fiction with what looks like a description of the world after an atomic war: much of the earth is desert and dangerous, human beings are deformed (perhaps from radiation) and have reverted to a primitive culture, riddled with superstition and half-understood remnants of twentieth-century civilization. In Anglo-Saxon England the ruins of Roman buildings were thought of as the work of giants; and to this future General Motors survive as the name of a ju-ju, and tin cans are treasure hoards left by mysterious dwarves. It will be a world without freedom or understanding or social progress: "Nor choice they have nor change know."

Such is the poem's argument (I shall revert to the final stanzas): because those unused to Auden's later poetry may find his allusive style unfamiliar, it seemed best to begin with a brief account of its train of thought, though it is not, on acquaintance, an obscure poem. Its picture of the emptiness of modern life is neither peculiar to Auden nor new in his work, and it is not difficult to set the poem against others that treat the same theme.

We can go right back to *The Ascent of F.6*, a verse play first performed in 1937, and choose part of the dialogue of Mr and Mrs A. The central event of the play is the climbing of a mountain by Michael Ransom, an act which is given both a political and a psychological significance, and Auden introduces two ordinary citizens as a kind of chorus whose drab lives are given new meaning as they eagerly follow the story of Ransom's expedition on the radio. Here is their first appearance.

*Mrs A.*   Evening.   A slick and unctuous Time
Has sold us yet another shop-soiled day,
Patently rusty, not even in a gaudy box.
I have dusted the six small rooms:

The parlour, once the magnificent image of my freedom,
And the bedroom, which once held for me
The mysterious languors of Egypt and the terrifying
    Indias.
The delivery-vans have paid their brief impersonal
    visits.
I have eaten a scrappy lunch from a plate on my knee.
I have spoken with acquaintances in the Stores;
Under our treble gossip heard the menacing throb of our
    hearts
As I hear them now, as all of us hear them,
Standing at our stoves in these villas, expecting our
    husbands:
The drums of an enormous and routed army,
Throbbing raggedly, fitfully, scatteredly, madly.
We are lost. We are lost.

*Mr A.*    No, nothing that matters will ever happen;
Nothing you'd want to put in a book;
Nothing to tell to impress your friends—
The old old story that never ends:
The eight o'clock train, the customary place,
Holding the paper in front of your face,
The public stairs, the glass swing-door,
The peg for your hat, the linoleum floor,
The office stool and the office jokes
And the fear in your ribs that slyly pokes:
Are they satisfied with you?
Nothing interesting to do,
Nothing interesting to say,
Nothing remarkable in any way;
Then the journey home again
In the hot suburban train
To the tawdry new estate,
Crumples, grubby, dazed and late:
Home to supper and to bed.
Shall we be like this when we are dead?

Mr and Mrs A. are clearly inhabitants of the *City without Walls;*
though as we compare the play with the later poem we can see that
Auden has not written about them in the same way. Indeed, there is
a contrast within this dialogue. Mr A. speaks with the flatness that
characterizes his world:

> Nothing interesting to do,
> Nothing interesting to say,
> Nothing remarkable in any way . . . .

This is pure doggerel. Its relation to the world it describes is one of pure imitation: the verse is as empty as Mr A.'s life. This is effective, but it is a dangerous method for any poet to use, for too faithful an imitation of the trivial and the monotonous will itself be monotonous; and just as no play Mr A. could write would interest us very deeply, so the mere voice of Mr A. will soon pall. In the case of Mrs A., Auden has offered us something more. There is mere imitative doggerel ("I have spoken with acquaintances in the Stores"), but there is more. "The delivery-vans have paid their brief impersonal visits" the word here that would in fact have been beyond Mrs A.'s powers is "impersonal", in which she is seen saying something *about* her situation, not merely thrusting it on us. More interesting are her opening lines, which have a real expressive power. The brilliantly sordid image of the shop-soiled day has a lyrical quality: it captures an emotion, though the emotion is (of course) depressing and even repellent. It is the language of T. S. Eliot's *Preludes*

> The burnt-out ends of smoky days . . .
> The worlds revolve like ancient women
> Gathering fuel in vacant lots . . .

What do we find in Mrs A.'s lines (and in Eliot's) that is absent from the mere flatness of the doggerel? The answer surely is, a greater degree of articulateness. The Mrs A.'s of real life could not themselves find the words, but what the lines are expressing is exactly what they feel. It is a perfect example of the function of poetry as stated in Pope's famous line, "What oft was thought but ne'er so well expressed".

In *City without Walls* however, we have moved further from Mr and Mrs A. The speaker of this poem is not merely articulate, he is sophisticated at analysis—he is in fact much more like Auden himself, the well-read civilized man with a sense of history and the ability to use abstract concepts. He is not content to express the dullness of the week-end, he places it in a context: holidays were once holy days, now they are mere relaxation time, "free still but a feast no longer"; street violence is seen in terms of historical comparison, so that New York after dark is the marches (an archaic term for a border area of uncertain boundaries, where violence is likely), and the brutality and dishonesty of the police is given a medieval analogy, robber barons being those who use legitimate authority to steal for themselves.

The fact that the speaker of this poem has all the knowledge and sophistication of the poet himself is no doubt responsible for the self-conscious ending. The purpose of that ending is clearly to step back from the voice who has so far spoken and view it critically. Everything in the poem, we are being told, was said by one voice; and so far we've been invited to take him quite seriously. But it turns out that there is another part of the poet who refuses to do this—the "sharp voice" who complains that the whole thing sounds like a literary exercise, an imitation of those two famous denouncers of their fellow men, the Roman satirist and the Old Testament prophet, and because it is a literary game, which he enjoys, the misery itself gives him pleasure (the meaning of *Schadenfreude*). If the poem ended there, the final distancing would have given us an ironic twist, but Auden wants a more complicated irony, and so the original voice is allowed to reply, accusing the other of being a *pococurante* (one who doesn't care) and of being too moral in the probing of motive; and we then end on the third voice who seems to represent the simple need of the body for sleep, a basic self to whom such arguments mean nothing.

It is not difficult to see why Auden wrote this ending: it is to disarm the reader. If the reader already feels that the poem is enjoying its own gloom, he may be reassured to see that the poet himself is capable of this comment; he is being asked not to mind, since perhaps the jeremiad should not be taken wholly seriously. But Auden is not willing to give his whole poem away to the pococurante reader, so a riposte put him in his place too, and the final lines suggest that we should not take that dispute too seriously.

That clearly is the purpose of the ending; but to describe the purpose is not to claim that it is justified, and I must now confess that I think the ending was a mistake artistically. There is an early poem by Tennyson, a meditation on religious doubt and the meaning of life, called *Supposed Confessions of a Second-rate Sensitive Mind*, which employs in the title the same self-deprecating devices that Auden uses at the end, and here, where the trick is obvious, we can see how little it is worth. If this book is not successful in achieving its aim, matters would not be improved by calling it "An Inadequate Introduction to English Poetry", and if we feel dissatisfied with Tennyson's poem, it is not rendered any better by the presence of the word "second-rate" in the title. Because Auden's self-deprecation is more involved, my criticism of it needs spelling out a little more fully: what corresponds most closely to the "second-rate mind" label is the final stanza, for the bored voice seems to feel that neither the dispute nor the poem are important; and to end on this dismissive shrug seems a wholly negative act, that does nothing to enhance the poem. The "sharp voice" who, I have suggested, represents the hostile reader is not being quite so dismissive and his comment is perhaps meant to offer us a perspective we can use on re-reading the poem. For that is, of course, the value of such distancing irony at the end: the fact that it enables us to see all that has gone before in a new and even an enriching way. Here I must speak for myself, and say that I do not find this successful either. The main poem *is* meant to be taken seriously and the rather cursory comment of the sharp voice does not bite into it in enough detail to change our response significantly.

Perhaps the main reason I cannot dismiss the speaker of the poem is the fact that he so obviously is Auden. The sophisticated, analytic witty mind, constantly concerned to probe, compare and analyse, is a mind we know from many of his other poems—from *Prologue at Sixty* for instance, the concluding poem in the volume of which this is the title poem, which treats the same theme in the same verse form, and is so similar that several stanzas look as if they could belong to either poem.

> Already a helpless orbited dog
> has blinked at our sorry conceited O,
> Where many are famished, few look good,
> and my day turned out torturers
> who read Rilke in their rest periods.

The launching of satellites, the concentration camps: the greatest technological achievement of our century, and its greatest disgrace— the first made slightly ridiculous, the second doubly disturbing because of the evidence that the torturing was done not only by thugs but by cultured and educated men. This complex, worried analysis keeps the same witty tone, but there is no distancing device at the end of *Prologue at Sixty*.

What sort of a man speaks in these poems and in what terms does he see the world? He is a man who reads the newspapers and worries about contemporary culture, and the concepts he uses are those of sociology and anthropology. What he notices are behaviour patterns and rituals, religious observances and those individual habits that speak the controlling influence of social *mores*. The cell meetings are seen as tribes, their speech is "palaver" (a term appropriate to primitive peace-making), their vocabulary is tribal jargon. Adam and

Eve are understood best by observing how they spend their days, for their timetable reveals the cultural patterns they exemplify.

This is not the only way of seeing society, and it has not always been Auden's. Here for instance is a sonnet from his sequence *In Time of War* (written in 1939, and the war is that between China and Japan).

> But in the evening the oppression lifted;
> The peaks came into focus; it had rained:
> Across the lawns and cultured flowers drifted
> The conversation of the highly trained.
>
> The gardeners watched them pass and priced their shoes:
> A chauffeur waited, reading in the drive,
> For them to finish their exchange of views;
> It seemed a picture of the private life.
>
> Far off, no matter what good they intended,
> The armies waited for a verbal error
> With all the instruments for causing pain:
>
> And on the issue of their charm depended
> A land laid waste, with all its young men slain,
> The women weeping, and the towns in terror.

In this poem we seem to be present at a political conference, whose outcome will determine peace or war—a conference between civilized educated men ("the highly trained") in a world of violence and slaughter. There is a shocking discrepancy then between the apparent calm of the "exchange of views" (a newspaper phrase for a meeting of politicians) and the consequence of its decisions. (It is not quite clear if the "highly trained" are planning a war or holding a peace conference that breaks down—in either case the discrepancy is there.) Now it is not difficult to recognize that it is by the same poet as *CWW*, but there is a difference. This sonnet sees society as divided into classes, and the shrewdness of observation has gone to show us the gap between the gentlemanliness of the cultured rulers, and the sharp cynical eye of their servants, who notice the trappings of wealth, not the content of diplomatic conversations. Nor is this an accident: for this society is torn by war and oppression and the rulers are seen as responsible. The exact nature of their responsibility depends on our reading of the phrase "verbal error". If it is ironic, then they decided to lay the land waste, and we are shown the terrifying power under their suavity, a suavity that will later shrug off responsibility. If it is to be taken straight, as the poet's comment, then they were helpless to control the armies that simply waited for them to say something that could be used as an excuse for continuing the war; and we are being shown the ineffectiveness of well-meaning politicians rather than the malice of tyrants. In both cases, the point is the reality of power under the mask of polished talk.

In what way does this view of the world differ from that of *CWW*? Briefly, through the presence of politics. Here we have a society where conflict causes suffering; and it is very important what happens, for some outcomes may kill innocent people. It is a world of actions and decisions, where we ought to take a moral stand and choose the right side. There is no indication in this sonnet what the sides are or which one we should take, but it is well known that the pre-war Auden had Marxist leanings, and many of his early poems offer a Marxist analysis and choose the side of the Left. But in *CWW* there is not a right and a wrong side, in fact there is no sense of crucial actions and decisions taking place. A society is a set of habits and rituals that lead its members to behave in certain observable ways.

In 1948 Auden published his long poem *The Age of Anxiety*, a meditation on modern man in the form of a conversation between four strangers who meet casually in a New York bar in wartime. It is quite clear, as we read this work, that the transition from the political to what we may call the sociological Auden has taken place. The speakers have a vision of arriving in an unfamiliar city, and one says—

> Well, here I am but how, how, asks the visitor,
> Strolling through the strange streets, can I start to discover
> The fashionable feminine fret, or the form of insult
> Minded most by the men? In what myth do their sages
> Locate the cause of evil?
> How are these people punished?

Could any poet get more anthropological than that? Arriving in a city, the speaker assumes it will be unfamiliar, and asks about conventions, habits, social patterns that will be common to all the inhabitants. A politically minded speaker would assume that a good deal in the society was familiar, and would ask about what was *happening*—what the issues and conflicts were, what decisions were being taken that would affect the distribution of power and the happiness of the citizens. This is what is meant by saying that in his later poetry Auden turned away from politics.

Let us now try a comparison—another modern poet satirizing urban life and the time he lives in, and in non-political terms.

## Middlesex

Gaily into Ruislip Gardens
Runs the red electric train,
With a thousand Ta's and Pardon's
Daintily alights Elaine;
Hurries down the concrete station
With a frown of concentration,
Out into the outskirt's edges
Where a few surviving hedges
Keep alive our lost Elysium—rural Middlesex again.

Well cut Windsmoor flapping lightly,
Jacqmar scarf of mauve and green
Hiding hair which, Friday nightly,
Delicately drowns in Drene;
Fair Elaine the bobby-soxer,
Fresh-complexioned with Innoxa,
Gains the garden—father's hobby—
Hangs her Windsmoor in the lobby,
Settles down to sandwich supper and the television screen.

Gentle Brent, I used to know you
Wandering Wembley-wards at will,
Now what change your waters show you
In the meadowlands you fill!
Recollect the elm-trees misty
And the footpaths climbing twisty
Under cedar-shaded palings,
Low laburnam-leaned-on railings,
Out of Northold on and upward to the heights of Harrow hill.

Parish of enormous hayfields
Perivale stood all alone,
And from Greenford scent of mayfields
Most enticingly was blown
Over market gardens tidy,
Taverns for the *bona fide*,
Cockney anglers, cockney shooters,
Murray Poshes, Lupin Pooters
Long in Kensal Green and Highgate silent under soot and stone.

*John Betjeman*

Elaine is Auden's Eve—the completely ordinary citizen, a young
girl working as a secretary in London commuting home to the part

of Middlesex where she lives, and where the poet himself used to wander when the landscape was unspoilt. But now it's the home of Elaine, the dainty urban miss, who leads a trivial life concerned with fashion, make-up and television. There is something in common between Auden's subject and Betjeman's but how utterly different the poems are. We have stepped into another poetic world, and the contrast is a forcible reminder that poems are made of words and not of ideas, and that the language of Betjeman sees Elaine as the conforming product of a society of mass-produced consumer goods. To keep us in the world of that society, he uses the trade-marks of all Elaine's favourite products—sometimes even as rhymes, as with Innoxa—and the result is mildly comic. He is making fun of Elaine, but gently, for the language of the first two stanzas never gets too far from hers.

> With a thousand Ta's and Pardons
> Daintily alights Elaine.

She is vulgar we realize, her daintiness is affected and a bit ridiculous, but there is nothing in these lines at which Elaine could easily take offence—she might not even be sure, if she read the lines, that she was being laughed at. The sensibility of the poet never leaves her sensibility too far behind.

Auden's theoretical interests however have left their stamp on his language. He uses jargon freely, especially sociological jargon ("sub-cultures", "built-in obsolescence") or the technical terms of the mass media ("newsprint and network"). There is a particularly interesting linguistic touch in stanza fourteen of *CWW*.

> Small marvel, then, if many adopt
> cancer as the only offered career
> worth while.

Career? It is a strange way to think of cancer. Sure no one *adopts* illness as he might adopt medicine or law as a profession? The idea is startling, almost witty—and the alliteration emphasizes it for us. Now the idea did not originate with Auden. Here is a short extract from *Asylums* by Erving Goffman:

"Traditionally the term *career* has been reserved for those who expect to enjoy the rises laid out within a respectable profession. The term is coming to be used, however, in a broadened sense to refer to any social strand of any person's course through life. . . Such a career is not a thing that can be brilliant or disappointing;

it can no more be a success than a failure. In this light, I want to consider the mental patient."

Goffman analyses the life of the inmate of an asylum in terms which draw on the resemblance between that life and the pattern of a career. Such a parallel ignores the purpose of the institution (to cure illness) in order to describe its functioning in a way that will show the similarities to apparently quite different institutions. This method has keen followers and severe critics, and it is clearly not possible to discuss its advantages and disadvantages here; what we can notice is that Auden has encapsulated the point into the language of the poem, in the apparent wit of his use of a "career". It is not just that Auden uses sociological ideas; what is of far more importance to his poetry is that he has developed a feel for sociological vocabulary.

There is another very different but equally striking quality to the language of *CWW*; that is the archaisms and learned terms. In the description of comedy in stanza sixteen the bridal pairs are rustic and oppidan—an unusual word meaning "belonging to the town", and they perform "stately bransels"—an extremely out of the way word for dances. This is a common habit of Auden, and it can produce two very different effects: either disdain, reminding the reader of his ignorance, or nostalgic delight ("look at all these lovely old words people used to have"). If it is the latter it makes of the speaker a rather attractive personality, but one can understand why the sharp voice accuses him of playing fun and games.

If we turn to the last two stanzas of *Middlesex* we find another revealing contrast with Auden. These stanzas take us back to a past that contrasts with the suburban present, but what a mild contrast it is! Rural Middlesex was not very wild, with its railings and market gardens. The "taverns for the *bona fide*" are presumably a reminder that the cockney anglers and cockney shooters were genuine in a way Elaine no longer quite is, but they sound very much like her equivalents a generation or two earlier. Lupin Pooter, son of the hero of *The Diary of a Nobody*, George and Weedon Grossmith's comic story of a well-meaning lower middle-class family, is as typical a young person of his world as Elaine is of hers. Just as the first two stanzas never got too far away from Elaine in their language, the last two never get too far from the Middlesex of the time of writing.

How much stronger is Auden's contrast with the past. For his past is remote and primitive, vividly different from the present, and the contrast is central to the effect of the poem. And now it is necessary to say something about the poem's form. It is written in Anglo-Saxon alliterative metre, the metre of *Beowulf* and of Old English lyric poetry. Alliteration is common enough in later verse for decoration or to achieve particular effects, but in this metrical form it is used as a structural principle, instead of rhyme. Every line has four beats with a marked break or caesura in the middle, and either one or both of the beats in the first half alliterates with one of those in the second half. Thus the alliterative pattern of stanza one runs:

$$FF \ / \ Fx$$
$$BB \ / \ Bx$$
$$xH \ / \ Ux$$
$$xP \ / \ Px$$
$$DD \ / \ Dx$$

(the third line alliterates because all vowels and syllables beginning with H are regarded as the same sound). Now we happen to know that Auden, who studied Anglo-Saxon poetry when an undergraduate at Oxford, is very fond of this metre and has often used it in other poems: you may have noticed that it is used in *Prologue at Sixty,* and it is also the normal metre of *The Age of Anxiety* (though not as it happens in the lines quoted above). In *CWW,* however, the metrical form has a greater importance than elsewhere, for the subject of the poem is the loss of traditional culture, and by using so archaic a form the poem is making a declaration of allegiance to the old, a more powerful declaration than anything it says explicitly. Stanza twelve is particularly significant here.

> Against Whom
> shall the Sons band to rebel there,
> where Troll-Father, Tusked-Mother,
> are dream-monsters like dinosaurs
> with a built-in obsolescence?

The hygienic world of computers lacks the rich overtones of those deep-seated conflicts that are at the root of the psyche. There will no longer be a folk-lore of monsters based on the rebellion of the son against his parents. How this point is transformed by being stated in a metre that belongs to the world of myth and superstition, the world of trolls and tusks!

That world makes a more sustained appearance, as we have already seen, in stanzas seventeen to twenty: but these are not about the past but the future. This is a paradox and one of great importance in the poem. The present is being condemned for its smooth efficiency, the loss of the old rhythms, fears and holiness that formed the culture. The emptiness of this new world is terrifying, and may lead everything to "go phut", replacing our civilization by a strange and terrifying world whose inhabitants are stunted in stature, strangely deformed. Here the Old English metre is terribly appropriate: we are back in the world of Beowulf, our modern security gone. The future has reverted to the far past. The paradox is, of course, that the two fears—our age as inhumanly efficient, and our age as dangerous, doomed to revert to the primitive—ought logically to cancel each other out. Fear does not obey logic, so one can easily imagine both being held at the same time, but this assimilation of the feared future to the lost past gives a powerful, paradoxical quality to the whole—and makes the continuity of the metre especially appropriate.

Betjeman's metre in *Middlesex,* a rhyming jingle with some ingenious, not quite comic rhymes, suggests the world of clever, light verse. It may have a mildly satiric effect—the sort of poetic form that even Elaine might appreciate—but if so the satire is very mild, for Betjeman himself seems to enjoy it. Perhaps it is the metre Lupin Pooter would enjoy too. There is, we realize again, no such violent contrast as Auden is making.

*CWW* raises one important point for the reading of poetry on which I shall conclude. The subject of this poem is topical and urgent: it raises just the sort of question, about modern civilization and the future, that most of us worry and argue about. The thoughtful newspaper-reader, the young radical, the responsible teacher or scientist, are all deeply concerned over the Asphalt Lands, the boredom of spirit, the glare of Nothing. The poem springs from the concern of our everyday prose.

This presents us with two dangers. On the one hand, we may find ourselves so involved with the issues themselves that we forget we are reading a poem. We may treat it as part of an ongoing and important debate we are taking part in, setting a point by Auden against one by Goffman or Goldmann, Hoggart or *The Times* editorials. This is to keep poetry in touch with life, but it is to forget what makes poetry unique. On the other hand we may firmly exclude any discussion of the subject-matter itself, confining our comments to questions of metre and literary influence, structure, imagery and literary tradition, comparing it only with other poems. This is to remember what makes a poem a poem, but at the price of treating it as a literary exercise, a self-contained aesthetic experience that never engages with life outside.

No one can say which of these dangers is greater. If you feel that a poem should above all be real, or true, or urgent, or wise, you will incline to the first. If you feel it should above all be beautiful, that poetry is a matter of language and its possibilities, you will incline to the second. Auden himself often mentioned this dilemma, and usually put himself in the second camp; but perhaps this was partly because he realized that his poems were so concerned to be true and wise. To conclude the essay, I suggest we should see this dilemma as a possibility rather than a danger; we should realize that the splendour of poetry is precisely that it offers both appeals and we simply need to avoid the untenable extremes of each position. This essay is an attempt to do just that.

# Conclusion:

# Interpreting a Poem

One question has worried me all through this book; and the aim of this conclusion is to bring it to the surface. How far should there be a standard pattern for the essays? Ought not an introduction to the study of poetry to contain some guidance on how to articulate and express one's reaction to a poem? Ought it not to offer help to the reader who wants to try his hand at discussing some other poems? Ought it not in short, to concern itself with how to write a critical essay on poetry, perhaps by suggesting a series of questions, or a method of interpretation that can be applied to any poem? It is clear that it ought, but I feel a strong reluctance to do it, for to impose a paradigm on each essay would be to betray the poems. I felt on each poem that I knew what I wanted to say, and it was often quite different from what I had said on the previous one. Not to follow this feeling would have been to leave out what really mattered, for what one must above all do is follow in the direction in which the poem is leading. This conclusion, then, is an attempt to resolve this dilemma: to suggest some general ideas on the writing of the essays that will be firm enough to offer the reader some genuine guidance, and that are at the same time flexible enough to respect the differences between poems.

And we must of course start by reiterating (it can never be said too often) that the poem must speak for itself. That until one has got to know a poem well, and allowed it to take on its own life in our minds, one should not even begin to think about discussing it. And once having reached this point, what then?

First, we should notice the difference between an intrinsic and an extrinsic approach to poetry. To explain this, let me describe the two very different critical methods that have dominated the academic study of literature. In the early years of this century, literature was taught as if it consisted of periods, movements, metrical forms, perhaps authors, illustrated occasionally with a few lines of verse. Lecture courses on the history of English Literature would describe what Augustan poetry was about, and who the main Augustan poets were; would talk about satire, the heroic couplet, the imitation of the classics, the character-sketch, the *topos*, the Pindaric Ode, and into this magisterial survey would be inserted quotations from Dryden, Pope and Johnson. Such courses were not a total waste of time: they gave to the students a general view and a sense of historical continuity that they could not easily have got otherwise, and to the student who was already an eager reader of Augustan poetry, they probably did nothing but good. But it meant that you began with the historical process as something ready-made: you had to believe what the lecturer told you. And the great central truth that was in danger of disappearing was that English poetry consists of English poems.

The extreme reaction to this was known as the New Criticism. This insisted on studying poems as self-contained entities. The reading of a poem was seen as the direct impact of the words on the receptive reader, with no interference from outside sources. A really purist "new critic" might even want to conceal from his students the name of the author and the time when a poem was written, so that nothing would sully the effect of the words on the page. The result of this was a sensitive, sophisticated awareness of the nature of the reading experience—poems regained their individuality—but a complete loss of historical sense, of the awareness of a continuing literary tradition.

This controversy is more or less over now; and the growing interest in the way poetry relates to the whole society that lies behind it has introduced further complications. Nor was it ever quite as clear-cut as I have indicated, for most historical scholars and most new critics were (and are) less single-minded than the paradigm. But the contrast in approach is a real and permanent one; and each method has its advantages. One of the poems in this book, *The Bunch of Grapes* is actually, as I have tried to show, about this very question: a single poem, like a single deed, is small renown.

On the one hand, there is no substitute for the poem itself: unless we have read it and responded to it, we have nothing to move out from. So there is a sense in which the intrinsic approach has to be primary, and in each essay there is a part of the discussion which draws on nothing but what the poem offers. Such a discussion should be within the reach of every reader, since it requires sensitivity and understanding rather than knowledge, though our ability to point to what it is in the poem's technique that produced some effect we have been moved by is naturally something that grows with experience. It may be that the most natural way to write a critique of a poem is to begin with the intrinsic, and more often that not this is what I have done; but not always. In the case of *The Lie,* I have discussed the nature and purpose of the poem, and of that kind of poem, before turning to details of execution; *To Mr Fortescue* is an imitation of a poem by Horace, and if we start from Horace we put ourselves in a position closer to that of Pope's ideal reader; *Elegiac*

*Stanzas* is an occasional poem, and to begin from the occasion offers a valuable way in (but not the only way in: *The Picture of Little T.C.* is also an occasional poem, but there I saved the occasion for the end); *Johannes Agricola in Meditation* deals with a theological position, and we handicap ourselves if we do not begin by understanding that position; *To an Old Philosopher in Rome* is so difficult that some help, if only over the identity of the philosopher and what the poet thought about him, seems almost essential to the reader unfamiliar with Stevens. In each case there seemed good rhetorical reasons for beginning the discussion with the extrinsic. In each case it would have been possible the other way round. One rule however has been unvarying: there is both an intrinsic and an extrinsic discussion for every poem, and each of them occupies about half the essay.

In the extrinsic discussion, the kind of material used for comparison naturally varies, though here again there is a general rule: to talk about, and to quote from, at least one other poem. Usually I have quoted at least one other complete poem, so as to place the reader on more nearly equal terms, but in the cases of Pope and Wordsworth the most appropriate comparisons were with rather long and very well-known poems, so I have contented myself with simply quoting extracts. In the case of *Clerk Saunders* the nature of ballad texts makes it more useful to quote other versions rather than complete different ballads (though the joining together of two separate ballads in this case does provide us with an automatic comparison). This rule, however, still leaves great variety and freedom over the kind of comparison made. If the poem is part of a series (like the Shakespeare sonnet or, to a lesser extent, *To Mr Fortescue*), then it is clear where we have to look; though we can look further afield as well. Sometimes another poem by the same author offers the best comparison, whether a similar poem (as with Browning) or a contrasting poem (as with Herbert); sometimes we can offer something more like a glimpse of the whole work of an author (as with Milton or Auden), though that must never get too far from particular poems. Sometimes I have used other poems in the same tradition (as with Marvell or Shelley): this draws our attention away from the individual poet to a wider poetic context, but can often serve to make us sharply aware of that poet's individual contribution. In one case (Raleigh) I have used a reply to the poem whose appropriateness makes up (or almost makes up!) for its inferior quality. We must let each poem reach out in its own way.

Another very general rule can arise out of the remarks already made on genre. With a poem, as with anything else, it seems best to start by asking what kind of thing we are faced with; and to identify this is to see what questions will take us to the centre of the poem's aim. If it is a meditation, we must start from the argument: the only way to an understanding of *The Bunch of Grapes* or *City without Walls* is to establish the train of thought and reasoning. If it is a lyric, we can best describe its nature by identifying the emotion expressed—the anger of Raleigh, the struggle between complaint and patience in *On his Blindness*. Of course there is anger and anger: no two good lyrics express quite the same emotion; but to give a general name seems to be an essential first step before going on to the nuances. Sometimes the search for the best way of naming the emotion may produce a critical discussion that tells us something important about the poem, as I tried to show with the *Stanzas written in Dejection*. If the poem is dramatic, we will ask ourselves what sort of person is speaking, as we did at some length with *Johannes Agricola in Meditation*, and more briefly with *The Ruined Maid*. If it is narrative we may want to discuss both the story itself (is it traditional? is it an episode in two or more interacting lives, or the whole biography of an individual?), and its telling (how dramatically is it told? how selectively? are we kept in suspense? do we double back on what has already been told? and so on). And finally— this needs saying with great emphasis—though many poems are clearly of one single kind, many are not. How far are the *Elegiac Stanzas* a meditation, and how far a pure lyric of grief? Is not Wordsworth at his most impressive (but also, sometimes, most tedious) when he moves beyond the purely lyrical? And in the essay on *The Dream* I have tried to show how important is the mingling of lyric, narrative *and* dramatic in the work of this great complex poet.

Next to be discussed is form. The formal aspects of a poem are almost unlimited, and if we were to go through them all systematically the resulting essay would be interminable and tedious. We can describe the metre and stanza form, and look for all the irregularities; or the pattern of imagery; or the diction (is it formal or colloquial, Latinate or Saxon, restricted or not?); or the syntax (is it mainly simple or very complex, or, as in the case of much modern poetry, disintegrated?); or the tone (the poet's attitude to his reader); the use of irony; repetition or ellipsis; the presence and function of descriptive detail; and so on and so on. We ought to be able to talk about all these technical points, as we ought to know all the words in a language we have learnt; but we are not likely to need many of them at any one time. What matters in any poem is its impact, and technical elements matter in so far as we realize on reflection that they have contributed to this effect. Metre is almost certain to be important, though it will not always be used with the subtlety of Shakespeare or Pope. Irony is crucial in *The Dream* and *The Ruined Maid*, non-existent in *On his Blindness* or *Stanzas written in Dejection*. Tone is all-important in *The Picture of Little T.C.* and *To Mr Fortescue*, but of no particular interest in *Stanzas written in Dejection* —where the poet is not conscious of his reader—and a more or less meaningless concept in the case of purely narrative or dramatic poems. Imagery is important in the *Stanzas Written in Dejection* and potentially important in the *Elegiac Stanzas* (which is the kind of poem in which imagery tells, but it has very little); the use and then the disappearance of imagery in the Shakespeare sonnet is crucial, as the essay tries to show; whereas in *To Mr Fortescue* there is hardly any imagery. No rule can tell us which elements matter in a particular poem: that is why we must start from our response, and from our reflexions on that response.

Finally, and trickiest of all, is the question of evaluation. I believe all fifteen of these poems are very fine, and would not have chosen them if I didn't; but suppose one or two seem to you greatly inferior to the others. Does that make them less suitable as examples of that kind, or that period, or that poet? Or can the essay remain more or less unchanged even for those who don't share my high opinion of the poem? Furthermore, can we show in an essay what there is in any poem that makes it better or worse than another? Perhaps we should ignore value judgements, and confine ourselves to interpretation, discussing what each poem means, what kind of poem it is, what technical devices it employs. This is the crucial question for any student of literature, that sooner or later he must ask himself: how central is evaluation to what he is doing?

I believe the place of evaluation in literary studies is a paradoxical one. No one, surely, would study literature unless he believed that some poems are better than others. We study it because literature *matters*: because of the power with which a poem speaks to our condition, or the haunting beauty of its language. If we did not value what the poem offers, why should we bother to read it again? To write a critique of it would then seem a barren academic exercise. But though value judgements may be central to literary appreciation, this does not mean they can be demonstrated. Shakespeare is certainly a finer writer of sonnets than Spenser, and far far better than Barnaby Googe; I believe Auden to be certainly a finer poet than Cecil Day Lewis, and far, far better than Mary Wilson. But to show this difference beyond the possibility of doubt is so difficult that one often feels it to be impossible. However carefully you describe just what gives such power to a Shakespearean sonnet, it is hard to be quite sure that your description won't fit some sonnet by Spenser or even Googe which we all recognize to be inferior. Evaluative criticism always has to rely on the reader accepting our point because he has himself recognized the merit of the poem; you cannot, as Wordsworth remarked, argue people into liking a poem. But interpretation can argue: if there are two views on what a poem means, it is possible to look for evidence in the text to settle the dispute.

Most of the essays in this book lie somewhere between the two: they are interpretations, with a touch of evaluation. I have been mainly concerned with the kind and meaning of each poem, and in comparing it with others have aimed to sharpen awareness of what it is like. None of the essays is primarily built round the question, Why is this poem so good? But I have never pretended that I don't admire the poem, and in discussing its aim and technique I have inevitably been trying to show wherein its merit lies. Sometimes (but not often: for I believe we should mostly discuss good poems only) I have introduced a comparison with a similar and less successful poem, as a foil. Poetic excellence is like happiness: the way to capture it, even the way to capture a description of it, is not to go looking for it, but to steal up on it unawares while looking for the poem.

# Suggestions for Reading

The reading list is constructed in the following way. First comes a recapitulation of the names of those poems quoted (wholly or in part) and discussed in each essay: this is for the benefit of those readers who would like to read through these before beginning the essay (a procedure I advise). Then come the names of further poems by the same poet, or in the same tradition, for the benefit of those who would like to carry further the ideas developed in the essay: here I have concentrated on poems that arise out of the comparisons already offered, while making sure that some at least of that poet's best work are mentioned. Then come critical books or articles that discuss the poem, or the work of the poet, in a way that follows from (or contrasts with) the essay: I have included only critical works which I recommend, but it by no means includes all the good criticism of that poet or that genre. Sometimes this third section opens out into wider, but related issues. The whole list is designed to follow the reading of this book, and makes no claim to completeness of any sort.

## 1   Clerk Saunders

i   All the versions discussed can be found in Child's *English and Scottish Popular Ballads,* vol. 2, as can the versions of *Sweet William's Ghost.* Another version of *Clerk Saunders* can conveniently be found in the *Faber Book of Ballads,* ed. Hodgart.

ii   *Sir Patrick Spens, Thomas the Rhymer, The Wife of Usher's Well, Fair Annie, Fair Margaret and Sweet William.* (Most or all of these will be found in Child or Hodgart, as well as in the following convenient collections: *The Oxford Book of Ballads, The Oxford Book of English Verse* (ed. Quiller-Couch) nos. 367–92.)
Scott: *Proud Maisie, Jock of Hazeldean.*

iii   F B Gummere: *The Popular Ballad;* M J C Hodgart: *The Ballads;* G H Ferauld: *The Ballad of Tradition.*

## 2   Sonnet 34

i   Sidney: *Astrophel and Stella* no. 15 ("You that do search for every purling spring")
Shakespeare: Sonnets 33, 35, 42.

ii   Shakespeare: the complete sonnets, and especially nos. 17, 18, 60, 63–5, 87–9, 127–52.

Sidney: *Astrophel and Stella,* and especially nos 7, 31, 47, 54, 78.
Daniel: *Sonnets to Delia,* especially "Fair is my Love, and cruel as she's fair"; "The star of my mishap imposed this pain"; "Beauty, sweet Love, is like the morning dew"; "Let others sing of knights and paladins."
Drayton: "Since there's no help, come, let us kiss and part."

iii   Edward Hubler: *The Sense of Shakespeare's Sonnets;* C L Barber: Introduction to the Laurel edition of *The Sonnets of Shakespeare.*

## 3   The Lie

i   Raleigh: "Praised be Diana's fair and harmless light."
Spenser: *Colin Clout's Come Home Again.*
Tourneur: *The Revenger's Tragedy.*
Anon: "Go, Echo of the Mind" (in *The Poems of Sir W Raleigh ,* ed. Agnes Latham, p 159).
Shakespeare: *Macbeth* Act V scene v, "Tomorrow and tomorrow and tomorrow"; sonnet 66.
D H Lawrence: "Vengeance is Mine", from *More Pansies.*
Anon.: *Totus Mundus in Maligno Positus* (*Tottell's Miscellany* no 284).

ii   Raleigh: "If all the world and love were young"; *Farewell to the Court* ("Like truthless dreams, so are my joys expired"); *A Poesie to Prove Affection is not Love* ("Conceit begotten by the eyes"); *The Passionate Man's Pilgrimage;* "What is our life?"; "Even such is Time"; *The Ocean to Cynthia.*

iii   Peter Ure, "Two Elizabethan Poets, Daniel and Raleigh", in *The Pelican Guide to English Literature,* vol. 2; Rosamund Tuve, *Elizabethan and Metaphysical Imagery,* chs. 10 and 11; Philip Edwards, *Sir Walter Raleigh;* Laurence Lerner: *The Uses of Nostalgia,* ch. 6 ("City Troubles: Pastoral and Satire").

## 4   The Dream

i   Donne: *The Relic.*
Thomas Campion: "Come O Come my Life's delight."

ii   Donne: *Songs and Sonnets,* especially *The Good-Morrow, The Sun Rising, The Canonisation, The Anniversary, Love's Alchemy, The Apparition.*
Campion: "Rose-cheeked Laura", "My sweetest Lesbia", "Follow thy fair sun, unhappy shadow", "When thou must home to shades of underground".

iii   Joan Bennett: *Four Metaphysical Poets;* C S Lewis: "Donne an Love Poetry in the seventeenth century" (conveniently available i

*Donne: Songs and Sonnets. A Casebook,* ed. J Lovelock); Patrick
Cruttwell: *The Shakespearean Moment* (especially chs. 2 and 3);
J B Leishmann: *The Monarch of Wit;* Barbara Hardy: "Thinking and
Feeling in the Songs and Sonnets", in *John Donne: Essays in
Celebration,* ed. A J Smith.

## 5   The Bunch of Grapes

i   Herbert: *The Collar, Affliction I* ("When first thou didst entice
to me thy heart").

ii   Herbert:*Jordan* I and II, *Love* III ("Love bade me welcome"),
*Affliction* IV ("Broken in pieces all asunder"), *The Pearl, The Holy
Scriptures* II ("Oh that I knew how all thy lights combine").
Donne: *Holy Sonnets,* and especially "Batter my heart, three-
personed God" and "Death be not proud."
Marvell: *The Coronet.*
G M Hopkins: "No worst there is none", "Thou art indeed just,
Lord."

iii   Rosamund Tuve: *A Reading of George Herbert;* Erich Auerbach:
"Figura", in *Scenes from the Drama of European Literature;* H Cap-
lan: "Scriptural Interpretation" in *Speculum* 1929; Rosemary
Freeman: *English Emblem Books;* Gabriel Josipovici: *The World and
the Book,* ch. 2.

## 6   On his Blindness

i   Milton: *Paradise Lost,* and especially Book 5 lines 743-end, and
Book 3 lines 1–55; "How soon hath Time the subtle thief of Youth."

ii   Milton: Sonnets, and especially *To the Lord General Cromwell,
On the Late Massacre in Piedmont, To Mr Cyriack Skinner upon his
Blindness,* "Methought I saw my late espoused saint"; *Lycidas,
Samson Agonistes.*

iii   E M W Tillyard: *Milton*; David Daiches: *Milton*; Leo Spitzer:
"Understanding Mitlon", in *Essays on English and American
Literature,* ed. A Hatcher (on this sonnet); A D Nuttall: Introduction
to *Milton's Minor Poems in English* (Macmillan).
Autobiographical passages from Milton's prose are conveniently
gathered in J H Hanford's *Milton Handbook,* and in *Aeopogitica and
other Prose Works* (Everyman's Library).

## 7   The Picture of Little T.C.

i   Marvell: *To his Coy Mistress.*

Horace: *Odes* III 26.

Spenser: *Amoretti* 12 ("One day I sought with her heart thrilling eyes".)

Matthew Prior: *To a Child of Quality*.

ii   Marvell: *Clorinda and Damon, A Dialogue between Thyrsis and Dorinda, The Nymph Complaining for the Death of her Fawn, The Mower to the Gloworms, The Garden*.

Robert Herrick: *To Dianeme, Corinna's Going a-Maying, To the Virgins to Make Much of Time, To Daffodils*.

iii   M C Bradbrook and M G Lloyd Thomas: *Andrew Marvell;* Laurence Lerner: *The Uses of Nostalgia*, ch. 9 ("Nature in Marvell"); Rosalie L Collie: *My Echoing Song*.

## 8   To Mr Fortescue

i   Pope: *Epistle to Dr Arbuthnot, On the Use of Riches* (Moral Essay no. 4: To Bolingbroke), *Epilogue to the Satires*.

ii   Pope: *The Moral Essays* (or, *Epistles to Several Persons*); *Imitations of Horace*.

Dr Johnson: *London, The Vanity of Human Wishes*.

iii   Dr Johnson: *Life of Pope;* Lytton Strachey: *Pope*; Peter Dixon: *The World of Pope's Satires*.

## 9   Peter Grimes

i   Crabbe: *The Village*

Keats: *Lamia*

Pope: *Pastorals, To Mr Fortescue*.

ii   Crabbe: *The Borough*, Letter 1 (General Description); *The Frank Courtship, The Mother, Advice*, or *The Squire and the Priest, The Confidant*.

Wordsworth: *Michael, The Thorn, The Excursion Book I*.

iii   *The Life of George Crabbe*, by his son; Howard Mills: Introduction to *Crabbe: Tales 1812 and other Selected Poems;* John Lucas: Introduction to *A Selection from George Crabbe;* Lilian Haddakin: *The Poetry of George Crabbe*.

## 10   Elegiac Stanzas

i   Wordsworth: *Elegiac Verses in Memory of my Brother John Wordsworth, Tintern Abbey, Ode on Intimations of Immortality*.

ii   Wordsworth: *The Prelude*, and especially Books 1, 2, and 8.

Coleridge: *Kubla Khan, Dejection, Frost at Midnight.*
Shelley: *Hymn to Intellectual Beauty.*
Keats: *Lamia,* "Ever let the Fancy roam."

iii    J S Mill: *Autobiography,* ch. 5; F L Lucas: *The Decline and Fall of the Romantic Ideal;* M H Abrams: *The Mirror and the Lamp;* F W Bateson: "The Approach to Romanticism" (ch. 8 of *A Guide to English Literature*); A E Powell: *The Romantic Theory of Poetry.*


## 11    Stanzas written in Dejection

i    Shelley: "A widow bird sat mourning for her love."
Whitman: "Out of the cradle endlessly rocking".
Herman Melville: *Billy in the Darbies.*
Coleridge: *The Pains of Sleep.*

ii    Shelley: *Ode to the West Wind, To a Skylark,* "When the lamp is shattered", *Epipsychidion, Adonais.*
Coleridge: *Dejection: an Ode, Work without Hope.*
Keats: *Ode to a Nightingale, Ode on Melancholy,* "When I have fears that I may cease to be".
Matthew Arnold: *Dover Beach, The Youth of Man; To Marguerite, The Scholar Gispy.*

iii    A C Bradley: *Oxford Lectures on Poetry;* Herbert Read: *The True Voice of Feeling;* Graham Hough: *The Romantic Poets;* C S Lewis: "Shelley, Dryden and Mr Eliot" (conveniently reprinted, along with several other interesting essays on Shelley, in *The English Romantic Poets,* ed. by M H Abrams).


## 12    Johannes Agricola in Meditation

i    Browning: *Porphyria's Lover, Fra Lippo Lippi,* St Paul's Epistle to the Romans, and especially chapters 3, 8, 11.
Donne: The Second Anniversary, lines 179–213.

ii    Browning: *Creon, An Epistle . . . of Karshish the Arab Physician, Up at a Villa, Down in the City, Soliloquy in a Spanish Cloister, My Last Duchess, Caliban upon Setebos, The Bishop orders his Tomb.*
Ezra Pound: *Mesmerism, Marvoil, Altaforte, Pierre Vidal Old.*

iii    Yvor Winters: "Problems for the Modern Critic of Literature", in *The Function of Criticism;* Robert Langbaum: *The Poetry of Experience;* Thomas Blackburn: *Robert Browning;* Philip Drew: *The Poetry of Browning.*

## 13    The Ruined Maid

i   Hardy: *Ballad of Love's Skeleton.*
Broadside Ballads: *The Oldham Weaver* (in Mary Barton, by
Elizabeth Gaskell, ch. 4), *The Red Wig, My Master and I,* The
*Coal Owner and the Pitman's Wife, The Lass of Islington* (all in *The
Common Muse,* ed. de Sola Pinto and Rodway).

ii   Hardy: *The Sergeant's Song, The Levelled Churchyard, Her Late
Husband, A Woman's Fancy, On Stinforth Hill at Midnight, The
Fight on Durnover Moor, Reluctant Confession.*
John Gay: *The Beggar's Opera* (and especially, among the songs,
"Through all the Employments of Life", "Since laws were made,
for every degree" and "Thus I stand like a Turk.")
Shaw: *Arms and the Man, Mrs Warren's Profession.* W H Auden:
*Miss Gee, Victor,* "O what is that sound that so thrills the ear?"

iii   Irving Howe: *Thomas Hardy,* ch. 8, "The Lyric Poems".
C Day Lewis: *The Lyric Poetry of Thomas Hardy* (British Academy
Warton Lecture 1953); David Craig: *The Real Foundations,* ch. 3,
"Songs of the Bleak Age"; Martha Vicinus: "The Study of 19th
century British Working-class Poetry", in *The Politics of Literature,*
ed. Kampf and Lauter; A L Lloyd: *Folk Song in England.*

## 14    To an Old Philosopher in Rome

i   Stevens: *Le Monocle de Mon Oncle, Esthetique du Mal* (part 3),
*Sea Surface full of Clouds,* "The house was quiet and the world was
calm."

ii   Stevens: *Sunday Morning, Credences of Summer, Of Heaven
considered as a Tomb.*
Keats: *Ode on a Grecian Urn.*
Tennyson: *Tithonus, Ulysses.*

iii   Frank Kermode: *Wallace Stevens;* Randall Jarrell: *Poetry and
the Age,* pages 124-36; L L Martz: "Wallace Stevens—the World as
Meditation", *Yale Review* XLVII (1958) pages 517-36; R H Pearce:
"Wallace Stevens: the Life of the Imagination", *Publications of the
Modern Language Association of America,* LXVI (1951) pages 65-89.

## 15    City without Walls

i   Auden: *The Ascent of F.6* (with Christopher Isherwood), *Prologue
at Sixty, In Time of War,* no. 19.
John Betjeman: *Middlesex.*

ii    Auden: *The Age of Anxiety, In Time of War* (especially nos. 12, 14 15, 16, 27) *The Shield of Achilles*.
T S Eliot: *Preludes*.
Philip Larkin: *Church Going*.

iii    Richard Hoggart: *Auden, an Introductory Essay;* Monroe K Spears: *The Poetry of W H Auden;* Barbara Everett: *Auden;* Auden: *The Dyer's Hand,* and especially "Making, Knowing and Judging", "The Poet and the City", "Christianity and Art".

# Index of authors and titles

(Anonymous works are listed under titles)